D0537149

MICHEL GUÉRARD'S CUISINE GOURMANDE

By the same author

Michel Guerard's Cuisine Minceur

MICHEL GUÉRARD'S CUISINE GOURMANDE

BY MICHEL GUÉRARD

Translated and with Editors' Notes by
Philip and Mary Hyman

WILLIAM MORROW AND COMPANY, INC.
New York

Color photography by Didier Blanchat
BOOK DESIGN BY SALLIE BALDWIN, ANTLER & BALDWIN, INC.

Library of Congress Cataloging in Publication Data
Guérard, Michel, 1933-
Michel Guérard's Cuisine gourmande.
Translation of La cuisine gourmande.
Includes index.
1. Cookery, French. I. Title.
TX719.G81713 1979 641.5'944 79-17165
ISBN 0-688-03508-6

Printed in the United States of America.

First Edition
1 2 3 4 5 6 7 8 9 10

Prologue

As a child in Vétheuil, I had my first gastronomic experience at the age of five. I remember going daily to the local restaurant, only a couple of éclair lengths from my home, and stationing myself by the kitchen window. There I would sing at the top of my lungs until my friend the chef appeared at the window and threw me some of the pastries left over from the previous day. I never really knew whether this was a spontaneous act of generosity on his part or just a way to stop my singing.

Sundays were always special in the village where I grew up; the children of the town (all the boys in short pants) would wait on the icy steps of the town hall for "the nice lady" (*la belle dame*) to appear. This generous woman would come and take us all to the local bakery and treat us to the pastry of our choice. The first time I participated in this taste-tempting excursion, my career as a young gastronome almost came to an abrupt end. All week long, in anticipation of the awaited Sunday, I pressed my nose to the window of the bakery shop to study the choices that would be offered to me. Finally I decided in favor of a pastry overflowing with a white, creamy filling, not because it was beautiful to look at but because it was the biggest thing there. So when on Sunday I went with the others to the shop with the nice lady, I designated the aforementioned pastry as my choice. When I had it in my hands, I closed my eyes with excitement and took a giant mouthful. I immediately felt my stomach violently revolt against this matter I was introducing into it—it was demonstrating its disapproval of what turned out to be a *bouchée à la reine*, not hot as it should be but repulsively cold and inedible! Imagine how embarrassed I was, having to refuse to eat this treat so generously offered by the nice lady. I suddenly understood that heaven had condemned me to a sensitive palate and that there was nothing I could do about it.

I became a *chef-gourmand*, and how could it have been otherwise with such childhood memories: A grandmother who simmered hearty, warming stews for me on winter evenings, always prepared with love and so delicious? I will never forget the wild-almond fragrance of the ripe apricots of summers gone by. Such apricots! Made into preserves or in caramelized rows covering a tart hot from the oven—the same oven my grandmother used to bake stuffed potatoes which I watched swelling ever so slightly from the heat as they cooked. Later, in Normandy, my mother taught me the secrets of making a *daube*, how to know by the touch of a finger the degree to which meat has cooked, to roast rabbits, and a hundred other things.

Then the war came and I made my first attempts both at cooking and being a soldier. Every Thursday, when there was no school, my friends and I set up the Camp of the Golden Flag. We made tents out of old potato sacks and the like, and I would treat them to little cakes I had secretly made the day before with the skin that forms on the top of boiled milk. We'd wash down these little delicacies with the juice of wild blackberries, which we also used afterward to stain our faces in outrageous patterns, like Indians in war paint. What risks we took! Without giving a second thought to the danger, we then sneaked out in search of the metal bodies of downed airplanes—to make into canoes.

After the war, I was faced with a choice of possible careers. At first, I was tempted to break all connections with cooking, since I was leaning toward a vocation in the Church. I would become a priest. No, more than that, I wanted to be a bishop. Then I changed my mind: The stage! That was the thing for me, I'd become an actor! And then reality intervened.

Prologue

My adolescence truly ended when I began working as a cook's helper and apprentice. It was a hard, jolting experience, brightened here and there by the excitement of learning, but full of moments of despair and struggles between discipline and rebellion. Then I moved on to work and learn with new teachers who were masters of the art of cooking and who communicated their enthusiasm and love of the profession to me. First among these master chefs for me was Kléber Alix, who taught me the importance of pleasure in cooking and how to please one's guest. More than that, he preached the importance of humility, patience, and a sense of humor. When I went on from there, it was with a different attitude toward my profession. The next period in my career was marked by the appearance of what I will call my cooking godfathers: those who treated me like a son or younger brother and welded enduring ties between us that have become strong and lasting friendships. These were people like Jean Delaveyne, Paul Bocuse, the Troisgros brothers; and *all the others* . . . my friends!

You now understand that cooking is not just a profession—it is a matter of love. Cooking, in which a magical enthusiasm reigns among the true professionals and rigorous limitations are in fact the means to explore endless possibilities and creative experiences. Cooking, a profession exercised behind clouds of fragrant vapors, that lives and grows through the spontaneity and creativity of its practitioners.

In a later life, when I am forced to abandon this world for another, where I and my friends will meet among other clouds at the table of the heavenly host, I will perhaps dare to ask Him to grant me the rank of apprentice for all eternity in the kitchen of the angels. But I will also ask, especially, that He let me taste *His* latest creation!

MICHEL GUÉRARD

Acknowledgments

We would like to thank Narcisse Chamberlain and the Publisher for permission to use information she included in *Michel Guérard's Cuisine Minceur* which we felt was pertinent to this book as well. We also thank Michel Guérard for his help in suggesting substitutions for hard-to-find ingredients and his cordial willingness to consult with us on so many details concerning the American edition of his book.

P.H./M.H.

Contents

Contents

PART TWO

Contents

In the
beginning
there was the earth,

then man,
who
discovered
fire,

and then he began
to
cook . . .

Editors' Preface

Before and after Michel Guérard's famous sideline, the slimming *cuisine minceur*, his true fame as a chef was due to *cuisine gourmande.* This is the name he has given to his own style of cooking which is, at this moment, still evolving in the kitchens at Eugénie-les-Bains. *Cuisine gourmande* is what has made Guérard one of the most highly respected and admired "*nouvelle-cuisine*" chefs of France. What makes Guérard different? What is his style of cooking all about?

First of all, Michel Guérard is an inventive and adventurous chef. Not only is he willing, even eager, to experiment, but he has a masterly sense of balancing and dosing ingredients, so that his creations are always subtle and refined. Another important element in Guérard's *cuisine gourmande* is his emphasis on purity, purity meaning that the taste of foods is never masked or distorted, but rather highlighted through the use of light sauces and judiciously chosen garnishes. The overall effect of any *gourmande* dish or dinner is one of lightness and delicacy. This is achieved through his extraordinary attention to details and his impeccable palate. Salads, sauces, and garnishes are characteristically made with small quantities of a variety of ingredients, carefully chosen to produce an effect of perfectly harmonious combinations, pleasing to both the palate and the eye.

As in *cuisine minceur*, Michel Guérard frequently uses cooking techniques that were either previously neglected or unknown in France. A method such as steaming is experimented with and used in some surprising situations, such as in making soups; see **Vegetable soup from Christine's garden (81).** The electric blender is employed to purée ingredients, not just in making vegetable granishes, as in **Green bean purée (269)**, but in thickening sauces without the addition of flour, starch, or any other "foreign" thickening agent, as in **Chive sauce (69)**. Another important technique directly related to the idea of purity, is that of cooking at very high temperatures for short times. This is traditionally associated with frying or sautéing, but Guérard achieves marvelous results in the oven by roasting at high heats just long enough to seal in and cook juices that otherwise would have been lost, as in **Roast saddle of hare with beet sauce (229)**. Pan juices form the basis for many sauces in the best French tradition, and tastes are often concentrated through reduction. Butter or cream is often added by "swirling it in," to produce a creamy result that retains the full flavor of these ingredients, often lost through overheating or prolonged cooking. A thorough description of these and other *gourmandes* techniques is given in detail in his introductory section, "The Methods of Cooking."

All in all, *cuisine gourmande* represents nothing less than the finest French cooking today. It is subtle, refined, inventive cooking, producing dishes that often appear deceptively simple and whose taste is foreshadowed by the beauty and symmetry of their presentation.

All great chefs have a style of cooking that is identifiably their own. Michel Guérard has developed a style combining ancient traditions and modern ideas in the imaginative recipes of his *cuisine gourmande*. All cooks with a sense of adventure as well as those with profound respect for the best French traditions should be grateful to Michel Guérard for this, his latest contribution to French gastronomy.

PHILIP AND MARY HYMAN

Part One

Color Pictures

⚜ **NOTE:** All the recipes are numbered. When a recipe is referred to in text or in a list of ingredients, its name and number are printed in **boldface** type. The numbers of the recipes for the dishes in the following color pictures are entered below at the end of their English titles:

Salade de jambon d'aile de canard aux pois de jardin
I **Duck "ham" and green-pea salad (32)**

Feuilleté d'asperges au beurre de cerfeuil
II **Puff pastry with asparagus and chervil (43)**

Les coquilles à la coque de Didier Oudill
III **Didier Oudill's shell-baked scallops (55)**

Tournedos de veau à la crème de ciboulette
IV **Veal steaks with chive sauce (86)**

Dorade en croûte de sel
V **Sea bream or porgy baked in salt (63)**

Perdreaux sur un lit de chou
VI **Partridge on a bed of cabbage leaves (82)**

Crêpes soufflées
VII **Crêpes with soufflé filling (136)**

Granité au vin de Saint-Émilion
VIII **Bordeaux red-wine ice (130)**

I Duck "ham" and green-pea salad

II Puff pastry with asparagus and chervil

III Didier Oudill's shell-baked scallops

IV Veal steaks with chive sauce

V Sea bream or porgy baked in salt

VI Partridge on a bed of cabbage leaves

VII Crêpes with soufflé filling

VIII Bordeaux red-wine ice

Les cuissons

THE METHODS OF COOKING

Whatever method is used, either a traditional method—such as in a fireplace or on an outdoor grill, roasting, in an oven or on a spit, sautéing, frying, steaming, "encased" cooking, in a crust, braising, stewing, poaching—or some method not yet discovered, food passes from the raw to the cooked state, a phenomenon that changes its outward appearance, its color, its texture, its flavor, and creates aromas that stimulate the appetite. Heat, the agent that causes the transformation, comes from many sources: wood, coal, gas, electricity, microwaves. . . .

The Two Main Principles

Cooking by "sealing": *Saisissement*

With browning: This method retains all the juices and nutritive elements of foods by caramelizing their exterior surfaces over heat, with or without the addition of fat, as when broiling (or grilling), roasting, sautéing, or frying.

Without browning: The same result can also be achieved without browning by cooking the food in boiling liquid, steaming it, or using a nonstick pan, as when poaching eggs, fish, poultry, meat, and vegetables, and in cooking pastas.

Cooking by "interchange": *Echange*

With browning: This method is used for pot-roasting or braising meat, poultry, game, and variety meats. First the food is sautéed quickly in hot fat (to retain the juices and nutritive elements), then liquid (wine or stock) is added to half-cover, and the food is then simmered slowly on top of the stove or in the oven. The juices within the food are gradually released and mix with the cooking liquid, and the food is enriched in turn by the various elements in this liquid, hence the term "interchange."

Without browning: The procedure is the same as above except that the food may be sautéed in fat, but not browned, i.e., simmered in butter as for a fricassee. Some foods are first soaked in cold water to remove any traces of blood (this is done for veal, sweetbreads, and brains) and parboiled for a few minutes, if necessary (this is also done for sweetbreads, brains, tripe, etc.). Then the food is sautéed, the moisturizing element (which will become the basis of the sauce) is added, and the "interchange" occurs as described above while the food cooks.

Unlike braised meats, braised fish are not sautéed, but simply placed in a baking dish (buttered or not), and cold fish stock, white wine, or red wine is added to half-cover before cooking. The fish is then placed in the oven, sometimes covered with parchment paper or aluminum foil, to keep it from burning. This is a perfect example of cooking by "interchange without browning": As the fish cooks, its juices and aromas mix with the stock, which becomes richer and makes for a tender and juicy final dish.

Cooking in a Fireplace or on an Outdoor Grill

Man began to cook over a wood fire, and this is still the best way to gain an understanding of the use of heat in the art of cooking. This chapter was written specifically and affectionately for those who cook on a hearth, to all outdoor cooks and Sunday cooks. I want to show them that **with a little ingenuity, they are not limited to simply broiling or grilling, but can make use of the entire range of cooking methods.**

⚜ **Cooking on a grill:** This is an outdoor version of cooking by "sealing with browning."

The heat is provided by burning wood or prunings (from grapevines, wood from fruit trees, or other nonresinous wood), or charcoal, over which the grill is placed. There are modern grills that function with gas or electricity or infrared heat, as well as ridged or corrugated cast-iron griddles, slightly slanted, that are placed directly over the source of heat and can be used on top of the stove. But nothing can rival the savory woodsmoke flavor imparted to food cooked on an open grill!

⚜ **How to grill red meat:** The grill must be clean and very hot; the meat should be at room temperature and lightly coated with peanut or olive oil.

To grill meat very rare (*bleu*):

The meat is placed on the grill and seared, then shifted 90 degrees (without being turned over) to make a crisscross pattern of brown lines on its surface. Then the meat is turned over and the same thing is done on the other side.

After the meat has been on the grill for a very short time, and is still soft when pressed gently with a finger, it is ready to serve for those who like it very rare (*bleu*). At this stage the heat may not have penetrated to the center of the meat, so place the meat on a plate, cover, and keep warm for a little while longer to finish cooking (heat through).

To grill meat rare (*saignant*):

Grill the meat over the center of the fire until a few drops of pinkish blood appear on the upper surface. When you press the meat now, you will feel a little resistance, although the meat is still soft: This means it is rare (*saignant*) and can be served.

To grill meat medium-rare (*à point*):

If you continue the cooking somewhat longer, you must do it more slowly; therefore, keep the meat considerably farther from the main source of heat. More drops of blood will appear on the upper surface, and when you press the meat, it will be more resistant and firmer than before: It is now medium-rare (*à point*).

To grill meat well-done (*bien cuit*):
If you continue to cook the meat even longer, the drops of blood begin to form pinkish-brown trickles on the surface of the meat. You will find noticeable resistance when you press the meat: It is now well-done (*bien cuit*).

⚜ **How to grill white meats, poultry & feathered game, brochettes:** The fire should not be as hot as for red meat, but the grill must nevertheless be very hot before the food is placed on it. Never leave the food on the grill too long, or it will dry out; be careful to stop the cooking in time to preserve tenderness and juiciness. A chicken, for example, must retain some blood; it should be pale pink along the entire breastbone. This indicates that it is well cooked and tender. When you prick the breast with a fine skewer, it should sink in easily and release a trickle of almost colorless juice when the meat is done. The same test can be applied to lamb.

When cooking small pieces of meat on skewers, with garnishes such as mushrooms, green or red sweet peppers, and bacon, it is often best to parboil the garnishing elements in boiling water (omit salt if you are using bacon) before skewering. The meat, poultry, or fish is generally marinated (see "simple" marinade, page 39) before being skewered and cooked.

⚜ **How to grill fish:** Fat and moderately fat fish (sardines, mackerel, herring, salmon) is delicious grilled, since this process drains off some of the fattiness. After marinating the fish (page 38), baste it very lightly with oil. The grill must also be oiled so that the skin will not tear when you turn the fish over. The fire should be as follows for grilling fish:

Very hot for small fish.

Very hot for large fish, which—unlike small fish—are usually seared in a crisscross pattern on both sides, like red meat, then placed in the oven to finish cooking.

Hot for large fish that are cooked entirely on the grill.

Flatfish—American lemon or gray sole, turbot, skate, Dover sole, dab—are placed on the grill white-skin side down.

Fat, fleshy fish (herring, mackerel, red mullet, bass, sardine) are turned over on the grill backbone side, not slit side, down so as not to lose the juices inside.

Some large fish (salmon and halibut, especially) are cut into thick slices or "steaks" (*darnes*; the old word *dalle*—roughly, "slab"—seems more logical to me). However, rather than cutting a small salmon into slices, you can have it filleted and cut the fillets into strips 2 inches wide. It is essential to leave the skin on these pieces. Score the skin (that is, make slashes in it in a crisscross pattern with a knife), and place the fillets **skin side down** on the hot grill. Cook in this position, **without turning it over.** The grilled skin imparts a delicious taste of smoke to the fish and keeps its flesh moist and incomparably tender.

Oysters, sea or bay scallops, and hard-shell clams are placed in their shells directly on the grill and will open by themselves. They may be eaten as is, or with a little freshly ground pepper and whatever *fines herbes* you like.

HINTS:

Salt tends to extract juices and blood from meat and prevent it from browning. Therefore, it is always preferable to **salt small pieces of red meat halfway through the cooking.** When cooking a big piece of meat, which will be cut into slices afterwards, or a fish from which you will lift the fillets, it is best (not to say **essential**) **to salt the food a second time** after you have carved it. The salt will never flavor the center of the meat or fish. This applies to all large cuts, such as a leg of lamb, beef or veal rib roasts, saddle of lamb, etc.

When turning the meat during the cooking, use a spoon or spatula; be careful not to pierce it with a fork, which would allow the juices and blood to escape.

Large cuts of meat must be cooked more slowly than smaller ones so that the heat will penetrate to the center; do not cook over very high heat. To speed their cooking, score the skin in several places with a sharp knife (especially for leg of lamb and fish).

If the cut of meat is thinner at one end than the other, it can be evenly cooked by putting the small end farther away from the center of the fire than the large end.

If you are not afraid of excess calories, you can brush the meat or fish after it has been grilled with a little oil or melted butter. This will make it beautiful and shiny when served.

Grilled meat is usually served with the side cooked first uppermost.

After you have used the grill, and while it is still hot, scrape it with a metal-bristle brush to loosen anything that has stuck to it. Otherwise, the next time you use the grill, these particles will burn and give a bitter taste to the food.

⚜ **"Covered" cooking in a fireplace or on an outdoor grill:** Here the equivalent of cooking in a covered pan (*à l'étouffée*) is obtained by wrapping food in oiled parchment paper or in aluminum foil, and cooking it under the hot ashes.

"Dry" cooking (simply wrap and "bake"):

Vegetables: potatoes, mushrooms, asparagus.

Meats: small game birds, squab, young rabbit—seasoned with *fines herbes*, thyme, bay leaf.

Fruits: apples, bananas—together with vanilla beans to flavor them.

"Moist" cooking:

Place the food to be cooked on a piece of aluminum foil or parchment paper, fold up the edges, then add enough wine or stock to cover. Fold the foil or paper to completely enclose the liquid, and place the *papillote* on the grill or bury it under the glowing coals. The liquid will be completely absorbed by the food when cooked (it will also keep the parchment paper from catching fire).

⚜ **Steaming fish in a fireplace or on an outdoor grill:** On the grill, spread fresh seaweed soaked in seawater or moist wild grasses. Place the fish on this and cover it with more seaweed or grass. It will take no longer than 20 minutes to cook a 1½- to 2-pound sea bass.

⚜ **Cooking "the lazy way" in a fireplace or on an outdoor grill:** A large piece of meat such as a rib roast or a leg of lamb can actually be cooked in a fireplace or on a grill without a spit. All you have to do is to brown the meat well on all sides first and sear it in a crisscross pattern on the grill. Then put a piece of aluminum foil on the hot—but not red-hot—coals, and place the meat directly on the foil.

From time to time, turn the leg of lamb or whatever you are cooking, and don't be afraid to leave it there, very close to the heat, for 2 or 3 hours, depending on its size. Cooking this way takes longer than any other form of grilling, because the temperature is roughly the same as that of a warming oven—about 225° F. When you slice the meat, you will be amazed at its tenderness and even, rosy color.

⚜ **"SMOKING" IN A FIREPLACE:** This is not to be confused with the kind of "cold" smoking used to preserve and flavor certain foods after salting (such as salmon, goose, pork). Here, smoke is used as a cooking agent, not as a preservative. First build a blazing fire, and, when you have a nice bed of hot coals, heat the grill. Quickly sear the meat or fish on the hot grill, but do not cook it all the way through. Remove the food and cover the fire with damp branches or sawdust, preferably from oak or fruit trees—*never* from resinous woods. Replace the food on the grill, cover with a glass dome like those used for cheeses or cakes, and leave it to cook slowly in the smoke that will be trapped inside the glass. The food will be flavored by a thousand and one delicious tastes when smoked this way.

Roasting

To roast is to cook food by exposure to direct heat, without moisture, but with frequent turning. This is a version of cooking by "sealing with browning."

To brown and caramelize foods that are roasted, it is necessary to baste them—without overdoing it—with fat (two-thirds oil, one-third butter). Roasting is done in the oven, on a spit, or even, as a last resort, in an uncovered casserole or braising pan.

⚜ **IN THE OVEN:** The oven should always be preheated before anything is cooked in it. The temperature depends on the kind and size of the piece to be roasted; it should be hot enough—475° F to 550° F—to brown the surface of the roast and seal in all its juices.

Meat, poultry, game, or fish should all be very lightly brushed with some kind of fat, but not salted before roasting. Place the food in the oven either directly in a roasting pan (this is known as *façon ménagère*, "home style") or in a pan with a rack that will keep the food from resting in the drippings; or on a bed of bones that have first been cracked and lightly browned. Fish can be roasted on a bed of seaweed.

As soon as the roast has browned completely, lower the oven temperature a little, and baste often with the juices in the bottom of the pan (except if you are using seaweed) until the cooking is finished. Then you can salt the meat, bird, or fish.

As for red meats, the surface of white meats, poultry, game, and fat fish must be browned at a fairly high temperature, but finish the cooking at a lower temperature or they will become tough.

⚜ **On a spit—whether in the fireplace or in an electric rotisserie:** When food is roasted on a spit, either outdoors or indoors, it should be in the open air, not enclosed. Consequently, no moisture accumulates and, since the roast is constantly turning on the spit, a more savory result can be achieved than in any closed oven.

Browning and sealing are required as for roasting in the oven. It is still best to baste the food frequently with the fat that collects in the drippings pan.

⚜ **How to serve a tender roast:** Food roasted on a spit or in the oven is cooked by "sealing with browning." The high temperature and the fat on the outer surface produce the browning, keeping the juices and blood inside. Through its own circulatory system, the juices and blood are sent to the center of the roast, and it consequently cooks in its own juice without losing any nutritive elements. When a roast is carved immediately after being cooked, the resulting slices have a very well-done outer rim, another less well-done, and a center that is very rare (*bleu*) and contains all the blood—which then runs out.

You must let meat rest before carving it! After roasting, keep the roast warm on a platter or carving board covered with a roasting-pan lid, a large bowl, or aluminum foil. Exterior heat will no longer exert pressure toward the center of the roast, and by reverse process the blood will now flow toward the outer layers of the meat, giving them an even color—rosy or red depending on how long it was cooked. At the same time, the muscle fibers, which have contracted because of the heat, expand and relax, producing the desired tenderness.

It is therefore best to finish cooking a leg of lamb, for instance, one hour before it is to be served.

HINTS:

Salt the roast halfway through the cooking time; then salt again on each slice as you carve, adding a little freshly ground pepper.

Avoid pricking the roast with a fork during the cooking.

Certain foods, especially game, need to be wrapped in a thin layer of barding fat before roasting; the fat is removed toward the end of the cooking to allow browning. Certain meats and some game (woodcocks, pheasants, hares, etc.) should be larded with strips of fat to avoid drying out when roasted.

If the food you are roasting is particularly delicate or sensitive to heat and begins to burn, cover it with aluminum foil. (This includes fragile parts such as the ends of the bones in a crown roast, the tail of fish, etc.).

⚜ **Sauces for roasts:** The best sauces or gravies (*jus*) for roasts are made at home by cooks who instinctively do what is simplest and best. Professional chefs often make elaborate, even sophisticated sauces which, in my opinion, cannot rival a well-made *jus.*

If you use a pan of the proper size for roasting (not too large), then the juices of meat, poultry, game, and even of fish will collect in the bottom and will make a simple but excellent base for the sauce or *jus.*

TIPS FOR MAKING A GOOD SAUCE:

When basting the roast with fat, use a mixture of oil and butter—1 tablespoon of the mixture per pound. Butter tends to separate and scorches at high temperatures; the addition of oil helps to prevent this. Use either half oil, half butter, or two-thirds oil, one-third butter for basting.

Add one or more whole unpeeled cloves of garlic, as you like, to the pan when you place the roast in the preheated oven.

As soon as the roast has browned well on one side, after about 10 minutes, baste it with the juices that will have accumulated in the pan. Turn it over. Repeat this operation. Then baste frequently for the remainder of the cooking time.

Take the pan out of the oven, remove the roast, and keep it warm and covered. The juices in the bottom of the pan should be caramelized. (**Be absolutely vigilant to avoid burning them**, which would give the gravy an irremediably bitter taste.)

Degrease (*dégraisser*) the pan: that is, pour off all but about one-quarter of the fat: the sauce will thicken when simmered with this fat.

Deglaze (*déglacer*) the pan: that is, add twice as much hot water as the total amount of sauce you want to have at the end, and, with a spoon, loosen all the caramelized juices sticking to the bottom of the pan so they will dissolve in the hot liquid.

Boil and reduce the sauce by half (allow 2 generous tablespoons of reduced sauce per serving). Pour it into a small saucepan and keep it warm.

If you want a slightly garlicky sauce, pour the sauce through a fine-mesh strainer into a saucepan, and crush the garlic with the bottom of a spoon or a small ladle.

Finally, to mellow the sauce, pieces of softened butter can be swirled into it, or a few drops of a good red-wine vinegar may be added; the vinegar will enliven and bring out the character of the sauce.

To enrich the *jus* of a roast *during* the cooking, lightly brown in advance, in the roasting pan, cracked veal bones for a beef or veal roast, lamb bones for a leg or saddle of lamb, cut-up poultry carcasses for a fowl, etc., and place the roast on these as suggested earlier.

And, when deglazing the pan, instead of using hot water, a light stock or bouillon of veal, lamb, or poultry may be used to enrich the sauce.

Sautéing

Sautéing is a very quick way of preparing a dish in a savory sauce. This method of fast cooking by "sealing" is similar to both grilling and roasting in that it first involves quick browning of the food. It is best done in a high-sided frying pan (*sauteuse*), but an ordinary frying pan can fill the bill equally well. The food is cut into small pieces —meat, variety meats, poultry, game, or fish, and sometimes vegetables —and cooked in 1 tablespoon, in all, of oil and butter, mixed together, per serving being made. Since the food being sautéed is in constant contact with the hot fat, it will caramelize and brown, thus trapping all the juices and nutrients inside.

⚜ **General procedure for sautéing:** After the food has been sautéed to a light brown on both sides, salted, and cooked to your liking— very rare, medium, or well-done, as in grilling—take it out of the pan and place it on a hot platter close to the heat. If the food is left in the pan when the deglazing and reduction occur, the result is a stew (*ragoût*) and not a *sauté*. It is essential that the food be removed from the pan while making the sauce.

Degrease (*dégraisser*) the pan as described earlier, then deglaze (*déglacer*), that is, pour into the pan the liquid named in the recipe— a white or red wine, vinegar, madeira, port, sherry, vermouth, armagnac, cognac—allowing 2 teaspoons of a brandy or 2 tablespoons of a wine per serving. Bring this liquid to a boil, stirring constantly; it will dissolve the caramelized juices sticking to the bottom of the pan. Simmer it to reduce it by three-quarters of its original volume.

Then, depending on the sizes of the pieces of meat, fish, or vegetable, and the number of servings, add 3 to 5 spoonfuls of veal, poultry, game, or fish stock. Reduce the sauce again by one-half.

Away from the heat, or over very low heat, and while shaking the pan to make the sauce spin around the sides, add pieces of softened butter (2 tablespoons per serving) or 3 tablespoons of *crème fraîche* (see page 352) or heavy cream per serving. This will bind and finish the sauce.

The idea is not to drown the *sauté* in the sauce but rather to serve it with a concentrated liquid that just covers and delicately surrounds it. Here is a typical example of a *sauté*:

Pièce de boeuf sautée au bordeaux
1 STEAK WITH RED-WINE SAUCE

Ingredients for 2 servings:

- 1 sirloin steak weighing approximately 1¼ pounds
- Butter to brown the meat
- 1 tablespoon finely chopped shallots
- 4 tablespoons red wine, preferably bordeaux
- 8 tablespoons stock
- 4 tablespoons softened butter

Brown a steak in a frying pan over high heat. Remove from the pan and make the sauce as follows:

Add the shallots to the pan and stir over medium heat; they will begin to soften. Deglaze the pan with the red wine, then boil until three-quarters of the wine has evaporated. Add the stock to the pan and continue boiling to reduce the liquid by half, then swirl in the 4 tablespoons of butter. Serve the sauce immediately, spooned over the meat. The sauce can be strained before serving and the meat garnished with two pieces of poached bone marrow.

Note: Veal scallops can be sautéed and served with a sauce made in a similar way. Simply omit the shallots and deglaze with either dry vermouth or port. Add 3 tablespoons of *crème fraîche* (see page 352) or heavy cream per person instead of stock, and boil to reduce the sauce by half; no butter is added.

HINTS:

The size of the pan must be right for the amount of food to be sautéed. If the food does not completely cover the bottom of the pan, the fat will quickly burn in the empty spots and will give the sauce a bitter taste when you deglaze the pan.

Small cuts (*tournedos*, chops, veal scallops) should be cooked quickly in an uncovered pan. Larger pieces (dark meat of poultry, pieces of rabbit) take a little longer to cook after browning, and are therefore covered after browning and then cooked more slowly.

⚜ **The proper way to cook a fish à la meunière:** The technique known as *à la meunière* (lightly floured; literally, "as the miller's wife does it") is reserved for fish (trout, pike, sole, whiting, etc.) or other foods with similar texture, such as brains. It is a form of sautéing, but it stops before the deglazing stage. Let us take trout as an example:

In a skillet or an oval pan just large enough to hold the fish, heat a mixture of half oil, half butter; the combination will keep the butter from browning too quickly. Use 1½ to 2 tablespoons in all. Add a clove of garlic, unpeeled, to the pan; the aroma of the garlic thereby remains muted and imparts a subtle nuance to the dish as a whole. Put the pan on the heat.

Dry the fish with absorbent paper or a clean cloth. Salt and pepper it, then very lightly dust both sides with flour. Tap it to remove the excess flour.

Put the fish in the hot fat. Let it cook without too much heat for about 4 minutes on each side, until it is a nice golden brown. If this is done properly, the small amount of fat that remains in the pan will remain a pale brown. Take the fish from the pan and keep it warm.

Raise the heat and add 3½ tablespoons of fresh butter to the pan. When this browns to a nut-brown color and no longer sizzles, the water it contains has evaporated and it has cooked enough. Squeeze the juice of a lemon into the butter (this will make it foam), remove the clove of garlic, and immediately pour the butter over the fish.

It is imperative that the fish be cooked in a minimum of fat. A fish must retain its flavor of the sea or freshwater stream and is not to become a "sponge for butter."

Deep-frying

Deep-frying is a form of cooking by "sealing with browning." The food is plunged into a bath of hot fat, which may be peanut, olive, or vegetable oil; lard; or the rendered kidney fat (suet) of beef or veal. The fat is heated to a maximum of 340° F and the temperature is maintained until the cooking has been completed. Butter and margarine must not be used because they decompose at high temperatures.

For this process to succeed, the food should be well dried and cut into pieces small enough to cook through quickly. Fry only a small quantity at a time; otherwise, the temperature of the fat drops too rapidly when the food is added to it.

Foods are fried with or without an outside coating. The foods that are fried without an outside coating include potatoes, eggs, parsley or sorrel for garnishing, tiny game birds, and various forms of pastry (*pâte à chou, pâte brisée, pâte à brioche*). Coatings vary for deep-frying. Foods coated with flour include small fish and slices of fish (dipped in milk, salted, then coated with a little flour). Foods coated with bread crumbs, such as fish, chicken, or veal scallops, are first dipped in beaten egg mixed with a little oil, then coated with the bread crumbs. Fritters of different kinds are made by dipping food into a batter before deep-frying, and some things (*rissoles de truffes*) are deep-fried in puff pastry.

⚜ **How to make good french-fried potatoes:** Cut the potatoes (preferably a mealy variety) into small sticks of whatever thickness you prefer—from ⅜ inch for standard french-fried potatoes, down to ⅛ inch for matchstick potatoes (*pommes allumettes*). Rinse them in cold water, then pat them dry in a clean cloth or towel. Put them in the frying basket.

Heat the oil to a temperature averaging 300° F. Test it by dropping a piece of potato into it; if it boils up quickly and the potato rises to the surface within about 25 seconds, the oil is at the right temperature.

Plunge the potatoes into the oil and give them a preliminary cooking of about 7 to 8 minutes. If a potato stick that has been removed from the hot oil and allowed to cool can be crushed easily, it is done.

Lift out the frying basket and turn the potatoes out onto a plate covered with a towel or with absorbent paper.

Now raise the heat of the oil to 340° F, but be careful not to let it heat to the smoking point. Return the potatoes to the oil, shaking the basket to keep them from sticking together. In 2 or 3 minutes, they will be golden brown and crisp.

Take the potatoes out of the oil again, and turn them out onto the plate covered with a clean cloth or a fresh piece of absorbent paper. Sprinkle with salt or, better, with freshly ground coarse salt.

It is the second cooking in the hotter oil that seals and crisps the surface of the potatoes, which will also puff up because of the evaporation of the water still trapped inside. (This is the same principle used in making *pommes soufflées.*) It is essential to control the temperature of the oil with a deep-frying thermometer; it must not go above 340° F. If the oil gets hotter than this, it rapidly becomes toxic.

Covered Cooking: Steaming, "Encased" Cooking, Braising & Stewing

Covered cooking (*cuisson à l'étouffée*; literally, smothered cooking) can be a version of cooking by "sealing," or of cooking by "interchange," or sometimes by both principles.

⚜ **Steaming:** This form of covered cooking, *cuisson à la vapeur*, relies on "sealing." The food is cooked in the steam of a hot liquid, which may or may not be seasoned, and it imparts nothing to the liquid in return. You can use the simplest of broths with steaming—salted water. There are two methods of steaming:

Use a pot or pan with a closely fitting lid and of a size and shape just large enough to hold the food to be cooked: a saucepan with a footed steaming rack (see page 358) a round or oval casserole, or a covered roasting pan with its own perforated rack (which may be raised above the level of the water with metal jar tops placed underneath); a two-part steamer or couscous pot (see page 358), or a fish poacher. Fill the pan one-quarter of the way up with bouillon, seasoned or not, or with stock or water, depending on the circumstances. If a rack is used, it should be just above the level of the boiling liquid.

Here is another, more unusual method of steaming: In a utensil of the appropriate size, with a tightly fitting lid, place a saltwater fish on a bed of seaweed, or a freshwater fish on a bed of wild meadow grass. Then cover the fish with another layer of seaweed or grass moistened with a ladleful of water to start the cooking and create the steam; see **Bass cooked in seaweed (62).** The same method can be used to cook a leg of lamb covered with hay.

When the steam is generated from a meat- or poultry-based stock, this stock can be used to make an accompanying sauce. This cannot be done when you use seaweed or hay.

⚜ **"ENCASED" COOKING:** There are various forms of this technique; all are variations of "smothered" cooking by "interchange."

Cuisson en vessie: This method is one in which a food is sealed inside a pig's bladder (*vessie*); often chickens, sometimes stuffed, are cooked this way. This is how it is done:

The bladder should be thoroughly washed and turned inside out. (This means that any unpleasant odor will evaporate away from the food during cooking.)

The food (chicken, beef—even a leg of lamb) is placed inside the bladder and the bladder tied closed with a string. The bladder is pricked in several places with a pin or the point of a sharp knife to avoid too much pressure building up inside it during cooking.

The filled bladder may be cooked in a large pot of hot water; in this case a string should be attached to it and tied around one handle of the pot to keep it suspended in the liquid, off of the bottom of the pot, while cooking. Or, the bladder is steamed in the upper part of a couscous pot or steamer or in a pressure cooker. Both of these last methods, using steam, are easier and quicker than the first. In a steamer, a chicken weighing 5½ pounds is perfectly cooked and tender after cooking for 45 minutes to an hour.

Cuisson en papillote: This form of encased cooking is done with either parchment paper or aluminum foil. It can be used for leftover or previously cooked foods as well as for raw ingredients.

In either case, the food is wrapped inside a round or heart-shaped piece of paper, of which the border is folded tightly, then tied closed. It is usually baked in a hot oven or in the embers of a fire. When using leftover or precooked foods such as sweetbreads, sausages, veal cutlets, pigs' feet, etc., cover the meat with a little mushroom purée and add some finely sliced vegetables (*mirepoix*) before wrapping and heating; see **Salmon papillotes (61)**. Raw ingredients can also be used. Fish and shellfish, *foie gras*, small game birds, vegetables, mushrooms, and various fruits can all be cooked this way. An easy dessert can be made by peeling and coring an apple, then placing it on a piece of foil with a little sugar, rum, and a piece of vanilla bean. The foil is folded over the fruit and the edges are pinched closed, then the *papillote* is baked in a hot oven for about 15 minutes.

All types of encased cooking have the advantage of concentrating the aromas and flavors of the food being cooked. Foods served encased in this way are delicious complete meals since all the main elements and the garnish are cooked together. The flavors of the different ingredients delectably interpenetrate when cooked in this way.

Cuisson en croûte: As with encased cooking, this type of cooking will concentrate the flavors sealed inside either an edible or inedible shell.

EDIBLE-SHELL COOKING:

The food is first browned to seal in its juices, then allowed to cool before being wrapped in a sheet of dough and baked. A beef fillet, boned leg of lamb, chicken, and game birds can all be cooked in either puff pastry, brioche dough, or short pastry dough, and baked. Foods can be wrapped in dough when raw, as when making a *pâté en croûte*. Whenever dough is used, one or two holes should be cut in the top of it to serve as "chimneys." Into these holes, a rolled strip of paper or foil, about the size of your little finger, is inserted to let steam escape from the meat while baking, and avoid damaging the crust with the bubbling juices. The dough should be lightly brushed with beaten egg, to help browning, before baking.

INEDIBLE-SHELL COOKING:

The inedible crust most frequently used is a paste of coarse salt mixed with a little flour and dampened with water. The food is encased in this paste and is cooked in the oven. A rib roast of 5 or 6 ribs may be cooked *sous le sel*: After a preliminary browning, it is entirely encased in the salt paste and roasted slowly in a moderate oven, producing a tender, juicy, evenly cooked roast.

This is an excellent variation of the technique for roasting a chicken: Line an oval, ovenproof casserole with aluminum foil and line the foil with a thick layer of coarse salt. Put in a trussed 3- to 3½-pound chicken, and bury the chicken completely in more coarse salt. Sprinkle with a little water, then bake the chicken, uncovered, in a hot 450° F oven for about one hour. When you break open the salt crust, you will find a chicken more tender than if it had been conventionally roasted, with all its juices retained inside.

⚜ **Braising and stewing:** Braising is the example *par excellence* of cooking by "interchange." A piece of meat for braising may be larded and marinated in advance (see page 38). Then all surfaces of meat or poultry—but not of fish—are first sealed by light browning. The meat or bird is removed; diced vegetables (*mirepoix*) are added to the pot and briefly cooked in the juices. The meat or bird is placed back in the pan on top of the *mirepoix*, and a flavorful liquid (bouillon, wine, veal or chicken stock) is added to half-cover the piece.

An appropriate utensil is a heavy-bottomed, cast-iron pot with a tightly fitting lid. Even better is the deep, oblong braising pot called a *braisière* which has a lid that fits down closely over the sides of the pot.

In braising, the cooking must be gentle, long, and even. The cooking is done either in a slow oven or on top of the stove. (The latter requires an asbestos mat or other heat-diffusing device to protect the bottom of the pot.) As its fibers are tenderized, the meat or poultry exudes juices that heighten the flavor of the braising liquid, which is thereby gradually transformed into a rich and fragrant sauce. At the end, this sauce is usually carefully strained.

The braising of fish is handled a little differently. The fish is not cooked in a pan covered with a lid, but rather placed in a buttered baking dish. Seasonings are added, and the fish is sprinkled, most usually, with minced shallots. A mixture of half fish stock and half wine (white or red, as specified by the recipe) is added, and the dish is baked in the oven. The cooking time is much shorter than for meat or poultry. Instead of using a lid to shield the fish against the heat, a sheet of buttered parchment paper, or of aluminum foil, is placed over the baking dish. In some instances, even this protection is not necessary and may prevent the braising liquid from reducing sufficiently.

As a general rule (including the braising of fish particularly), to preserve the moisture in braised foods, the top part of which is not immersed in liquid, the piece should be basted often with the braising juices—with a large spoon, a small ladle, or a bulb baster—throughout the entire cooking time.

Even when braised foods are cooked for a very long time, properly cooked they will always remain moist and tender. Meats can be allowed to cook virtually to shreds, to the point where they could be eaten with a spoon—hence the expression *à la cuiller* in the names of some braised dishes and *daubes.* This is why, toward the end of his life, the Duc de Richelieu, who had lost most of his teeth but who was an incurable *gourmand,* demanded that even squab be prepared for him by braising.

Stews (*ragoûts*) are cooked in the same way as braised dishes, starting with browning at the beginning. The principal difference is that the meat or fowl is cut into pieces (as in *boeuf bourguignon, navarin* of lamb, veal Marengo, *coq au vin*). After the pieces have been sealed and browned, they are sometimes *singés,* that is, sprinkled with flour (preferably browned flour, see page 51) that will eventually bind the final sauce. A higher proportion of liquid eliminates the need for basting in stews.

Poaching

Poaching is cooking by immersing a food in a liquid (such as water, broth, meat or fish stock, *court-bouillon,* or a sweet syrup). The poaching liquid at the start may be cold, simmering slightly, or boiling vigorously.

⚜ **Starting with a cold liquid:** This is a form of cooking by "interchange with or without browning."

Beginning with a cold liquid prevents "sealing" and consequently makes it possible to release the flavors of the food to the enhancement of the broth in which it is cooked. This is the situation in a *pot-au-feu,* in which the meat enriches the broth but loses much of its own flavor. A similar richness is achieved in a veal stock (using bones that have first been browned in the oven) or in a fish stock (*without* browning the fish bones).

For the opposite result, that is, to preserve the flavor and aroma of the food, you must enrich the bouillon by incorporating into it seasonings, vegetables, wine, juices of meat or fish, etc.—all of which will "pay back" flavor to the food that cooks with them. For example, poach fish in *court-bouillon* or fish stock; poach a stewing hen in chicken stock or bouillon; poach brains in a *court-bouillon* containing vinegar.

If the foods thus cooked are to be served cold, it is best to let them cool in their cooking liquid; if this is done, reduce the cooking time a little.

All dried beans, lentils, split peas, etc., are cooked starting with cold water. Dried beans should be soaked overnight before cooking. Season the water with salt, pepper, a *bouquet garni*, diced carrot, and onion.

⚜ **Starting with a hot liquid:** This is a form of cooking by "sealing without browning." Beginning with a hot liquid makes it possible to preserve intact virtually all the flavor and nutritive elements.

Green vegetables should be cooked, uncovered, at a rapid boil in a large quantity of salted water; allow 1 to 2 generous teaspoons of coarse salt per quart of water.

In cooking fish *au bleu*, the live fish is given a sharp blow on the head, gutted, sprinkled with vinegar, and plunged into simmering, not boiling, *court-bouillon*.

Noodles and rice are cooked in boiling liquid. They should then be rinsed in warm or cold water to remove any excess starch and to keep them from sticking.

HOW TO COOK GREEN BEANS:

Certain vegetables, among them green beans, contain organic acids which, when they come into contact with heat, produce a change in the color of the vegetable from its original fresh garden green to various shades of yellow or even brownish green.

These acids are also volatile, therefore they can be dispersed rapidly before the color of the bean is damaged. To do this, proceed as follows: In a large pot or saucepan, enameled or otherwise stainless, bring a generous quantity of water, salted with 2 generous teaspoons of coarse salt per quart of water, to a rolling boil. Add the beans, young ones, first snapped and stringed if necessary, and boil them, uncovered, over high heat until they are crisp-tender, testing often as they cook. A fine, small green bean will cook in 4 or 5 minutes; larger beans will necessarily take longer cooking, but the object is to boil them for the minimum time possible. Not only color but also flavor and vitamins will be preserved.

Drain the beans in a colander, then turn them out into a bowl of ice water, and leave them there for 10 seconds. This operation not only stops their cooking, it also "desalts" them, since they were cooked in heavily salted water (heavy salting played its part in their rapid cooking without discoloration).

HOW TO COOK ASPARAGUS:

As we all know, the whole asparagus stalk rarely gets eaten; the tip is tender, the base is stringy and is often left on the plate. Here is a way to improve matters; it depends on a homemade asparagus cooker:

Wash the asparagus, cut off all the woody part of the bottoms of the stalks, and peel the asparagus, running the knife (or a vegetable peeler) from close to the tip downward to the bottom.

The homemade cooker is a tall tin can, such as a fruit-juice can, in which you have poked holes all over the bottom and sides with an ice pick, turning it into a virtual sieve. Stand the asparagus in the can (tying them together loosely if the can is too large for the amount of asparagus).

Put the can in a tall, narrow stockpot, and pour in enough boiling water to come one-third of the way up the asparagus; boil for 3 to 5 minutes, depending on the size of the asparagus. Then add more boiling water to come two-thirds of the way up, and boil for the same length of time. Finally add water to the top of the tips and boil again.

If the asparagus are fresh and of medium size, each stage of the cooking will be about 3 minutes, so that the tough part of the stalk gets 9 minutes of cooking time, the middle 6 minutes, and the tip 3 minutes.

Marinades

Marinades are an alchemy handed down from an earlier age. They were first of all an ingenious means of preserving meats, retarding spoilage, and also considerably enhancing flavor at the same time. Today these *bains épicés* (spice baths) are still useful to flavor both meat and game. They tenderize game (wild boar, deer, etc.) and impart a vigorous "wild" taste to domestic beef and lamb. During the process of slowly impregnating the meat with the flavors of a marinade, keep it in a cool place and turn it over frequently.

Often the marinade is also used as the cooking liquid and in the final preparation of the sauce that will accompany the marinated meat.

⚜ **The traditional uncooked marinade:** The ingredients for an uncooked marinade (*marinade crue*) are 1 onion, 2 shallots, ½ carrot, and a 3-inch piece of celery, all peeled and thinly sliced.

Thyme, bay leaf, 1 clove of garlic, 2 cloves, 6 peppercorns, 6 whole grains of coriander, and a good pinch of salt.

And, 2 generous cups of white or red wine, a scant ⅔ cup of vinegar, and 5 tablespoons of oil.

In a deep dish, such as a baking dish, of a size just large enough to hold the meat comfortably, spread a bed of half of the sliced vegetables. Put in the meat and spread the rest of the vegetables over it. Add the wine, white or red depending on the final recipe, the vinegar, herbs and spices, and then the oil.

⚜ **The traditional cooked marinade:** A cooked marinade (*marinade cuite*) accelerates the process of tenderizing meat. It is made with the same ingredients as the preceding uncooked marinade. But first, in a saucepan, heat a little olive oil and cook the sliced vegetables in it gently until they give off some of their liquid. Then add the wine, vinegar, and herbs and spices, and simmer the marinade over low heat for 30 minutes. Let it cool completely before using.

⚜ **Marinades for fish:** In the South Pacific, raw fish is marinated, or macerated, in a little lemon juice and pepper which gives the effect of partial cooking, and the fish is eaten raw and very thinly sliced.

When fish are to be grilled, they may be macerated in a "simple" marinade. The base is a little oil. The flavorings, depending on the fish and the effect wanted, are thin slices of peeled lemon, thyme, bay leaf, fennel, parsley stems, basil, thinly sliced onion, minced shallot, salt, pepper, saffron, etc.

In northern Europe, fish are marinated in an interesting way: Once the bones are removed from the fish fillets, fresh dill is spread over the fish. Then the fish is buried in a mixture of a generous ½ cup of coarse salt, 1⅓ cups granulated sugar, and 4 tablespoons peppercorns, coarsely crushed. A weight is placed on top and the fish is left to marinate for 24 hours.

HINT:

The wine that usually serves as the base for a marinade can be replaced by an infusion of water or stock in which aromatic herbs (rosemary, thyme, marjoram, basil) have been simmered. Such infusions can also be used for cooking various white meats in flavored steam (*à la vapeur*).

Les herbes & les épices

HERBS, SPICES & CONDIMENTS

All herbs, spices, and condiments should be used with great discretion since their overabundance can unbalance and ruin a dish. It is almost impossible to counteract or repair the damage done by their indiscriminate use in cooking. Remember that heat increases the flavor of many herbs, and that their flavor should always be secondary to that of the food being cooked. These observations apply to desserts and pastries as well, where vanilla, cinnamon, orange and lemon peels are used to spice and flavor them.

The following list is far from complete; it includes only herbs and spices frequently used in French cooking—many more could have been included.

Herbs

Parsley

Fresh parsley is too often thought of as something purely decorative, when it is a delicious garnish (especially deep-fried) for fish and other foods.

Garden-fresh parsley has a wonderful flavor and aroma. Finely chopped parsley leaves are used to flavor many dishes; the stems can be saved and used for a *bouquet garni.*

Chervil

This herb has a fine and delicate flavor. It is used chopped with other herbs to make *fines herbes*, or alone sprinkled into soups and salads.

Tarragon

Freshly chopped, this is another of the herbs used in the *fines herbes* mixture. Tarragon is used in **Béarnaise sauce** (**5**) and many others. Fresh tarragon can be stored in a jar of vinegar for use when it is out of season.

NOTE: *If it is stored in vinegar, be sure to rinse the tarragon off under cold running water briefly before using. Ed.*

Basil

The fragrance of this herb is almost heady and it should be used sparingly; but what sunny memories its aroma evokes! Basil is the primary ingredient used in making *pistou*, a mixture used both in the South of France and in Italy to flavor soups and pasta.

Fresh basil can be puréed with olive oil in an electric blender and stored in a tightly closed jar in the refrigerator. Parsley can be puréed and stored in the same way, but a tasteless oil like peanut oil should be used instead of olive oil.

Rosemary

This herb is almost synonymous with the Mediterranean coast, where it grows wild and perfumes the air with its powerful aroma. Although this herb is often used in *cuisine minceur*, especially as an infusion, it is rarely used in *cuisine gourmande* or traditional French cooking except in marinades, *civets*, or with roast pork.

Don't use too much rosemary in cooking; a little goes a long way. Especially avoid covering grilled meats with it; it tends to "burn" the taste of the meat away.

Mint

Wild mint, spearmint, or peppermint all have an incredibly fresh taste. Mint is used alone in desserts, or mixed in small quantities with other herbs for cooking.

Ever popular in Arab countries, mint infusions were experimented with in *cuisine minceur*.

Mint sauce, an English classic, is often served with lamb or mutton.

Thyme

One of the three components of a *bouquet garni,* thyme can be used alone to flavor roast meat, especially rabbit, but use it with discretion. Thyme is also delicious with lamb, and is used to season certain stuffings and pâtés.

Bay leaf

Another component of the classic *bouquet garni,* bay leaves are a powerful flavoring ingredient, and half of a fresh leaf is usually enough for most dishes. Don't confuse bay leaves with the leaves of the cherry laurel, which, though used to flavor some puddings, can be poisonous if employed too often or in too large quantities.

Fresh and dried fennel

A fresh or dried branch of fennel can be used to grill fish or flavor fish soups. The bulb of fresh Florence fennel is a vegetable that can be cooked like celery or made into salads.

Sage

The taste of sage, slightly bitter, makes me think of autumn.

This herb can be used to flavor fresh broad beans or peas and to season pork or wrap around game birds before roasting.

The young sprouts of this plant can be eaten raw in salads.

Juniper berries

These berries are striking because of their piercing yet pleasant flavor. They are used when marinating game, making sauerkraut, or cooking small game birds, especially thrush. Juniper berries give gin its characteristic taste, and are also used in making other *eaux de vie.*

Bouquet garni

This bundle of herbs is the constant companion of salt and pepper, used to flavor almost all types of stews. It is made with several branches, or stems, of fresh parsley, thyme, and a bay leaf (very little of the last two is needed). To this classic combination can be added a branch of celery, or fresh herbs such as basil, tarragon, or chervil, depending on your personal taste. All the herbs are tied together into a little bundle before being used in cooking. The *bouquet garni* is never served; always remove it and discard it after cooking.

NOTE: *The size of a* bouquet garni *varies with the amount of liquid it is used to flavor. Usually a small* bouquet garni *is sufficient; this is made with half a bay leaf, a finger-size sprig of thyme, and 3 sprigs of fresh parsley.*

If sprigs of thyme are not available, and powdered thyme or thyme leaves must be used, tie them in a little cheesecloth with the broken bay leaf and use like a bouquet garni *(1/4 teaspoon of thyme leaves is about the same as the small sprig of thyme described above). When this is done, the sprigs of parsley are tied together and later removed with the* bouquet garni *bag. Ed.*

Spices

Pepper

Ground, coarsely crushed, or as whole peppercorns, this spice is used constantly in cooking. It is always best to season with pepper just before a food has finished cooking; this way the flavor of the pepper is not lost.

Green peppercorns with their mild, strange, and subtle flavor have a personality all their own. They should be used discriminately to create interesting and unusual dishes. Dried, these same green peppercorns can be placed in a pepper mill, ground, and used like ordinary black or white pepper.

Paprika

This spice, sometimes called "pink pepper," is used primarily to prepare dishes *à la hongroise* (Hungarian-style)—goulash—or to accentuate the reddening of shellfish that are baked in the oven.

Cayenne or chili pepper

Powdered, and in very small doses, this hot and peppery spice can be used in many dishes and sauces instead of pepper; in a mayonnaise, for example.

Nutmeg and mace

The nutmeg is the fruit of a tropical tree, and mace is the lacy envelope that surrounds the nutmeg. Nutmeg is always grated, whereas mace is generally ground or pounded in a mortar before use. Personally, I prefer mace to nutmeg, since its flavor places it somewhere between the taste of nutmeg and cinnamon. Powdered mace, used very discreetly, is the ideal seasoner for white sauces, stuffings, and marinated *foie gras.*

Saffron

Saffron is made from the dried stamen of a particular variety of crocus. Its flavor is at once heavy and strong, as well as full and fruity. It is used in bouillabaisse, fish soups, and rice dishes, but can be added to many foods to give them an interesting and unusual flavor; chicken with mussels is an example.

Cloves

Cloves are the dried flowers of the clove tree. They have long been thought to have strong antiseptic powers. Cloves are a powerful spice and should be used sparingly; an onion stuck with one clove will flavor a whole stew.

Coriander

This spice is especially good in cold sauces, or dishes made with olive oil. I use it in my **Fresh tomato and herb sauce (9).**

Ginger

Ginger, fresh or dried, white or gray, is used in the Far East to flavor meat dishes, but is rarely used in anything but desserts and jellies in French cooking.

Cinnamon

This spice, from the bark of a tropical tree, lends its fine, warm, sweet taste to that of sugar to enliven and enrich many excellent desserts.

Condiments

Salt

Salt, whether coarse or fine, mined or from the sea, is the only mineral used in cooking. Salt is the seasoner *par excellence* and is used in almost everything man cooks.

NOTE: *Coarse salt is often called for in these recipes. When used in small quantities (such as salting water to boil a small quantity of vege-*

*tables), ordinary salt may be used instead although coarse salt is preferable. When food is packed in salt before being cooked—***Sea bream or porgy baked in salt** (63)*—coarse salt must be used. Ed.*

Acid seasoners

In this category are such varied ingredients as lemon juice; vinegars made from red wine, sherry, champagne, or cider; pickles and capers, as well as many other foods preserved (pickled) in vinegar.

NOTE: *Sherry vinegar is frequently used. This is available in specialty food stores; its special flavor is essential to many recipes. Ed.*

Oils

Unless otherwise specified, cooking oils or salad oils are of the tasteless varieties, such as peanut oil for cooking and soybean or sunflower-seed oil for salads.

When olive oil is called for, use only the best first cold-pressed oil. Ed.

Sweeteners

First comes sugar in all of its various forms, then honey, and various flavorings often associated with sweeteners such as vanilla, coffee, chocolate, cinnamon, etc. Sweeteners, though most often used in desserts, are sometimes used with vegetables (such as peas and lettuce); meats (such as duck in orange sauce); sweet-and-sour sauce, so popular in the Far East; or *sauce gastrique* (a reduction of sugar with vinegar used in *cuisine minceur*).

Red fruit jellies, traditionally served with game, and vanilla beans, whose flavor is unrivaled when making desserts, should both have their place in any kitchen cupboard.

Mixed spices and condiments

These carefully blended mixtures have flavors all their own; some prominent examples are:

Curry powder, made from coriander, tumeric, chili peppers, and other spices, is used to season dishes *à l'indienne*—mainly rice, lamb, and chicken.

NOTE: *Curry powders used in France are always quite mild. Use French curry powder or other very mild curry powders in French recipes. Ed.*

Liquid mixtures include soy sauce, Worcestershire sauce, ketchup, etc.

Wine as a condiment

When wine or alcohol is evaporated, usually after deglazing a pan, its flavor is concentrated into an essence that seasons and enlivens many dishes.

Garlic, onions, and shallots, etc.

To the three most prominent members of the onion tribe should be added such relatives as scallions, chives, leeks, and others.

When roasting meat, rather than larding it with pieces of garlic, try placing whole, unpeeled cloves of garlic around the meat instead. Once the meat is cooked, the garlic can be crushed and mixed with the juices in the roasting pan to make a subtle sauce that is easy to digest and delicious as well.

Freshly chopped garlic can be stored if covered with olive oil. Freshly chopped shallot can be stored covered with white wine.

NOTE: *If shallots are not available, scallions or even onion, though quite different, can be used instead. Use 1/4 of a medium onion, or the white of 2 scallions, for each shallot. Ed.*

Les fonds, les liaisons & les sauces

STOCKS, LIAISONS & CLASSIC SAUCES

The renown of French cuisine is born of its sauces. The metaphors used to describe the nature of sauces draw heavily upon the vocabularies of alchemy and magic, botany and horticulture, chemistry and architecture—indeed, any vocabulary including that of poetry.

The *saucier*, sauce chef, is a magician dealing in alchemy, his craft a culinary sleight-of-hand in which well-made stocks become the roots from which sauces, like plants, grow. Binding sauces, with *liaisons*, makes them unctuous and voluptuous, and rounds them out. The great sauces of France must be described as the cornerstones of cuisine.

Stock

Commercially produced canned stocks of real excellence—whether of veal, chicken, or fish—do not exist in France, any more than they do in the United States. To a Frenchman, this is a gross omission in his own country, for were they available and properly made, French housewives could sensibly achieve a sometime dream—to concoct the sauces they eye with envy and apprehension in the books of *grande cuisine.*

Until commerce finally remedies the situation, take heart. A fine stock is not really so difficult—no more so than the annual ritual of canning, preserving, and jam- and jelly-making which has once again become popular. I invite you ladies—and gentlemen—to supposedly "waste" a few weekend afternoons in making a supply of stock.

Note: *Great restaurants always have several stocks on hand for cooking and making sauces. To simplify things, Michel Guérard uses only one kind of stock in the* gourmande *recipes in this book—chicken stock. This basic stock can be made easily at home, but for convenience, a second stock recipe is given as an acceptable shortcut. Ed.*

Fond blanc de volaille I
2 CHICKEN STOCK

Ingredients for approximately 3 quarts stock:

Approximately 4½ pounds chicken carcasses (*see Note*), cut up, or a large stewing hen
2 large carrots, peeled and sliced
½ pound fresh mushrooms, cleaned and sliced
2 shallots, peeled and chopped
2 leeks, trimmed and washed
1 large stalk celery
2 large or 4 small cloves garlic, unpeeled but crushed
⅔ cup dry white wine
4 quarts water
2 small onions, peeled, each stuck with 1 clove
Bouquet garni

Put the cut-up chicken carcasses or stewing hen in a soup pot with the carrots, mushrooms, shallots, leeks, celery, and garlic. Add the white wine and boil for 15 minutes or until almost all of the liquid has evaporated.

Then add the cold water, the onions, and the *bouquet garni.* Simmer the stock gently, partially covered, over low heat for about 3 hours. During this time, skim off any foam that rises to the surface.

Strain the stock—there should be about 3 quarts—through a large sieve into a large bowl. Allow to cool, skim off the fat, then store in a covered container in the refrigerator.

Note: *A restaurant kitchen evidently will have a constant supply of chicken carcasses which can thriftily be made into stock; the home cook cannot count on this. It is convenient—and more economical than buying a whole bird—to buy chicken wings and backs from a market that sells chicken in parts. Ed.*

Fond de volaille II
SHORTCUT CHICKEN STOCK 3

Note: *Michel Guérard has studied the time-consuming aspects of making large quantities of stock in the home kitchen. He worked with several cans of American-made chicken broth which he freshened up simply by simmering the broth with fresh vegetables and giblets—as many American cooks also do—to make this shortcut chicken stock. Ed.*

Ingredients for 3 cups stock:

- 3½ cups canned clear chicken broth
- 1 cup water
- 1 medium onion, peeled and coarsely chopped
- 1 small carrot, peeled and coarsely chopped
- 1 stalk celery, coarsely chopped
- 1 leek, white part only, washed and thinly sliced
- 1 or 2 large fresh mushrooms, cleaned and coarsely chopped
- Several sprigs parsley
- ½ bay leaf
- A pinch of dried thyme or a small sprig fresh thyme

If you are making a chicken dish the same day, you may also have available the *abbatis*, that is, the gizzard (cut it up), heart, and neck, plus wing tips and fresh chicken bones that you might otherwise throw away. Add these to the ingredients if convenient.

Combine everything in a saucepan, and simmer, partially covered, over low heat for ½ hour. Strain the stock through a sieve, allow to cool, then store, covered, in the refrigerator.

Note: *This stock is significantly different from the real thing in that it contains no gelatin. Ed.*

The Principles of Binding Sauces (Liaisons)

It is much easier to make successful sauces if you understand how they work and why. The objective is to bind and enrich a light stock or liquid to make a thickened sauce. Classically, this is done in the following ways:

⚜ **Binding with flour:** This is being done less and less today. Nevertheless, handled with finesse, binding with flour is better for you than the enrichment of sauces with outlandish quantities of butter and reduced cream. However, my personal views about sauces lead me not to make much use of either of these methods, even in *cuisine gourmande* and very rarely in *cuisine minceur.*

Binding with cooked flour: *Les roux*

This is one of the ways of binding a liquid through the action of starch in flour. Whether the *roux* is to be brown, light brown, or white, it is made with equal amounts, *by weight,* of flour and butter—although half the amount of butter can be used to make a lighter sauce.

Ordinary flour is usually used, but cornstarch, arrowroot, potato starch, rice flour, etc., may be used instead. The liquid may be milk, chicken, veal, or beef broth or stock, fish *fumet* or stock, red or white wine, etc.

A standard example, to make a *roux blanc* for approximately 1 quart of sauce:

5 tablespoons butter (2½ ounces)
½ cup flour (2½ ounces)
1 quart liquid

The process, well known to all, is to melt the butter, add the flour, and stir very briskly with a whisk until, thanks to the elasticity of the gluten in the flour, you get a smooth, light paste which you then simmer very gently for 5 or 10 minutes. The mixture is not allowed to color at all.

The *roux* is allowed to cool a little. The liquid, boiling hot, is poured over the *roux* and beaten with a whisk to eliminate all lumps. The mixture is brought back to a boil and simmered for 20 minutes. Heavy at first, the sauce will become lighter as it cooks.

Traditional uses for *roux blanc* are for *sauce béchamel* and for chicken and fish *velouté* sauces.

NOTE: *Cold liquids may also be added to a* roux. *In this case, do not allow the* roux *to cool before adding the liquid. Ed.*

For a *roux blond*, the butter and flour are allowed to color together lightly. For a *roux brun*, they are allowed to brown. They must be stirred often with a whisk. The remainder of the process is the same.

An improvement can be made in the *roux brun* by first spreading the flour on a baking sheet and letting it brown lightly in the oven (*farine torréfiée*). The butter then will not have to cook as long for the *roux* to achieve its color.

Similar in spirit to the *roux* is the technique of dusting with flour (or browned flour) the pieces of meat that are sautéed and browned in fat before the liquid is added to make *ragoûts*, stews, *estouffades* (very slowly cooked stews), and brown fricassees.

Binding with uncooked flour: *Liaisons à cru et à froid*

With potato starch: When a sauce seems too thin, it can be bound with a mixture of potato starch dissolved in cold water or white wine. Pour the mixture gradually into the boiling sauce, beating rapidly with a whisk. Use from 2 tablespoons to ½ cup of starch for each quart of liquid, and boil for 15 minutes.

With *beurre manié* or *crème maniée:* Again for a sauce that seems too thin, cream together either butter or *crème fraîche* with flour (which amounts to the same thing as an uncooked *roux*) in the proportion of 1 part flour to 2 parts butter or cream. Beat the mixture bit by bit into the simmering sauce with a whisk until you achieve the consistency you want. The sauce starts to thicken almost immediately.

⚜ **Binding with egg yolks:** The yolks are first beaten with a whisk (cream may then be added), then beaten into a cupful of the hot liquid to be thickened into a sauce. This mixture is then stirred into the saucepan of hot liquid. Continue heating the sauce, still whisking, but of course do not attempt to boil it to make it thicken further. Above 160° F, the yolks will begin to harden and the sauce will curdle.

Traditional uses for *liaisons* with egg yolks are in *velouté* soups, *sauce poulette, blanquettes,* etc.

Binding with egg yolks and water: *Le sabayon léger*

Beat together with a whisk egg yolks and cold water in the proportion of 4 egg yolks to 6 tablespoons of water. As air is beaten into the mixture, it foams and grows in volume. When it has foamed up as much as it will, whisk it rapidly into the boiling soup or sauce you want to thicken. The egg yolks, in suspension with the water, "set" when they come into contact with the hot liquid and give it added volume and an effect of great lightness.

⚜ **Binding with the blood of the meat:** This is done with the blood of pork and game, and also of fish and lamprey eel, and (the same principle) with lobster coral and tomalley (all sometimes mixed with *crème fraîche*) replacing the yolks of eggs. The sauce is not allowed to boil.

Traditional uses are in *coq au vin, civets* of game and fish, *matelotes* (freshwater fish stews), and lobster *à l'américaine.*

⚜ **Binding with fat:** This includes butter, cream, and *foie gras.*

Binding with butter or cream: *Liaison au beurre ou à la crème fraîche*

The expression is *monter une sauce au beurre,* to finish or "build" a sauce with butter. The aim is not only to thicken but especially to enrich the sauce. The method is, over very low heat, to swirl one by one small pieces of cold butter into the hot sauce by shaking the pan so that the sauce spins around the sides of the pan.

One may also boil the sauce over brisk heat, add butter, and continue boiling until the butter has melted; see Comment in the recipe for **Foamy butter sauce (6).** The sauce is then more shiny, less creamy.

To thicken a sauce with cream, simply bring the sauce and cream to a boil together and simmer until the sauce is reduced to the desired consistency.

Binding with *foie gras*

This is somewhat similar to a *liaison* with butter. In an electric blender, purée together a mixture of 2 parts *foie gras* and 1 part *crème fraîche.* Off the heat, beat the *foie gras* mixture into the hot sauce with a whisk.

⚜ **Binding by emulsion:** This also includes the use of fat. Binding by emulsion is the successful marriage of two ingredients that do not mix of their own accord, such as water with oil, cream, or butter, for which a third ingredient such as egg yolk or mustard serves as matchmaker or catalyst to make the union possible.

The best-known cold emulsified sauce is mayonnaise. The famous sauces emulsified over heat are the *béarnaise* and hollandaise sauces and their derivatives, and also **Foamy butter sauce** (*beurre blanc*). Many cooks find these sauces difficult to make. The techniques are described in the section on classic sauces that follows.

⚜ **Binding with vegetable purées:** This *liaison* is made with a precise amount of very finely puréed cooked vegetables (easily done in an electric blender). Depending on the recipe, the vegetables may either be cooked with the meat or fish for which they will later bind the sauce, or they may be cooked separately. These binding purées (*purées de liaison*) have a high vitamin content and the vitamins are all the more easily absorbed because the cellulose in the vegetables is broken down in the puréeing process.

The subtle and flavorful vegetable mixtures of which these *liaisons* are composed are based on new and delicious combinations. It is also possible to create other flavorful sauces with judicious combinations of fruits and vegetables.

Classic Sauces

Here are a few recipes dear from time immemorial to the cooking of France: mayonnaise, *béarnaise*, and foamy butter sauce (*beurre blanc*).

Sauce mayonnaise
4 MAYONNAISE

Ingredients for approximately 1 cup sauce:

- 1 egg yolk
- 1 teaspoon Dijon mustard
- A pinch salt
- A pinch white pepper or cayenne
- 1 cup oil (peanut, olive, or other oil, as you prefer)
- A few drops wine vinegar, or lemon juice if using olive oil

In a bowl and with a wire whisk, beat together the egg yolk, mustard, salt, and pepper. Then, a few drops at a time, slowly begin adding the oil, beating it into the other ingredients. As the mixture thickens, the oil may be added in a very thin stream. Bit by bit, add either the vinegar or lemon juice to thin out the sauce a little. When all the oil has been added, taste and adjust the seasoning if necessary.

COMMENTS:

The egg yolk and oil should both be at room temperature.

It is important to add the oil very slowly, especially in the beginning.

If the mayonnaise curdles, put a small spoonful of mustard in another bowl and bit by bit whisk the curdled sauce into it.

Mayonnaise should be stored in a cool place, but preferably not in the refrigerator. Some oils (such as olive oil) will harden under refrigeration and the sauce will separate.

Serve this sauce with cold meats or fish. Use to make salads with cooked vegetables or meats.

VARIANTS:

Sauce aïoli—Mayonnaise made with olive oil to which cooked mashed potato and several crushed cloves of garlic have been added.

Sauce antiboise—Mayonnaise made with olive oil, garlic, coriander, chervil, and parsley.

Sauce andalouse—Mayonnaise to which tomato paste and chopped green pepper or pimiento are added.

Sauce tartare—Mayonnaise to which capers, pickles, onions, parsley, chervil, and tarragon are added.

Sauce vendanger—Mayonnaise to which red wine and shallots are added.

Sauce Vincent—Mayonnaise to which sorrel purée, parsley, chervil, water cress, chives, and hard-boiled eggs are added.

Sauce béarnaise
BÉARNAISE SAUCE 5

NOTE: *In making all emulsified sauces over heat, there is constant manipulation of the heat so that the sauces will not curdle or separate. The usual dodge of the amateur cook is to make the sauces over hot water; this is convenient, and it works, but it takes much longer than whisking the sauces over direct heat.*

Over direct heat, the tendency is to fiddle constantly with the control knob of the stove to control the heat, which is a nuisance and does not work very well. What chefs and experienced cooks know instinctively (and therefore often neglect to mention in their recipes) is that you can leave the heat at a moderate, or even surprisingly high, level and control the temperature of the sauce as you whisk it merely by holding the saucepan up away from the heat to lower the temperature, or by bringing the pan down closer to the stove to raise the temperature. Ed.

Ingredients for 8 servings:

- 6½ tablespoons red-wine vinegar
- ⅓ cup finely chopped shallot
- 1 teaspoon coarsely crushed peppercorns
- 2 tablespoons fresh chopped tarragon (*see Comment*)
- 1 teaspoon chopped fresh chervil or parsley
- A pinch of salt
- 5 egg yolks
- ⅝ pound softened unsalted butter (or 2½ sticks), broken into pieces, or 1⅓ cups *crème fraîche* (*see p. 352*) or heavy cream

Additional freshly chopped tarragon and chervil or parsley (optional)

UTENSILS:

Small heavy-bottomed saucepan
Whisk
Saucepan of warm, not boiling, water (*bain-marie*)
Sieve (optional)

In the heavy-bottomed saucepan place the vinegar, shallot, pepper, tarragon, chervil, and salt. Boil over medium heat, uncovered, for about 5 minutes or until the liquid is reduced to about three-quarters; there should be a soft, juicy, but not liquid "marmalade" left. Allow to cool.

Off the heat and with the whisk, beat the egg yolks into the vinegar-shallot reduction. Put the saucepan back over low heat and heat, whisking constantly, until the mixture thickens and becomes creamy. It must not heat too much; although hot, you should be able to touch it with the back of your finger without feeling a burning sensation. The yolks have thickened enough when the movement of the whisk exposes streaks of the bottom of the pan.

Still whisking, add the butter bit by bit; the sauce is ready when the last piece of butter has been absorbed and the whole is thickened —creamy but not heavy. Set aside over warm water; beware of too hot water in the *bain-marie.*

The sauce may be served as is, or it may be strained through a sieve, in which case you then add a little more chopped fresh tarragon and chervil.

COMMENTS:

When fresh tarragon is not in season, use 4 teaspoons of chopped tarragon preserved in vinegar or 2 scant teaspoons of dried tarragon.

The essential point in making a *béarnaise* is the whisking, which equalizes the temperature of the egg yolks as they coagulate and also beats air into the sauce to lighten it.

Some things may go wrong:

The egg yolks become too thick. The heat is too high; lower it and add a few drops of cold water.

The egg yolks foam but do not thicken. The heat is too low.

In the end, the sauce curdles. This can happen if it has cooled too much or if it has gotten too hot. If it is too cold, put a little hot water in a bowl and gradually whisk the sauce into it. If it is too hot, do the same thing with a little cold water in the bowl. This will rescue the sauce, though it will not regain the lightness it should have had.

This sauce can also be made in a blender. Once the egg yolks have been heated and thickened, place them in a blender and add the butter or cream little by little. You are guaranteed a perfect sauce.

Serve this sauce with poached eggs, poached or grilled fish, grilled meats, or asparagus.

VARIANTS:

Sauce Choron—Béarnaise to which 2 tablespoons of peeled and diced tomatoes are added (for ⅝ pound of butter).

Sauce arlésienne—Same as Choron, plus anchovy purée.

Sauce Foyot—Béarnaise to which a little *glace de viande* is added.

Sauce paloise—Béarnaise made with fresh mint instead of tarragon.

Sauce tyrolienne—Béarnaise made with oil instead of butter, to which a little tomato paste is added.

Sauce hollandaise—Béarnaise in which cold water is used instead of the aromatic reduction when thickening the egg yolks (1 teaspoon of cold water per egg yolk). The sauce is flavored with the juice of half a lemon (for ⅝ pound butter).

Variants of the hollandaise are *sauce mousseline,* to which whipped cream is added at the end; *sauce maltaise,* to which a *julienne* of parboiled orange peel is added; and *sauce moutarde,* in which Dijon mustard is added to the hollandaise.

Sauce au beurre blanc
6 FOAMY BUTTER SAUCE

This is a cousin of the other emulsified sauces in which the egg yolk has been dispensed with.

Ingredients for 4 servings:

3 tablespoons water
3 tablespoons wine vinegar
2 heaping tablespoons finely chopped shallots
½ pound softened butter, broken into little pieces
1 teaspoon lemon juice
Salt and pepper

UTENSILS:

Small saucepan
Wire whisk

SERVE WITH:

Lobster, spiny lobster, or crayfish in court-bouillon (60)
Salmon papillotes (61)
Broiled sole with oysters and chive sauce (67)
Mixed seafood steamed with seaweed (68)

Place the water, vinegar, and shallots in a small saucepan and bring to a boil. Let the liquid reduce until the shallots have softened and there are only 2 tablespoons of damp shallots left in the saucepan. Remove the pot from the heat and allow to cool for 2 to 3 minutes; the shallots should still be warm. Begin adding the butter little by little, whisking the sauce constantly. Test the temperature of the sauce with your finger. It should never be allowed to cool completely and should always be warm to the touch (see Note at the beginning of **Béarnaise sauce (5)**. Leave the saucepan directly on the burner and whisk vigorously while adding the last third of the butter, then add the lemon juice, salt, and pepper, remove from the heat, and keep the sauce warm in a *bain-marie* or double boiler over warm, not hot, water if not serving immediately.

COMMENTS:

Foamy butter sauce may also be made without whisking, using the same ingredients given above but proceeding as follows:

Reduce the water/vinegar/shallot mixture only by two-thirds and add all the butter (cold) in one piece to the rapidly boiling mixture in the pot. Continue boiling rapidly until all the butter has melted. The sauce is ready to serve.

Four tablespoons of cold water may be whisked into this version of the sauce once the butter has melted; this will make the sauce foamier and lighter.

Both versions of this sauce may be strained before serving to remove the chopped shallots. I personally prefer serving the sauce with the pieces of shallot in it.

This sauce can be varied by the addition of 1 heaping tablespoon of lemon or lime peel just before serving. The peel should have previously been dropped into boiling water for 2 minutes, cooled, and cut into very fine *julienne* strips before being added to the sauce.

In another variation of this sauce, 1 cup, tightly packed, of fresh sorrel leaves cut into fine *julienne* strips may be added instead of lemon or lime peel.

⚜ **SOME GENERAL COMMENTS ON SAUCES:** For a sauce that is based on a flavorful stock but still seems somewhat flat, add an ingredient with an incisive taste that will wake it up, such as a squeeze of lemon juice or a few drops of vinegar.

For a sauce that has acquired a slightly bitter or even acid taste, add a pinch of sugar or a dash of a fortified wine such as port, with, if necessary, a little cream.

It is often preferable when using wine in sauces to reduce them by boiling to diminish their volume and to evaporate their alcoholic content. For white wine, reduction lessens its acidity. For red wine, reduction heightens its flavor.

The same thing applies to brandies. However, fortified wines such as sherry or port, whose flavor is easily destroyed, usually do their work best unheated and added at the last minute.

Remember also for sauces based on a *roux* that any acid ingredient, such as lemon juice, must be added after the cooking and thickening of the sauce—in, for instance, a *blanquette* or *sauce ivoire.* If added at the beginning, it will interfere with the action of the *liaison* and thin out the sauce as well.

In emulsified sauces, on the contrary, lemon juice activates the coagulation of the egg yolks.

If the sauce contains milk, vegetables cannot be cooked in it because their acid content will curdle the milk. Exceptions are spinach, cabbage, and cauliflower.

Part Two

Les sauces

SAUCES

Sauce rouille
"RUST" SAUCE 7

Ingredients for 6 to 8 servings:

2 eggs
2 anchovy fillets
1 clove garlic, peeled
1 teaspoon tomato paste
2 egg yolks
Salt and pepper
1 teaspoon Dijon mustard
1 cup olive oil
1 teaspoon lemon juice
A pinch of powdered saffron
¼ teaspoon hot red-pepper paste (*or 1 teaspoon Tabasco; Ed.*)

UTENSILS:

Saucepan
Electric blender
2 bowls
Wire whisk

SERVE WITH:

Lobster, spiny lobster, or crayfish in court-bouillon (60)
Bouillabaisse of salt cod (66)
Mixed seafood steamed with seaweed (68)
All broiled or grilled fish

Cook the 2 eggs in boiling water for 8 minutes, then cool under running water. Shell the eggs and remove the yolks. Place the cooked egg yolks in a blender with the anchovy fillets, garlic, and tomato paste. Blend for 1 minute, then pour the mixture into a bowl and reserve.

In another bowl place the 2 raw egg yolks and the salt, pepper, and mustard. Beat together with a whisk, and make a mayonnaise by adding the olive oil a little at a time, whisking constantly. As the sauce thickens, add a little of the lemon juice, then, still whisking, continue adding the oil and lemon juice until both have been completely incorporated into the sauce. Once all the oil has been added, mix the reserved blended ingredients into the sauce with a spoon. Finally stir in the saffron and add hot red-pepper paste or Tabasco to taste; the sauce should be pale rust color when finished.

NOTE: *If you are making less sauce than the amount indicated here, the anchovies, hard-boiled egg yolks, garlic, and tomato paste must be pounded to a purée in a mortar, not in a blender. Ed.*

Nage ou court-bouillon pour crustacés et poissons
8 COURT-BOUILLON

Ingredients for making 5½ cups:

2 carrots, peeled and thinly sliced
White part of 1 leek, thinly sliced
8 baby onions, peeled and thinly sliced
2 shallots, peeled and thinly sliced
5½ cups water
2 teaspoons coarse salt
Zest of ½ lemon

2 unpeeled cloves garlic
1 teaspoon green peppercorns
1 clove
Bouquet garni, including a sprig of fresh fennel
1 cup dry white wine

UTENSILS:

Large pot
Large bowl

USED IN MAKING:

Crayfish soup (26)
Roast lobster (59)
Lobster, spiny lobster, or crayfish in court-bouillon (60)
Seafood pot-au-feu (69)

Place all the ingredients listed above (except the wine) in a pot and simmer together uncovered for 30 minutes (the vegetables should remain slightly firm). Add the wine, bring the mixture to a boil, boil for 30 seconds more, then remove from the heat. Remove the *bouquet garni,* garlic, lemon peel, and clove. Pour the liquid and remaining vegetables into a bowl and allow to cool, then store in the refrigerator until needed.

COMMENT:

Adding the wine at the end of the cooking time gives a fresh taste to the *court-bouillon.*

Note: *The vegetables that are left in the* court-bouillon *should not be strained out or mashed. They often become part of the garnish or sauce in recipes where* court-bouillon *is called for. Ed.*

Sauce vierge
9 FRESH TOMATO AND HERB SAUCE

Ingredients for 1⅔ cups sauce, or 4 servings:

3 large tomatoes
2 whole unpeeled cloves garlic
2 tablespoons freshly chopped chervil
2 tablespoons freshly chopped parsley
1 tablespoon freshly chopped tarragon
A pinch of powdered coriander
1 cup olive oil
Salt and pepper

UTENSILS:

Small saucepan

SERVE WITH:

Lobster, spiny lobster, or crayfish in court-bouillon (60)
Bass cooked in seaweed (62)
Sea bream or porgy baked in salt (63)
Mixed seafood steamed with seaweed (68)
Seafood pot-au-feu (69)

Peel, seed, and chop the tomatoes as explained in the recipe for **Raw diced tomatoes (96)**. Place the tomato pulp in a small saucepan with the rest of the ingredients. Simmer the sauce very slowly over low heat for 30 minutes. Serve either hot or cold. (Remove the cloves of garlic before serving.)

Sauce coulis de tomates fraîches
FRESH TOMATO SAUCE 10

Ingredients for a generous ¾ cup sauce, or 4 servings:

2 medium tomatoes
3 teaspoons olive oil
1 clove garlic, unpeeled but crushed
1 shallot, peeled and sliced
1 teaspoon tomato paste
¾ cup **chicken stock** (2) (3)
Bouquet garni
Salt and pepper

UTENSILS:

Small saucepan
Electric blender

SERVE WITH:

Foie gras pot-au-feu (52)
Boiled tongues with vegetables and tomato sauce (94)
The Pot-au-Feu Restaurant's pot-au-feu (95)

Peel, seed, and chop the tomatoes as explained in the recipe for **Raw diced tomatoes** (96).

Heat the oil in a small saucepan and add the garlic and shallot. Stir in the fresh tomato pulp, the tomato paste, and *bouquet garni.* Cover the pot and simmer the sauce for 20 minutes, then remove the *bouquet garni* and pour the sauce into a blender. Blend until the sauce is smooth, and taste for salt and pepper. Serve either hot or cold.

NOTE: *If it seems too thin, this sauce can be thickened after it is blended by boiling it over high heat for about 5 minutes, stirring constantly. Ed.*

11 *Sauce beurrée aux truffes* TRUFFLE SAUCE

Ingredients for 1 cup sauce, or 4 servings:

2 whole canned truffles (*for substitution, see Comment*)
2 teaspoons butter
3/8 cup heavy cream
Salt and pepper
1/4 pound softened butter, broken into pieces
1 teaspoon lemon juice

UTENSIL:

Small saucepan

SERVE WITH:

Foie gras pot-au-feu (52)

Drain the truffles and save 1/3 cup of their juice for this recipe. Cut the truffles into fine *julienne* strips. Heat the 2 teaspoons of butter in a small saucepan and sauté the truffles over low heat for 2 minutes, then stir in the cream and the reserved truffle juice. Salt and pepper lightly. Boil the sauce for about 6 minutes or until it is reduced by half, then lower the heat and add the remaining butter a piece at a time. While adding the butter, shake the saucepan continually, using a circular motion so that the sauce spins around the sides of the pan. The sauce will thicken and become creamy. Once all the butter has been added, add the lemon juice and taste for seasoning. The sauce can be served immediately or kept warm in a *bain-marie* or double boiler. If the sauce is allowed to cool, reheat it over very low heat.

COMMENTS:

Any fresh mushrooms may be used to make this sauce, but certain changes have to be made. If, for example, fresh white mushrooms are used, substitute 3 medium mushrooms for the amount of truffles given above. Once the mushrooms have been sliced like the truffles, they are sautéed in butter with 1 thinly sliced shallot. Instead of truffle juice, 2 tablespoons of red port or madeira, plus 1 teaspoon of finely chopped tarragon, are added to the sauce. The cream, butter, and lemon juice are added as described above.

Sauce crème de ciboulettes
CHIVE SAUCE 12

Ingredients for approximately 2 cups sauce, or 4 to 6 servings:

2 heaping tablespoons peeled and chopped shallots
¼ cup dry white wine
4 teaspoons **chicken stock** (**2**) (**3**)
1½ cups heavy cream
1 tablespoon **water-cress purée** (**102**)
3 tablespoons cold water
1 tablespoon finely chopped fresh chives
6½ tablespoons softened butter
1 tablespoon lemon juice
Salt and pepper

UTENSILS:

2 small saucepans
Electric blender

SERVE WITH:

Sea bream or porgy baked in salt (**63**)
Broiled sole with oysters and chive sauce (**67**)
Veal steaks with chive sauce (**86**)

Place the shallots and white wine in a small saucepan and boil slowly, uncovered, until almost all the wine has evaporated. Approximately 1 tablespoon of slightly damp, softened shallots should remain after evaporating the wine. Remove the pan from the heat.

In a second small saucepan, mix the stock and heavy cream. Boil, uncovered, until the mixture has reduced by one-third, or until it is rich and creamy. Remove from the heat.

In a blender, place the softened shallots, **water-cress purée,** cold water, chives, and butter. Blend for about 30 seconds, then add the stock-cream mixture and lemon juice. Blend for 30 seconds more, or until smooth. Taste and add salt and pepper if needed. Serve hot. The sauce can be kept warm in a *bain-marie* or double boiler, or reheat gently just before serving.

13 *Sauce coulis d'écrevisses*
CRAYFISH SAUCE

Ingredients for 3 cups sauce, or 6 to 8 servings:

¼ cup olive oil
¼ cup cooking oil
2¼ pounds live crayfish, approximately 32 (*for substitutions, see Comment and Note*)
2 medium carrots, peeled and finely chopped
1 large onion, peeled and finely chopped
1 shallot, peeled and finely chopped
1 clove garlic, unpeeled but crushed
Bouquet garni

3 tablespoons cognac or armagnac
3 tablespoons red port
1 cup dry white wine
3 raw diced tomatoes (96)
1 tablespoon tomato paste
Salt and pepper
1⅔ cups *crème fraîche* (*see p.* 352) or heavy cream
½ teaspoon finely chopped fresh tarragon

UTENSILS:

Large pot or *sauteuse* with cover
Slotted spoon
Mortar and pestle, electric blender, or food processor
Large sieve
Ladle or wooden spoon
2 bowls

SERVE WITH:

Puff pastry with crayfish and sweet onions (46)
Crayfish millefeuille (47)
Scallop mousse with crayfish sauce (56)

Heat the two oils in a large pot, add the live crayfish, cover, and shake the pot over medium heat for about 6 minutes. Uncover the pot and remove the crayfish with a slotted spoon. Using your fingers, remove the meat from the tail of each crayfish. Save the shells and heads for making the sauce. Place the tail meat on a separate plate and reserve. Place all the heads and crayfish shells in a large mortar, and pound until they are coarsely ground, or grind them in a heavy-duty blender or in a food processor.

Reheat the pot the crayfish were cooked in, and place in it the carrots, onion, shallot, garlic, *bouquet garni*, and crushed crayfish heads and shells. Simmer together, uncovered, for 5 minutes, shaking the pot occasionally, then add the cognac and port, and cover the pot. The liquid should boil very slowly and cook until it has been reduced by half. Then add the white wine, freshly chopped tomatoes, tomato paste, salt, and pepper. Continue boiling, uncovered, until the sauce has been reduced by one-third. Stir in the cream and the fresh tarragon, and continue boiling slowly for 10 minutes more.

Pour the contents of the pot through a large sieve into a bowl. Use a ladle or wooden spoon to squeeze as much sauce as possible out of the cooked shells and vegetables. The bowl containing the strained sauce may be kept in the refrigerator until needed. The crayfish tails should be kept covered in the refrigerator in a separate bowl; depending on the recipe, they will be added to the sauce or used separately. Reheat the sauce before serving.

COMMENTS:

Live, small swimming crabs or soft-shelled crabs may be used instead of crayfish. The crabs should be cut into four pieces before being sautéed in the oil.

NOTE: *If neither crayfish nor crabs are available, large whole shrimp may be used instead, but the flavor will be very different. Ed.*

Sauce mousse de cresson

14 WHIPPED WATER-CRESS SAUCE

Ingredients for 2⅔ cups sauce, or 8 to 10 servings:

- 1½ teaspoons gelatin
- 1½ tablespoons cold water
- 2 teaspoons butter
- 1 generous tablespoon finely chopped shallots
- 1 generous cup, tightly packed, cleaned water-cress leaves
- 1 tablespoon finely chopped fresh tarragon
- ½ teaspoon finely chopped garlic
- 2 tablespoons dry white wine
- ⅔ cup heavy cream
- Salt and pepper
- 1 teaspoon lemon juice

FOR THE WHIPPED CREAM:

- 1 cup cold heavy cream

UTENSILS:

- Small bowl
- Small saucepan with cover
- Wire whisk
- Electric blender
- 2 large bowls (preferably metal)
- Wooden spatula

SERVE WITH:

Eel terrine (42)

In a bowl, moisten the gelatin with the cold water. Melt the butter in a small saucepan and add the shallots. Cook for about 1 minute; they should soften but not color. Add the water cress, tarragon, garlic, and white wine. Cover the pan and simmer for 1 minute, then add the cream, salt, and pepper. Boil the sauce slowly, uncovered, for 10 minutes, stirring occasionally as the liquid evaporates. Remove the pan from the heat and add the gelatin, stirring the sauce constantly with a wire whisk. Pour the sauce into a blender, add the lemon juice, and blend for 1 minute or until the sauce is perfectly smooth. Pour the sauce into a large bowl and allow to cool before preparing the whipped cream.

While the water-cress mixture is cooling, place a mixing bowl (preferably stainless steel) in the freezer. When ready to make the whipped cream, remove the bowl from the freezer, pour in the cold cream, and whisk for about 1½ minutes. For the first minute beat gently, using a relaxed circular movement of the wrist. The cream will begin to puff up, and should grow by about one-third its original volume. During the last 30 seconds, beat the cream vigorously. It will become very thick and foamy, but it should not peak like egg whites when finished. If the cream is beaten too long and becomes too stiff, it will not be able to create the "creamy" texture that is desired when it is mixed with the water-cress purée.

Once the lightly whipped cream is ready and the water-cress mixture is cold, they can be mixed together. Pour the cream on top of the water-cress mixture and delicately fold it in as you would egg whites, that is, cut down the middle of the cream with a flat wooden spatula and gently life up one-half of the cream and water cress and fold them over the other half. Cut and fold the contents of the bowl in this way until you have a perfectly homogeneous mixture. The sauce may be served immediately or refrigerated before serving.

NOTE: *If stored for very long, the sauce will stiffen because of the gelatin in it. Simply stir it gently with a wire whisk before serving to restore its original creamy texture. Ed.*

Sauce mousse de tomate
WHIPPED TOMATO SAUCE 15

Ingredients and procedure are the same as in the previous recipe except the 3 heaping tablespoons of **Raw diced tomatoes (96)** plus 1 tablespoon of tomato paste are used instead of water cress when making this sauce.

SERVE WITH:

Carp or mackerel terrine (*see p. 122*)

COMMENTS:

Cold whipped sauces can be made with almost any vegetable. Leafy green vegetables (spinach, lettuce, or fresh herbs) may be used just like the water cress. Other vegetables (asparagus, leeks, celery, etc.) should be peeled and diced before being cooked to make this kind of sauce. Mixing vegetables can produce interesting results: fresh mint and leek sauce, broccoli and asparagus sauce, etc.

16 VINAIGRETTE GOURMANDE

Ingredients for 3 tablespoons sauce, or 2 servings:

A pinch of salt
A pinch of pepper
1 teaspoon lemon juice
2 teaspoons olive oil
2 teaspoons salad oil
1 teaspoon sherry vinegar
1 teaspoon finely chopped fresh chervil
1 teaspoon finely chopped fresh tarragon

UTENSILS:

Small bowl
Small wire whisk

SERVE WITH:

Salade gourmande (29)
Farmer's salad (27)
Salad from the parson's garden (31)
Duck "ham" and green-pea salad (32)
Smoked fish salad (33)

In a small bowl use a whisk to beat together the salt, pepper, and lemon juice, then add the two oils and lastly the sherry vinegar, chervil, and tarragon. Whisk well before pouring the sauce over a salad. The *vinaigrette* may be made several hours in advance.

COMMENTS:

Walnut oil (if available) may be used instead of salad oil, in which case red-wine vinegar should also be substituted for sherry vinegar. Parsley and chives may be used instead of chervil and tarragon.

Beurre vigneron
HERB BUTTER 17

Ingredients for ⅔ cup herb butter, or 6 to 8 servings:

3 tablespoons finely chopped shallots
¼ large clove garlic (or ½ small clove), peeled and finely chopped
3 tablespoons dry white wine
¼ pound softened butter
1 tablespoon finely chopped fresh parsley
1 tablespoon finely chopped fresh chervil
1 teaspoon lemon juice
1 scant teaspoon salt
Pepper
A pinch of nutmeg

UTENSILS:

Small saucepan
Small bowl
Fork

SERVE WITH:

Salt-roasted rib steak with herb butter (89)
Steak and bacon, country-style (88)

Place the shallots, garlic, and wine in a small saucepan and boil slowly for 2 minutes over low heat. The shallots will soften and about a teaspoon of liquid will remain in the pan. Pour the contents of the pan into a bowl and allow to cool. Once the shallots are cold, add all the remaining ingredients to the bowl and mix them all together with a fork; press the prongs of the fork repeatedly into the mixture until all the ingredients have been evenly blended into the butter. Serve immediately, or refrigerate, but then allow to soften before serving.

Les petits croûtons apéritifs

APPETIZERS

Les petits croûtons apéritifs
APPETIZER TOAST 18

The following seven recipes are for small appetizers all made with little pieces of toasted bread topped with different garnishes. The recipes only hint at the variety of interesting appetizers that can be made using a little imagination and the basic techniques described here. All these appetizers use toasted bread prepared in advance.

Ingredients for 8 small pieces of toast, or 4 servings:

8 slices bread, ¼ inch thick, cut from a small French-style loaf, or 8 circles, 2½ inches in diameter, cut out of slices of sandwich bread
2 tablespoons softened butter

Butter the pieces of bread on both sides and toast them on both sides under the broiler; or, fry them in the butter like *croûtons*. Garnish as described in one of the following recipes.

Note: *Eight of any of the following appetizers are usually sufficient for four servings, but it's best to make at least two different kinds, allowing one of each for each person. Ed.*

19 *Croûtons au fromage et au lard*
CHEESE AND BACON APPETIZERS

Ingredients for 8 small appetizers, or 4 servings:

1 cup grated Swiss cheese
1 tablespoon beaten egg
2 tablespoons *crème fraîche* (*see p. 352*)
Salt, pepper, and nutmeg
8 pieces **appetizer toast (18)**
8 pieces bacon each 1½ inches long

UTENSILS:

Electric blender
Baking sheet

Place the cheese, beaten egg, and cream in a blender. Blend for 1½ minutes, or until the mixture is perfectly smooth and homogeneous. Sprinkle in a little salt, pepper, and nutmeg. Spread this mixture over the eight pieces of toast, and top each with a piece of bacon. Place the garnished pieces of toast on a baking sheet, and broil for about 2 minutes just before serving. Serve hot from the broiler.

20 *Croûtons aux tomates et à la ciboulette*
FRESH TOMATO AND CHIVE APPETIZERS

Ingredients for 8 appetizers, or 4 servings:

Scant ½ cup **raw diced tomatoes (96)**
2 tablespoons *crème fraîche* (*see p. 352*) or heavy cream
1 tablespoon finely chopped shallots
2 tablespoons finely chopped fresh chives
1 teaspoon lemon juice
½ teaspoon Tabasco sauce (or to taste)
Salt and pepper
8 pieces **appetizer toast (18)**

Mix all the ingredients (except the toast) in a bowl, then place the bowl in the refrigerator for at least one hour to chill thoroughly. Spread the tomato-chive mixture evenly over the eight pieces of toast. Serve cold.

Croûtons à l'anchois
ANCHOVY APPETIZERS 21

Ingredients for 8 appetizers, or 4 servings:

2 eggs
2 small tomatoes
8 pieces **appetizer toast (18)**
Salt and pepper
2 teaspoons finely chopped chives
8 anchovy fillets
1 teaspoon wine vinegar

UTENSILS:

Saucepan
Serrated knife

Cook the eggs in boiling water for just 7 minutes. Cool them under cold running water, then shell them. Cut each egg into four slices and reserve.

Cut each tomato into four slices. Place a slice of tomato on each piece of toast, sprinkle with salt, pepper, and a few chives. Place one slice of egg on top of each tomato and top each appetizer with an anchovy fillet. Then sprinkle with a little vinegar (a drop or two per appetizer) and serve.

NOTE: *These appetizers are served cold and can be prepared in advance.*

Egg slicers are available that will cut eggs into perfectly even slices by means of wires strung across a small frame. If an egg slicer is used, place 2 slices of egg on each appetizer rather than one. Ed.

22 *Croûtons au saumon frais* RAW SALMON APPETIZERS

Ingredients for 8 appetizers, or 4 servings:

8 paper-thin slices of fresh raw salmon ($1\frac{1}{2}$ inches square)
Salt and pepper
1 teaspoon finely chopped shallot
1 teaspoon lemon juice
1 teaspoon olive oil
8 pieces **appetizer toast (18)**
16 green peppercorns

UTENSILS:

Large sharp knife
Plate

Place the salmon on a plate and salt and pepper lightly. Sprinkle with the shallots, lemon juice, and olive oil, and leave to marinate for 1 hour. Place one piece of marinated salmon on each piece of toast, and garnish each appetizer with two green peppercorns. Serve cold.

NOTE: *Cutting the fresh salmon into paper-thin slices can be difficult. Somewhat thicker pieces can be cut, then placed between two small sheets of plastic wrap or aluminum foil, and flattened by gently tapping them with the flat side of a cleaver or large knife. Ed.*

Les soupes
SOUPS

Soupe de tous les légumes du potager de Christine
VEGETABLE SOUP FROM CHRISTINE'S GARDEN 23

Ingredients for 4 servings:

Approximately 2½ quarts **chicken stock** (**2**) or (**3**)
1 medium carrot, peeled and quartered
½ very small turnip, peeled and quartered
1 small onion, peeled and quartered
1 teaspoon diced celery
1 small leek (white part only), cleaned and sliced
1 large shallot, peeled and halved
Salt and pepper

2 medium mushrooms, cleaned and quartered
1 cup, tightly packed, water-cress leaves, washed
½ tomato, peeled and seeded
½ head Bibb lettuce, washed and coarsely chopped
2 tablespoons peeled, seeded, and diced cucumber
½ cup string beans, broken into 1-inch pieces

½ clove garlic, peeled and finely chopped
1 tablespoon finely chopped parsley
1½ teaspoons finely chopped chervil
1½ teaspoons finely chopped chives
½ teaspoon finely chopped tarragon
1 cup heavy cream
1½ tablespoons softened butter
Salt and pepper

UTENSILS:

Couscous pot (steamer)
Electric blender
Saucepan
To serve: 4 hot soup bowls

Since some vegetables used in this soup cook more quickly than others, they are steamed in two steps.

COOKING THE VEGETABLES:

Place the stock in the bottom of the couscous pot or steamer. Place the carrot, turnip, onion, celery, leek, and shallot in the top of the pot. Salt and pepper the vegetables lightly. Cover, bring the stock to a boil, and steam the vegetables for 15 minutes.

Now add the mushrooms, water cress, tomato, lettuce, cucumber, and string beans to the top of the pot, and steam for 10 minutes more.

Measure out 1 cup of the stock to use in the soup.

MAKING THE SOUP:

Place the garlic, parsley, chervil, chives, and tarragon in the blender. Add all the steamed vegetables and purée for 30 seconds. Add half of the reserved stock. Continue blending for another 2 minutes, adding alternately some of the cream, the remaining stock, and the butter, little by little. All of these ingredients should be totally incorporated into the soup. Once it is blended, pour the soup into a saucepan and taste for salt and pepper. Heat the soup gently before serving —*it must not boil.* Ladle it into hot soup bowls and serve. Or after seasoning, simply place it in soup bowls and chill to serve cold.

COMMENT:

The number of vegetables used in this soup may seem exorbitant, but it is their very variety that makes it distinctive. It is important to use only small amounts of numerous fresh vegetables if the soup is to be a success (they are quite easy to prepare). Other fresh vegetables may be used in season, so long as the variety and relative proportions given here are respected.

Soupe de grenouilles à la laitue
FROGS' LEGS AND LETTUCE SOUP 24

Ingredients for 4 servings:

2 cups, tightly packed, Bibb lettuce leaves
1 tablespoon butter
2 generous tablespoons finely chopped shallots
1½ teaspoons finely chopped garlic
⅔ cup parsley leaves
4 tablespoons water
2⅔ cups heavy cream
3¼ cups **chicken stock (2) (3)**
2 generous tablespoons **water-cress purée (102)**
Salt and pepper
12 pairs large frogs' legs (*for substitution, see Note*)
2 egg yolks
1 tablespoon freshly chopped chives

UTENSILS:

Large saucepan
Wooden spoon
Skimmer or slotted spoon
Bowl
Wire whisk
To serve: 4 hot soup bowls

MAKING THE SOUP:

Wash and drain the lettuce, then remove the thick central stem from each leaf.

In a saucepan, over medium heat, melt the butter, then add the shallots and simmer for 1 minute, stirring constantly with a wooden spoon. Add the garlic, lettuce, parsley, and water. Cover and allow to boil gently for 1 minute more. Now add the cream, chicken stock, **water-cress purée,** salt, and pepper. Bring to a boil and add the frogs' legs, then cover the pot and cook gently for 4 minutes. At the end of this time, carefully remove the frogs' legs with a skimmer or slotted spoon, and set them aside on a plate to cool.

Boil the soup, uncovered, for 15 minutes, or until it has reduced by a third. During this time, detach the meat from the bones of the cooled frogs' legs. Place equal amounts of the meat in each of the soup bowls.

TO SERVE:

In a bowl, beat the egg yolks lightly with a wire whisk. Gradually add a few tablespoons of boiling soup, whisking constantly. Lower the heat, then, whisking the soup vigorously, pour the egg yolk mixture into it. Do not allow the soup to boil.

Remove the soup from the heat and taste for seasoning; add salt and pepper if necessary. Pour the hot soup over the frogs' legs, sprinkle with freshly chopped chives, and serve immediately.

COMMENT:

To add to the fresh taste of this soup, 3 tablespoons of cold, dry white wine may be added just before pouring into the soup bowls. The soup is equally good chilled and served cold.

NOTE: *A ¼-pound fillet of snapper, halibut, or other white-fleshed fish may be used instead of the frogs' legs. Cook as described, then break the fillet into small pieces to be distributed evenly among the soup bowls. Ed.*

Bouillon d'étrilles en gelée au cerfeuil
JELLIED CRAB CONSOMMÉ WITH CHERVIL 25

Ingredients for 6 to 8 servings:

4½ pounds live small swimming crabs or soft-shelled crabs
Salt and pepper
⅜ cup olive oil
2 carrots, peeled and diced
1 onion, peeled and diced
1 tablespoon finely chopped shallots
1 clove garlic, crushed but unpeeled
3 tablespoons armagnac or cognac
3 tablespoons port
1 cup white wine
2 tomatoes, peeled, seeded, and coarsely chopped
2 tablespoons tomato paste
1 small *bouquet garni*
8⅔ cups **chicken stock (2) (3)**

3 egg whites

3 tablespoons gelatin
½ cup cold water
9 ounces canned crab meat
2 tablespoons freshly chopped chervil
1 teaspoon freshly chopped tarragon

UTENSILS:

Large knife
Large frying pan
Large pot with cover
Large sieve
Small ladle or wooden spoon
Bowls
Fork
Wire whisk
Clean cloth
To serve: 6 chilled soup bowls or champagne glasses

MAKING THE CONSOMMÉ:

Cut the crabs into four pieces each with a large knife, then sprinkle with salt and pepper. In a large frying pan, heat half the olive oil and sauté the crabs over high heat for 8 minutes, making sure they are cooked on all sides.

In a large pot, heat the remaining olive oil, then add the carrots, onion, shallots, and garlic. Simmer, uncovered, for 5 minutes, then add the crabs, armagnac, and port. Boil over high heat for 10 seconds, then add the white wine and continue boiling rapidly until the total amount of liquid is reduced by half. Add the tomatoes, the tomato paste, *bouquet garni,* and chicken stock, cover the pot, and cook at a moderate boil for 15 minutes more. At the end of this time, strain the soup through a large sieve into a bowl, pressing all the juices out of the shells and vegetables with a small ladle or wooden spoon.

CLARIFYING THE CONSOMMÉ:

Salt the egg whites and beat them lightly with a fork. Place them in the rinsed pot, and pour the consommé over them, whisking rapidly with a wire whisk to mix the egg whites into the liquid. Bring just to a boil, whisking occasionally, then simmer, uncovered, for 20 minutes. A few minutes before the time is up, moisten the gelatin with the water, then stir into the boiling consommé.

Line a large strainer or sieve with a moistened cloth, then gently pour the consommé through it into a large bowl. Taste for seasoning and add salt and pepper if necessary. Chill for at least 2 hours or until set.

TO SERVE:

Cut the canned crab meat into small cubes and distribute it evenly among the chilled soup bowls or glasses. Sprinkle with half the chopped chervil and tarragon. Ladle the soup into the bowls, sprinkle with the remaining herbs, and serve immediately.

COMMENTS:

A few shredded lettuce leaves which have been parboiled for 1 minute, then cooled under running water and drained, as well as a few boiled new peas may be sprinkled over the consommé just before serving, in addition to the herbs.

This soup may be prepared a day in advance.

Soupe aux écrevisses de rivière
CRAYFISH SOUP 26

Ingredients for 4 servings:

4 tablespoons olive oil
4 tablespoons cooking oil
3¼ pounds live crayfish—approximately 32 (*for substitution, see Note*)
1 carrot, peeled and coarsely chopped
1 onion, peeled and coarsely chopped
1 shallot, peeled and coarsely chopped
1 small *bouquet garni*
1 clove garlic, crushed but unpeeled
Salt and pepper
3 tablespoons armagnac or cognac
3 tablespoons port
1 cup dry white wine
2 cups water
2 tomatoes, peeled and seeded
1 tablespoon tomato paste

1 cup **court-bouillon** (8)
1 teaspoon freshly chopped chervil
½ teaspoon freshly chopped tarragon
1 cup *crème fraîche* (*see p. 352*) or heavy cream
¼ pound plus 2 tablespoons softened butter
1 tablespoon freshly chopped chives

UTENSILS:

Large pot or *sauteuse* with cover
Skimmer or slotted spoon
Plate
Mortar and pestle, electric blender, or food processor
Large strainer or sieve
Large bowl
Small ladle or wooden spoon

Saucepan
Wire whisk
To serve: 4 hot soup bowls

MAKING THE CRAYFISH STOCK:

In the large pot or *sauteuse*, heat the olive oil and cooking oil, then add the live crayfish, cover, and sauté over high heat for 6 minutes. The crayfish should be completely red at the end of this time. Remove from the heat and lift the crayfish out with a skimmer or slotted spoon, then remove their heads and set the tails aside on a plate.

Crush the heads in a mortar or grind them in a blender or food processor. Put them back into the *sauteuse* and add the carrot, onion, shallot, *bouquet garni*, garlic, salt, and pepper. Cook, uncovered, over medium heat for 5 minutes, stirring frequently to prevent the vegetables from coloring. Add the armagnac and port, then cover the pot halfway and boil gently until the liquid has reduced by half. Now add the white wine, water, tomatoes, and tomato paste. Boil rapidly, uncovered, until this liquid has reduced by half, then strain the soup through a large strainer into a bowl, pressing as much juice out of the shells and vegetables as possible with a small ladle or wooden spoon. Set aside for later use.

TO SERVE:

While the soup is cooking, remove the meat from the crayfish tails and discard the shells. Place eight tails in each soup plate, then place the plates in a 325° F oven, with the door ajar, to keep them hot.

In a saucepan, bring the *court-bouillon* to a boil, then add the chopped chervil and tarragon and boil rapidly, uncovered, until the liquid has reduced by half. Add the cream, butter, and crayfish stock, beating gently with a wire whisk until all the elements are well mixed. Bring to a boil and cook for 30 seconds, taste for seasoning, and add salt and pepper if necessary. Then pour the soup into the soup bowls, sprinkle with chopped chives, and serve immediately.

This soup may also be chilled and served cold. In this case add the chopped chives just before serving.

Note: *This soup may also be made using large whole shrimp. Ed.*

Les salades

SALADS

Salade grande ferme
FARMER'S SALAD 27

Ingredients for 4 servings:

1 head of chicory
2 tablespoons butter
16 thin slices French bread, or 1½-inch squares cut from sandwich bread
1 large clove garlic, peeled
3 slices bacon, each cut into 12 to 15 small pieces (*lardons*)
⅜ cup **vinaigrette gourmande (16)** or simple *vinaigrette*
2½ ounces Roquefort, crumbled with a fork
1 generous tablespoon freshly chopped chervil or parsley

UTENSILS:

Colander
Salad bowl
Large frying pan

MAKING THE SALAD:

Remove any wilted or discolored leaves from the chicory, as well as any large dark-green leaves that seem tough. Separate all the other leaves and cut the longest ones into 2-inch lengths; then wash them carefully in a large basin of cold water (it may be necessary to wash the leaves twice). Drain the chicory in a colander, then pat it dry in a towel. Place in a salad bowl and set aside.

Butter both sides of each slice of bread, and brown in a frying pan, over high heat; or, simply melt the butter in the pan and add the slices of unbuttered bread. In either case, brown the bread on both sides. Stick the clove of garlic on the end of a fork and gently rub each *croûton* on one side as you take it from the pan. Place the *croûtons* on a plate and keep them warm in an oven preheated to 350° F. Leave the oven door ajar.

In the same pan the *croûtons* cooked in, sauté the bacon, over medium heat, until nicely browned and crisp, but do not let it dry out and harden. Lift out of the pan and drain.

TO SERVE:

Pour the *vinaigrette* over the chicory and toss the salad (I recommend using your hands to do this; the salad is more evenly mixed). Add the hot *croûtons*, the bits of bacon, and the Roquefort, mix them in lightly, then sprinkle with chopped chervil or parsley and serve.

Note: *This salad may also be made with escarole instead of chicory. Ed.*

28 *Salade de lentilles aux croûtons d'anchoïade* LENTIL SALAD WITH ANCHOVY CROÛTONS

Ingredients for 4 servings:

- 1 cup lentils
- 4½ cups cold water
- 1 teaspoon coarse salt
- 1 small *bouquet garni*

Pepper
½ large onion, peeled and diced
1 carrot, peeled and diced
½ clove garlic, peeled and finely chopped

4 salted anchovies, or 8 canned anchovy fillets in oil
1 egg yolk
6 tablespoons olive oil
12 thin slices French bread, or 1½-inch squares cut from sandwich bread

4 tablespoons salad oil
4 tablespoons wine vinegar
1 tablespoon shallot, finely chopped
Salt and pepper
1 tablespoon chopped capers

UTENSILS:

Colander
Saucepan
Large bowl
Clean cloth or towel
Electric blender
Small bowl
Pastry brush
Salad bowl

COOKING THE LENTILS:

Place the lentils in a colander and rinse them under cold running water. It is not necessary to soak them beforehand.

Put the lentils in a saucepan and cover them with the cold water. Bring to a boil, skim off any foam that rises to the surface, then add the coarse salt, *bouquet garni*, pepper, onion, carrot, and garlic. Lower the heat, cover the pot, and simmer for 35 minutes, or until the lentils are tender (they should *not*, however, be falling apart). When the lentils are cooked, drain them in a colander and remove the *bouquet garni*. Pour the lentils into a bowl and chill in the refrigerator for at least 2 hours.

MAKING THE ANCHOVY CROÛTONS:

If using salted anchovies, rinse them under cold running water, then lift the fillets off the bones. To do this, make a small slit at the tail end of the anchovy, then progressively pinch along the fillet with your thumb and index finger, working from the tail toward the head. The fillet will detach itself from the bone as you do this. When all the fillets have been detached, rinse them once more, then pat dry in a clean cloth or towel. If using canned anchovy fillets, simply use them as they come from the can.

Place the anchovy fillets and the egg yolks in the blender. Blend for 30 seconds, then add 4 tablespoons of olive oil, a tablespoon at a time. When the mixture is perfectly smooth, set aside in a bowl.

Brush both sides of each slice of bread with the remaining olive oil. Brown on both sides under the broiler, then spread one side of each *croûton* with a generous layer of the anchovy mixture.

TO SERVE:

Mix the salad oil, vinegar, shallot, and a little salt and pepper together in a salad bowl. Add the lentils and capers, and mix thoroughly with the dressing. Form the lentils into a dome, stick the anchovy *croûtons* into the salad like a crown, and serve.

COMMENTS:

A slice of tomato topped by a slice of hard-boiled egg and a canned anchovy fillet may be placed on each *croûton* instead of the anchovy paste described above. In this case, simply serve the *croûtons* on a plate, next to the salad.

To make this salad more colorful, white beans may be added to the lentils.

NOTE: *If you are using white beans, they must be prepared ahead of time. Be sure to soak them overnight before cooking. Cook them exactly as you would the lentils, but allow about 2 hours' cooking time. Ed.*

SALADE GOURMANDE 29

Ingredients for 2 servings:

6½ cups water
1 generous tablespoon coarse salt
½ pound small green beans, strings and ends removed
12 fresh or canned asparagus tips

3 tablespoons **vinaigrette gourmande (16)**
4 large lettuce leaves (preferably red *batavia* or *trévise*)
1 teaspoon finely chopped shallot
2 ounces *foie gras*, canned or fresh
1 large truffle, canned or fresh, cut into thin slices (*for substitution, see Comments*)

UTENSILS:

Large saucepan
Skimmer or slotted spoon
Large bowl
Colander
3 small bowls
Clean cloth or towel
To serve: 2 chilled plates

COOKING THE VEGETABLES:

In a large saucepan, bring the water to a boil, add the coarse salt, then the green beans. Cook for 4 to 8 minutes according to size—the beans should be cooked *al dente*. Lift them out of the boiling water with a skimmer or slotted spoon, and drop them immediately into a large bowl of ice water. Leave them there for 10 seconds, then drain in a colander. If using fresh asparagus tips, cook them after the beans, in the same way and using the same water, for 5 to 6 minutes.

MAKING THE SALAD:

Place the green beans, asparagus tips, and truffles in three separate bowls. Season each with a tablespoon of the *vinaigrette*.

Wash the lettuce leaves and pat them dry in a towel, then place two leaves on each plate. Place half of the green beans on each plate in a small mound, sprinkle with the chopped shallot, then plant six asparagus tips here and there in each mound of beans. Decorate the salads with the *foie gras* and truffle slices and serve.

COMMENTS:

Large green beans may be used instead of small (thin) ones, but they should be cut in half lengthwise before cooking.

A large fresh mushroom may be substituted for the truffle. In this case, cut the raw mushroom into very thin slices and sprinkle with lemon juice, then follow the directions given above for using the truffles.

30 *Salade chaude des dames landaises*
HOT DUCK SALAD FROM THE LANDES

Ingredients for 4 servings:

8 *filets mignons* of duck (*for substitution, see Note*)
Salt and pepper
3 tablespoons red wine
3½ ounces canned or fresh *foie gras* of duck (*for substitution, see Comments*)
2 cups, tightly packed, field salad (lamb's-lettuce)
2 cups, tightly packed, dandelion greens
2 large truffles, canned or fresh (*for substitution, see Comments*)
2 tablespoons olive oil
2 tablespoons lemon juice

UTENSILS:

Paring knife
Colander
2 clean cloths or towels
Salad bowl
Frying pan
Strainer

With a small sharp knife, eliminate the gristle that runs through the center of each *filet mignon* of duck, then place them in a shallow dish or soup plate, sprinkle with salt, pepper, and the red wine, and set aside while you prepare the other ingredients for the salad.

Cut the *foie gras* into small cubes a little less than ½ inch on a side.

Remove the roots from the field salad and dandelion greens, wash several times in cold water, drain in a colander, then pat dry in a clean cloth or towel.

Cut the truffles into slices 1/16 inch thick.

Mix the field salad, dandelion greens, and truffles together in a salad bowl, season with salt and pepper, then set aside.

Heat the frying pan over high heat (do not add any oil or butter). When very hot, sauté the cubes of *foie gras* in it for 30 to 40 seconds. They should be brown on all sides and give off quite a bit of fat. Pour this fat into the salad by holding a strainer over the salad bowl and pouring the contents of the frying pan into it. Set the strainer containing the *foie gras* cubes aside, and season the salad with 1 tablespoon of olive oil and the lemon juice. Mix the salad thoroughly.

In the same, very hot frying pan the *foie gras* cooked in, place the remaining tablespoon of olive oil and add the *filets mignons* of duck, after patting them dry in a towel. Sauté the *filets* for 15 seconds on a side, then lift them out of the pan, place them and the cubes of *foie gras* on top of the salad, and serve immediately.

COMMENTS:

If followed exactly, this recipe is of course very expensive to prepare. But with a little imagination, an excellent variation of it can be made with less expensive ingredients. Instead of using *foie gras*, ⅔ cup cooked ham, cut into small cubes, may be sautéed in 1 tablespoon of olive oil, and this oil and the cooked ham poured over the salad in place of the fat from the *foie gras*.

The truffles may be replaced by raw mushrooms, sliced as the truffles would be, and sprinkled with a little lemon juice.

The *filet mignon* of duck is a strip of meat that runs the length of the breast meat, next to the bone, of ducks specially fattened for making *foie gras* of duck. It is also found under the breast meat of other ducks, but is less developed than in the specially fattened ones.

The *filets mignons* alone may be cooked as described in the recipe and served as a light main dish for 2 servings. In this case, let them marinate for 1 hour before sautéing them in 1 tablespoon of olive oil. Serve with fresh butter or **Herb butter (17)** and garnish them with a salad or **Grenadine and onion "jam" (98)**.

NOTE: *The* filet mignon *of duck is extremely difficult to find, even in France, and of course you would have to have four ducks to start with, for this recipe. However, the breast meat of a duck weighing approximately 3 pounds, or simply 7 ounces of duck breast, will give the same amount of meat as that represented by the eight* filets mignons. *This meat should be cut lengthwise into eight thin strips, then marinated, etc., as described in the recipe. Ed.*

31 *Salade du jardin du curé*
SALAD FROM THE PARSON'S GARDEN

Ingredients for 4 servings:

- 1 cup *julienne* strips of carrots
- 1 cup *julienne* strips of celeriac (celery root)
- 1 clove garlic, crushed but unpeeled
- 8 peppercorns
- 1⅔ cups olive oil
- ⅔ cup, lightly packed, red *trévise* or *batavia* lettuce leaves
- ¾ cup, lightly packed, field salad (lamb's-lettuce)
- 1 cup, lightly packed, chicory or purslane
- ¾ cup, lightly packed, water-cress leaves
- 4 cups water
- 2 teaspoons coarse salt
- 1 cup soybean sprouts (*for substitution, see Comments*)
- 3 tablespoons fresh or frozen green peas
- 24 quail eggs (*for substitution, see Comments*)
- 2 cups water
- 2 cups red wine
- 3 thick slices bacon, cut into 12 to 15 small pieces each (*lardons*)

⅜ cup **vinaigrette gourmande (16)**
2 tablespoons freshly chopped chives
2 tablespoons freshly chopped parsley

UTENSILS:

Small *sauteuse* or saucepan
Skimmer or slotted spoon
Colander
Clean dry cloth or towel
Large bowl
Salad bowl, chilled
4 saucers
2 medium-size frying pans, or the *sauteuse* and a frying pan
To serve: 4 chilled plates

PREPARING THE VEGETABLES:

Place the carrots and celeriac in a small *sauteuse* or saucepan, add the garlic, peppercorns, and olive oil, and bring to a boil. Lower the heat and simmer for 10 minutes, then allow to cool. When cool, lift the vegetables out of the oil with a skimmer or slotted spoon. The olive oil may be stored and used again.

Remove any wilted or discolored leaves from the various types of lettuce and the water cress before measuring. Wash the leaves carefully, then drain in a colander and pat dry with a clean cloth.

Place the water and coarse salt in a saucepan, bring to a boil, then add the soybean sprouts. Boil for 2 minutes, then lift them out of the pot with a slotted spoon, place them immediately in a large bowl of ice water, then drain.

Cook the green peas in the same water used for cooking the bean sprouts. Cook for 15 minutes if using fresh peas, 6 minutes if using frozen ones. Cool and drain as described for the bean sprouts.

In a salad bowl, mix the salad greens and water cress. Sprinkle the bean sprouts, peas, carrots, and celeriac over them, then set aside in the refrigerator.

POACHING THE EGGS:

Break 6 quail eggs into each of four saucers and set aside. In a frying pan or the *sauteuse*, place the water and red wine and heat until almost boiling. *Do not salt!* Slide all the eggs, a saucerful at a time, into the simmering liquid, and poach for 1 minute, then remove from the heat and set aside to keep warm in the poaching liquid.

TO SERVE:

Heat a second frying pan over high heat. Do not add butter, oil, or any other fat. When it is very hot, place the pieces of bacon in the pan and sauté until golden brown (do not allow to dry out and become hard), then drain.

Pour the **vinaigrette gourmande** over the salad, add the bacon, and toss the salad. Now you can either divide the salad evenly among the chilled plates and place six poached eggs on top of each serving, or arrange them all on top of the salad in the salad bowl. Sprinkle the eggs with the chopped chives and parsley, and serve.

COMMENTS:

The quail eggs may be replaced by chicken eggs, but in this case, use only one per person, and poach them for 3 minutes before removing the pan from the heat.

The bean sprouts may be replaced by 2 ounces of spaghettini broken into 2-inch pieces and cooked *al dente* in boiling salted water.

This salad is delicious served with pieces of buttered toast on the side.

32 *Salade de jambon d'aile de canard aux pois de jardin* DUCK "HAM" AND GREEN-PEA SALAD

(color picture I)

Ingredients for 2 servings:

- 1 breast (*magret*) of a large, fat duck (weight of meat, 12 ounces; *see Note*)
- A pinch of thyme
- 1 small piece of bay leaf
- 4 coriander seeds, coarsely crushed
- 4 peppercorns, coarsely crushed
- 2 teaspoons coarse salt

2 cups water
1 teaspoon coarse salt
8 little onions, either new or dry, peeled

4 cups water
2 teaspoons coarse salt
Generous ½ cup green peas, fresh or frozen
½ head Bibb lettuce
3 tablespoons **vinaigrette gourmande (16)**

UTENSILS:

Small baking dish or platter
Piece of clean cheesecloth
String
Small saucepan
Skimmer or slotted spoon
Colander
Bowl
Small sharp knife
Sharp flexible-blade filleting knife
To serve: 2 chilled plates

MAKING THE DUCK "HAM":

Place the breast meat of the duck, skin side down, in a small baking dish or platter. Sprinkle the thyme, bay leaf, coriander, pepper, and salt over the top, and leave in the refrigerator for 24 hours.

The next day, lift the meat out of the salt and seasonings and wrap it in a clean piece of cheesecloth. Tie it up as you would a sausage or rolled roast, with several tight rings of string around the roll, and both ends of the cloth tied off. Hang the meat in a dry, draft-free place for 12 to 15 days. It is perfectly cured when it is firm, but by no means hard, to the touch.

PREPARING THE VEGETABLES:

In a small saucepan, place 2 generous cups of water and 1 teaspoon of coarse salt, bring to a boil, and add the onions. Boil gently, uncovered, for 7 minutes if using new onions, or 15 minutes if using dry ones, then drain, discarding the water.

In the same pot, bring to a boil 4 cups water and 2 teaspoons of coarse salt, add the peas, and cook, uncovered, for 15 minutes if using fresh ones, and 6 minutes if using frozen peas. Lift out of the water with a skimmer or slotted spoon and drain in a colander.

Remove two large, cupped leaves from the heart of the lettuce and set aside. Cook the rest of the lettuce for 4 minutes in the water the peas cooked in, then drain.

MAKING THE SALAD:

Detach the cooked lettuce leaves, and cut out the hard central rib from each leaf.

In a bowl, carefully mix the peas, onions, lettuce, and *vinaigrette.* Place one of the reserved, raw lettuce leaves in the center of each plate and fill with the mixed salad.

Unwrap the duck "ham" and cut off the skin around it with a small, very sharp knife; the fat left around the meat should be no more than 1/16 inch thick. Then, using a sharp filleting knife, cut the "ham" lengthwise into paper-thin slices—they should be almost transparent. Form a loose circle with each of these slices, then arrange the circles standing like the petals of a flower around the lettuce leaf on each plate (see color picture I). Sprinkle with a little freshly ground pepper, and serve.

COMMENTS:

Parma ham (*prosciutto*) may be used instead of the duck "ham" if you decide to make this salad at the last minute.

French-style canned peas, which are simmered with lettuce and onions and canned with their garnish, may be used instead of cooking these vegetables as described above. Drain the canned peas, rinse them under cold running water, drain again, then season with the *vinaigrette* and fill the lettuce leaves.

In the summer, slices of fresh cantaloupe or muskmelon may be placed around the salad with the slices of ham—the two tastes are delicious together.

NOTE: *Ideally, the breast meat* (magret) *from specially fattened ducks, used in making* foie gras *of duck, should be used in this recipe, but a very satisfactory version of this duck "ham" can be made using the breast meat of any duck of good quality. For the amount of meat called for in this recipe it would be necessary to have 1¼ pounds of duck breast with the bone. But we found that the ½ pound of* **meat** *from a breast weighing 12 ounces with the bone was sufficient for two people. Ed.*

Salade buissonière aux poissons fumés
SMOKED FISH SALAD 33

Ingredients for 4 servings:

1 cup *julienne* strips of carrot
1 cup *julienne* strips of celeriac (celery root)
1 clove garlic, crushed but unpeeled
8 peppercorns
1⅔ cups olive oil
¼ pound smoked salmon (*for substitution, see Comments and Note*)
¼ pound smoked sturgeon (*for substitution, see Comments and Note*)
Olive oil to brush on fish

¾ cup, lightly packed, field salad (lamb's-lettuce)
1 cup, lightly packed, red *trévise* or *batavia* lettuce
1½ cups, lightly packed, chicory
½ cup, lightly packed, water-cress leaves
2 small ripe avocados
⅜ cup **vinaigrette gourmande (16)**
1 tablespoon fine *julienne* strips of fresh ginger or lemon peel
1 tablespoon finely chopped shallot
48 green peppercorns
4 tablespoons fresh chervil or parsley leaves
24 fresh currants (optional)

UTENSILS:

Small saucepan
Skimmer or slotted spoon
Sharp flexible-blade filleting knife
Pastry brush
Clean cloth or towel
Vegetable peeler
Bowl
To serve: 4 chilled plates

COOKING THE CARROTS AND CELERIAC:

At least an hour before making the salad, prepare the carrots and celeriac. Place them in a small saucepan, add the garlic, peppercorns, and olive oil, bring to a boil, then lower the heat and simmer for 10 minutes. Remove from the heat and allow to cool in the pan, then lift the vegetables out with a skimmer or slotted spoon, drain, and set aside. The oil may be stored and used again.

MAKING THE SALAD:

Use a very sharp, flexible-blade filleting knife to cut the salmon and sturgeon into 24 slices each. Place them on a plate and brush with a little olive oil to make them shiny. Set aside.

Remove any wilted or discolored leaves from the different salad greens and water cress before measuring. Wash carefully, drain, then pat dry with a clean towel.

Peel the avocados with a vegetable peeler. Cut in half and remove the pit, then cut each half lengthwise into 4 slices. Place these slices on a plate and pour 1½ tablespoons of *vinaigrette* over them. Set aside.

If using lemon peel instead or ginger, parboil it for 7 to 8 minutes, uncovered, in boiling water, then cool under running water and drain.

In a bowl, mix the salad greens and water cress with the remaining *vinaigrette* and the shallot.

TO SERVE:

Arrange the slices of salmon and sturgeon in a circle just inside the border of 4 chilled plates. Sprinkle the salmon with the green peppercorns. Inside the circle of fish, make a second circle of avocado slices.

In the center of the plate, place a mound of the mixed salad, and place, here and there, little bunches of the cooked vegetables. Sprinkle with the ginger or lemon peel, the chervil or parsley, and the fresh currants, and serve.

COMMENTS:

Large slices of country-style bread, toasted and spread with a mixture of whipped cream and freshly grated horseradish, make an excellent accompaniment to this salad.

Marinated herring, herring fillets in oil, etc., are also very nice in this salad and much less expensive than salmon or sturgeon.

It is also fun to try smoking your own fish. Small smoking devices are sold which enable you to smoke the fish of your choice and experiment with all kinds of taste combinations this way.

Note: *Smoked mackerel and sprats (one of the best types of small herring) are particularly good in this salad. If you are using them, however, it is necessary to remove the skin (it peels off very easily) of the mackerel and lift the fillets off the bone. This is not really necessary with sprats—simply remove their heads and clean them. In using either of these substitutes, do not try to slice them as with the salmon and sturgeon; simply cut them into strips, then season and arrange them as described in the recipe. Ed.*

Salade de homard
LOBSTER SALAD 34

Ingredients for 2 servings:

4 cups **court-bouillon** (8)
1 live lobster weighing approximately 1 pound (*see p. 165*)

6 cups water
1 generous tablespoon coarse salt
6 ounces green beans, strings and tips removed
12 asparagus tips, fresh or canned

1 egg yolk
½ teaspoon Dijon mustard
3 tablespoons olive oil
3 tablespoons salad oil
Salt and pepper
1 teaspoon lemon juice
½ teaspoon tomato paste
½ teaspoon freshly chopped tarragon
A few drops armagnac (optional)

1 teaspoon chopped shallot
4 perfect lettuce leaves
1 tablespoon fresh chervil leaves

UTENSILS:

Large pot
Saucepan
Skimmer or slotted spoon
Large pair of scissors
Nutcracker or cleaver
Large bowl
4 small bowls
To serve: 2 chilled plates

COOKING THE LOBSTER:

In a pot put the *court-bouillon*, bring to a boil, then add the lobster and boil rapidly for 10 minutes. Lift the lobster out of the pot and set aside to cool. Save the vegetables of the *court-bouillon* for later use.

Detach the tail of the lobster, then cut the rings on the underside with large scissors and remove the meat. Cut the tail meat into 8 slices.

Crack the claws with a nutcracker or by hitting it with the blunt edge of a cleaver, then remove the meat. The head of the lobster will not be used in this recipe.

COOKING THE VEGETABLES:

Place the water and coarse salt in a saucepan, bring to a boil, and add the green beans. Boil rapidly, uncovered, for 4 to 8 minutes, depending on size. They should be cooked *al dente*. When done, lift them out of the pot with a skimmer or slotted spoon, and place them immediately in a large bowl of ice water. Leave them in the water for 10 seconds, then drain.

If using fresh asparagus tips, peel them, then cook them in the same water as the beans for 5 to 6 minutes. Drain and cool as described for the beans.

MAKING THE SALAD:

In a bowl, make a mayonnaise—see method under **Mayonnaise** (**4**)—with the egg yolk, mustard, olive oil, salad oil, salt, pepper, and lemon juice. When done, add to it the tomato paste, tarragon, armagnac, and 1 heaping tablespoon of chopped vegetables from the *court-bouillon.* This sauce will be more liquid than an ordinary mayonnaise.

Place the beans and asparagus in separate bowls and pour a quarter of the sauce over each of them. Sprinkle with chopped shallot.

Place two lettuce leaves on each plate. Make a mound of string beans in the center of each plate, then stick the asparagus tips here and there in the mound of beans. Place the slices of lobster around the beans, pour the remaining sauce over the lobster, then sprinkle the beans with the fresh chervil. Stand the meat from the lobster claws up on top of the mound of beans, the pointed end sticking up, then serve.

COMMENTS:

Instead of lobster, which tends to be expensive, mussels may be used.

A simple *vinaigrette*, seasoned with freshly chopped tarragon, is also very nice as a sauce for this salad.

Salade tiède de langoustines aux pois gourmands
SNOW-PEA AND LANGOUSTINE SALAD 35

Ingredients for 2 servings:

3 quarts water
2 generous tablespoons coarse salt
16 live *langoustines* (*for substitution, see Note*)

4 cups water
2 teaspoons coarse salt
¼ pound snow peas
12 asparagus tips, fresh or canned

¼ pound fresh morels, or ¼ cup dried morels
6 tablespoons water
Few drops lemon juice
Salt and pepper

5 tablespoons butter, broken into small pieces
1 teaspoon freshly chopped chervil or parsley

UTENSILS:

Large saucepan
Medium saucepan
Small *sauteuse* or saucepan
Skimmer or slotted spoon
Colander
To serve: 2 large hot plates

COOKING THE LANGOUSTINES AND VEGETABLES:

In a large saucepan, bring the 3 quarts of water and 2 tablespoons of coarse salt to a boil. Add the *langoustines*, cook for 1½ minutes, then remove the pan from the heat.

In a second saucepan, bring to a boil 4 cups of water and 2 teaspoons of coarse salt. Add the snow peas and asparagus tips, boil rapidly, uncovered, for 6 minutes, then remove from the heat. Keep the vegetables warm in their liquid.

Carefully wash fresh morels to remove any sand, then drain and pat dry in a clean cloth or towel. Cut each one into four slices lengthwise, place in a small *sauteuse* or saucepan, and add 6 tablespoons of water and the lemon juice. Salt and pepper, then cover the pot halfway and cook over medium heat for 10 minutes, or until the liquid is reduced by half.

MAKING THE SALAD:

While the mushrooms are cooking, lift the *langoustines* out of their cooking liquid with a skimmer or slotted spoon, and remove the tail meat from their shells.

Drain the snow peas and asparagus tips in a colander, then spread the peas over the bottom of the plates. Place the *langoustine* tails and asparagus tips over the snow peas. Lift the morels out of their cooking liquid and sprinkle them over the salad as well. Place the plates in a preheated 350° F oven to keep them warm and leave the oven door ajar.

Place the saucepan the morels cooked in back over medium heat. Add the butter to the mushrooms' cooking liquid. Bring to a slow boil and cook gently for 3 minutes, then remove from the heat and shake the saucepan with a circular motion to make the sauce spin around the sides. The sauce will thicken slightly as you do this.

Taste the sauce for seasoning, add salt and pepper if necessary, then stir in half of the chervil or parsley. Remove the plates from the oven, pour the sauce over the salad, sprinkle with the remaining chopped herbs, and serve.

COMMENTS:

Cooking the sauce at a slow boil with the butter is what actually thickens this sauce. Part of the water in the liquid evaporates and the butter mixes with the other elements in the sauce; the spinning motion helps add to the creaminess of the result.

This simple sauce may be flavored with various herbs, or with spices such as green peppercorns, saffron, etc., and can be served with a wide variety of dishes including poached or grilled fish and boiled or steamed vegetables.

This recipe may also be used in making a delicious puff pastry entrée, **Puff pastry with snow peas and langoustines.** Simply follow the basic recipe for one of the other puff-pastry entrées in this book (**recipes 43** to **46**) and use this salad to garnish the pastry.

NOTE: Langoustines *are small shellfish, about the size of a large crayfish. Only the tail meat is used. Since they are very hard to find in the United States, large shrimp may be used as a substitute. Cook them exactly as described above. Ed.*

Les entrées

ENTRÉES

Dame tartine

36 CHEESE TARTINES

Ingredients for 4 servings:

4 cups freshly grated Gruyère or Swiss cheese
2 tablespoons flour
¾ teaspoon salt
A generous pinch of pepper
2 eggs
1 tablespoon Kirsch
⅔ cup diced ham
3 tablespoons chopped onion
½ cup **raw diced tomatoes (96)**
1 tablespoon finely chopped fresh parsley
4 slices country-style bread, approximately ½ inch thick, 6 inches long, and 4 inches wide
2 quarts cooking oil (if deep-frying)

UTENSILS:

Electric blender
Large bowl
Deep fryer or large pot with frying basket, or baking sheet
Skimmer or slotted spoon

Place the cheese, flour, salt, pepper, and one egg in a blender. Blend for 30 seconds, then add the second egg and the Kirsch. Blend for about 2 minutes more, or until the mixture is perfectly smooth. Pour the mixture into a bowl and chill in the refrigerator for 1 to 2 hours, or until it has stiffened to the consistency of softened butter. Remove from the refrigerator and stir in the ham, onion, tomatoes, and parsley. Thickly spread the pieces of bread with this mixture and deep-fry them in hot oil for 1 minute on the garnished side, then 30 seconds on the other side; or, place the garnished pieces of bread on a baking sheet and bake in an oven preheated to 500° F for 6 minutes. Serve immediately, while hot.

COMMENTS:

This recipe can be prepared up to a day in advance. The garnished pieces of bread should then be kept refrigerated in a plastic bag.

Deep-frying the *tartines* gives the best results, but for those who prefer baking them, it is best to butter lightly the bottom of each slice before placing them in the oven.

The ham, tomato, and onion can be replaced with equal amounts of a variety of other ingredients such as capers, anchovies, mushrooms, etc.

Note: *If deep-frying, remove the* tartines *from the oil with a skimmer or slotted spoon and allow them to drain on a cloth or paper towel for a short time before serving. Ed.*

Brioche à la moelle au beurre rouge
BRIOCHE WITH MARROW AND RED BUTTER SAUCE 37

Ingredients for 4 servings:

- 12 ounces beef marrow (*see Note*)
- 4 cups cold water
- 2 teaspoons coarse salt
- 2 generous tablespoons finely chopped shallots

1 cup red wine
½ pound softened butter, divided into 20 pieces
Salt and pepper
1 tablespoon finely chopped fresh parsley
4 slices of a cylindrical brioche (*brioche mousseline*) each 4 inches in diameter and ¾ inch thick (*for substitution, see Note*)

UTENSILS:

Large bowl
2 saucepans
Wire whisk
Double boiler or *bain-marie*
Skimmer or slotted spoon
To serve: 4 hot plates

PREPARING THE MARROW:

A day ahead of time, ask the butcher to put aside 12 ounces of bone marrow; it should preferably be in long sausagelike pieces. Place the marrow in a large bowl of cold water and leave overnight before using. The next day, cut the marrow into rounds about ½ inch thick and place them in a saucepan with the cold water and coarse salt. Do not cook the marrow at this time; leave it in the cold salted water while preparing the sauce.

MAKING THE SAUCE:

Place the shallots and red wine in a saucepan and boil slowly until three-quarters of the liquid has evaporated; the shallots should be quite soft and a little wine still left in the bottom of the pot. Reduce the heat, or remove the pan from the heat, and wait until the shallot-wine mixture has cooled slightly (it should still be quite warm, however). Then add the butter a small lump at a time, beating the sauce constantly with a wire whisk as the butter is added. Test the temperature of the sauce with your finger; it should be warm but not hot. To keep the sauce at an even temperature, move the saucepan up and down over the heat; *see Note* preceding the recipe for **Béarnaise sauce (5)**. Replace the pan over the heat, and whisk vigorously while adding the last third of the butter. Then remove from the heat and stir in the salt, pepper, and parsley. Keep the sauce warm in a *bain-marie* or double boiler while cooking the marrow.

COOKING THE MARROW AND SERVING:

Place the slices of brioche under the broiler to toast them lightly, then place them on the hot plates.

Place the saucepan containing the marrow on the stove and bring to a boil. The minute the water boils, remove the pan from the heat and lift out the pieces of marrow, using a skimmer or slotted spoon. Place the pieces of marrow, which are now slightly translucent, on the pieces of toasted brioche, salt and pepper them lightly, then pour the sauce around (*not* over) the garnished pieces of brioche, and serve immediately.

COMMENT:

The marrow must be served immediately, while hot; once it cools it becomes gummy.

The sauce used in this recipe is basically the same as the **Foamy butter sauce (6).** The secret to making both sauces is that the sauce must be made over low heat; it should be very warm but you should be able to touch it with the back of your finger without the slightest sensation of burning. If the sauce is too cool or too hot, the butter will not be foamy, thick, and creamy as it should be.

NOTE: *The brioche used in this recipe is tall and cylindrical. If such a brioche is not available, slices of any egg bread will do. Even ordinary sandwich bread, buttered before being toasted, could be used.*

It may be difficult to buy bone marrow alone. If buying marrow-bones, 4 pounds of bones are necessary for 12 ounces of marrow. To remove the marrow from the bone, stand the bone on end and split it with a cleaver. Do not hit too hard, or the cleaver will slice the entire bone and marrow in half. When the bone has cracked, split it in half with your fingers and lift the marrow out. Ed.

Oeufs poule au caviar

38 SCRAMBLED EGGS IN THEIR SHELLS WITH CAVIAR

Ingredients for 4 servings:

- 8 very fresh eggs
- 2 teaspoons butter
- 1 tablespoon *crème fraîche* (*see p. 352*) or heavy cream
- ⅓ cup finely chopped onion
- ½ tablespoon finely chopped fresh chives
- Salt and pepper
- 4 ounces (8 tablespoons) caviar (*for substitution, see Comment*)
- 12 long thin pieces of toasted bread, or 12 fresh boiled asparagus tips

UTENSILS:

- Serrated knife or soft-boiled-egg cutter
- 2 bowls
- Small wire whisk
- Small saucepan
- Teaspoon
- *To serve:* 8 eggcups

PREPARING THE SHELLS:

Using a serrated knife or a soft-boiled-egg cutter, cut each eggshell about ½ inch down from its pointed end. Empty 6 of the eggs into a bowl. (The remaining 2 eggs will not be needed; use them for something else). Save the little tops as well as all the emptied shells, wash carefully in warm water, and turn upside down on a towel to dry completely.

COOKING THE EGGS:

Melt the butter in a small saucepan over low heat, then remove the pot from the heat. Beat the eggs lightly with a whisk, then pour them through a sieve to eliminate all filaments. Pour the beaten eggs into the warm butter and place over very low heat. Beat constantly with the whisk, and gradually increase the heat, until the eggs are thick and creamy, but not solid. Remove the eggs immediately from the heat and continue whisking while adding the cream, onion, chives, salt, and pepper.

TO SERVE:

Place the dried eggshells in eggcups. Using an ordinary teaspoon, carefully fill each shell three-quarters full with the creamed eggs, then finish filling each shell with 1 tablespoon of caviar; the caviar should be slightly domed on top. Place the little top of each shell on the caviar. Serve the eggs with strips of toasted bread or warm cooked asparagus tips, to be dipped into the egg and caviar and eaten with the fingers.

COMMENTS:

These eggs can be served hot or cold. If served cold, the eggs should be cooked and the shells filled in advance, then chilled, but the caviar should be added at the last minute, just before serving.

The caviar may be replaced by an equal amount of either black or red lumpfish caviar. Thinly sliced pieces of either smoked salmon or eel could also be used instead of caviar. A lighter, and more economical, version of this dish can be made simply by using the tomato and chive mixture given in the recipe for **Fresh tomato and chive appetizers (20)** instead of any of the previous suggestions.

Escargots en pots aux croûtons
SNAILS IN POTS WITH TOAST 39

Ingredients for 4 servings:

48 live snails (*see Comments*)
1 handful coarse salt
1 tablespoon flour
2 quarts water

2 cups water
2 cups dry white wine
1 carrot, peeled and sliced

1 onion, peeled and sliced
1 *bouquet garni*
1½ teaspoons salt
A pinch of pepper

FOR THE SNAIL BUTTER:

½ pound plus 2 tablespoons softened butter
6 large whole cloves garlic, peeled
2 cups, tightly packed, fresh parsley leaves
1 teaspoon Dijon mustard
2 tablespoons powdered almonds (optional)
1 teaspoon salt
¾ teaspoon pepper
A pinch of nutmeg
½ cup diced ham
1½ medium mushrooms, diced

FINAL GARNISH:

1 cup **cooked diced tomatoes** (**97**)
8 slices sandwich bread
3½ tablespoons butter

UTENSILS:

Small knife
Large bowl
Large colander
Large saucepan
Needle or pin
Electric blender
48 snail pots
Cookie cutter, about ⅝ inch in diameter
Small bowl

PREPARING THE LIVE SNAILS:

Scrape away the chalky substance sealing the shells or lift it off, using a small knife to detach it from underneath. Place the snails in a large bowl with the salt and flour. Stir them around, then leave for 2 hours, stirring them several times more. At the end of this time, thoroughly wash the snails several times in lots of cold water. Drain in a colander.

Bring 2 quarts of water to a boil in a large saucepan, add all the snails at once, and boil for 5 minutes, then pour them into a colander to drain. Use a small needle or pin to extract each snail from its shell. Cut off the black part at the end of the tail of each snail. Place the snails in a pot with 2 cups each water and the white wine. Add the carrot, onion, *bouquet garni*, salt, and pepper, Bring the liquid to a boil, then simmer slowly for 1½ to 2½ hours, depending on the size of the snails. They are done when a needle can be inserted into their flesh with no resistance. Leave the snails to cool in the cooking liquid.

PREPARING THE SNAIL BUTTER:

Place the butter, garlic, parsley, mustard, powdered almonds, salt, pepper, and nutmeg in the blender. Blend until all these ingredients are perfectly combined in a green paste. Remove from the blender and place in a bowl; stir in the ham and mushrooms.

TO BAKE AND SERVE:

Once the snails are cold, drain them on a cloth. Place ½ teaspoon of **cooked diced tomatoes** in each snail pot, then place a snail in the pot, and fill the pot to the brim with the snail butter. Fill all the pots in this manner.

Butter the slices of bread with the softened butter and use a small cookie cutter or knife to cut out 48 circles that are small enough to fit easily into each snail pot. Place the little pieces of bread on top of the filled pots.

Preheat the oven to 425° F. Bake the snail pots in the oven for 10 minutes. The pieces of bread should have begun to brown and the snail butter should be hot and creamy but *not* oily when the snails are removed from the oven and served.

COMMENTS:

The best time to eat snails is during the winter, when they have gone into hibernation. The instructions given above are for using these fat, hibernating snails. If snails are cooked at another time of the year they should be starved for days before they are prepared. The starving of the snails is a precaution used to make sure that any toxic plants they may have eaten have been eliminated from their bodies before they are cooked.

Canned snails, already cooked, are readily available and can be used instead of live snails.

The mustard and powdered almonds in the snail butter keep it from "decomposing" (turning to oil) when it is heated in the oven.

Note: *The snail pots used hold 1 tablespoon of water when filled to the brim. There are snail platters made out of earthenware or porcelain that have well-like indentations, each the size of an individual snail pot, which can be used instead of the individual ones.*

40 *Terrine ménagère aux foies de volaille*
FAMILY-STYLE CHICKEN-LIVER TERRINE

Ingredients for one *terrine*, or 5 to 6 servings:

1 pound chicken livers or a mixture of 12 ounces chicken livers and 4 ounces chicken hearts
6 ounces fresh pork belly
6 ounces sausage meat
⅜ cup armagnac or cognac
3 tablespoons red port
3 tablespoons sherry
1 tablespoon finely chopped garlic
⅔ cup finely chopped fresh parsley
1 teaspoon thyme flowers, or ½ teaspoon thyme leaves
1 teaspoon granulated sugar
A pinch of nutmeg
1¾ teaspoons salt
2 pinches of pepper

½ pound barding fat
4 whole bay leaves
4 small sprigs thyme

UTENSILS:

Small sharp knife
Large bowl
Oval *terrine* (ovenproof porcelain or earthenware) 6½ inches long, 4½ inches wide, and 2¾ inches deep (*see Note*)
High-sided roasting pan

SERVE WITH:

Grenadine and onion "jam" (98)
Pickled onions
Sour gherkins (*cornichons*)

TO MARINATE THE LIVERS:

Use a sharp knife to remove the white stringy gristle from the livers and cut off any parts of the liver that might have turned green from contact with the gall bladder. Cut the fatty top off of the hearts, and cut all of the hearts and livers in half.

Cut the pork belly into slices ¾ inch thick, then cut the slices into little rectangular pieces (*lardons*) about ½ inch wide. Place the pieces of pork, the chicken livers, and the hearts in a large bowl with the sausage meat. Add the armagnac, port, sherry, garlic, parsley, thyme, sugar, nutmeg, salt, and pepper. Use a fork to mix together thoroughly all the ingredients, then cover with aluminum foil and place in the refrigerator overnight to marinate.

COOKING THE TERRINE:

Line the bottom and sides of the *terrine* with the thin pieces of barding fat, reserving some of the fat for covering the top of the *terrine* once it has been filled. Stir all the ingredients that were marinated together, then pour them all into the *terrine*: It should be completely filled, with the meat filling slightly domed and higher than the sides of the *terrine* itself. Completely cover the top of the filling with the remaining barding fat, and place the whole bay leaves and sprigs of thyme on top.

Preheat the oven to 425° F. Place the *terrine* in a high-sided roasting pan or baking dish, and pour in enough boiling water to come about halfway up the sides of the *terrine*. Place in the oven and bake for 1 hour and 45 minutes. The top will be a light-caramel color by the end of the cooking time.

TO SERVE:

Remove the *terrine* from the oven and take it out of the pan of water. Let the *terrine* cool for 3 hours at room temperature, then place it in the refrigerator overnight before serving. Serve the *terrine* as it is: Cut it into thin slices at the table and serve with sour gherkins (*cornichons*), pickled onions, and **Grenadine and onion "jam" (98).**

Note: *The* terrine *can be kept for several days in the refrigerator before serving, and it will keep refrigerated once it has been cut for several more days without spoiling if covered with aluminum foil. (It is best to press the foil against the cut part of the* terrine.*)*

The size of the terrine *is important, no matter what shape it is. It should contain 3½ cups water when filled to the brim. Ed.*

41 *Terrine fondante de canard sauvage*
DUCK TERRINE WITH RAISINS

Ingredients for one *terrine*, or 8 servings:

2 young ducks (preferably wild) about 2¼ pounds each, dressed weight
Salt and pepper
1 tablespoon cooking oil
6 ounces fresh fatback, diced
⅔ pound chicken livers or duck livers, cleaned
1¾ teaspoons salt
1½ teaspoons pepper
A pinch of allspice
1 cup *crème fraîche* (*see p. 352*) or heavy cream
4 egg yolks
8 teaspoons armagnac or cognac
¼ cup golden raisins, washed in warm water and dried

UTENSILS:

2 roasting pans
Electric blender

Fine sieve
Bowl
Wooden spoon
Earthenware dish (*see Note*)

TO PREPARE AND BAKE:

Preheat the oven to 475° F.

Only the breast meat will be used in this recipe, so cut the legs of the ducks off (or ask the butcher to do it for you).

Leave the rest of each duck whole and place them in a roasting pan. Salt, pepper, and rub with the cooking oil, then place in the oven for 15 minutes; the duck should be rare when finished cooking. Allow the meat to cool, then take off the skin and carefully cut all the breast meat off the bone. Cut the meat into tiny cubes the size of very small peas.

Place the fatback and chicken livers, the salt, pepper, and allspice in the blender. Blend until creamy, then add the cream, egg yolks, and armagnac, and continue blending for 30 seconds more or until a perfectly homogeneous mixture is formed. Pour this mixture through a fine sieve into a bowl, pressing and rubbing with a wooden spoon to make sure all the filaments from the liver are removed. Add the raisins to the strained liver mixture as well as the tiny cubes of duck meat prepared earlier.

Heat the oven to 400° F. Pour the duck-liver mixture into the earthenware dish. Place the dish in a high-sided roasting pan, and add enough boiling water to the pan to come halfway up the sides of the dish. Cover with a piece of aluminum foil, then place in the oven and bake for 30 to 45 minutes. Remove from the oven. Take the earthenware dish out of the pan of water and allow to cool completely at room temperature. Then place in the refrigerator overnight before serving. Serve cold with slices of toast.

COMMENTS:

When I ask people what they think was used in making this *terrine*, they often answer *foie gras*!

A young duck has a beak and wings that are supple and give easily when pressed with the thumb and index finger. The legs of the duck can be used to make **Confit of duck legs preserved in goose fat (79).**

The duck meat can be cooked as much as a day in advance.

Note: *The size of the earthenware dish is important. Filled with water to the brim, it should hold about 5½ cups. The liver mixture should be about 2 inches deep when poured into the dish for baking.*

To test whether or not the terrine *is done, plunge a trussing needle or knife into the center. If it comes out moist but clean, it is done. If not, or if any liquid which comes out of the hole is red, cook a little longer.*

The terrine *can be kept for several days in the refrigerator without spoiling if covered with aluminum foil. Ed.*

42 *Terrine d'anguilles au vin de Tursan*
EEL TERRINE

Ingredients for one *terrine*, or 8 servings:

FOR THE MARINADE:

1 pound eel fillets taken from 2 large eels, boned and skinned (*for substitution, see Comments*)
Salt and pepper
1 cup dry white wine
3 tablespoons armagnac or cognac (optional)
1 tablespoon freshly chopped tarragon
1 tablespoon freshly chopped chervil
1 tablespoon freshly chopped chives

FOR THE FISH-MUSHROOM MIXTURE:

1½ tablespoons butter
3½ cups diced mushrooms
1 tablespoon finely chopped shallot
1 tablespoon finely chopped fresh parsley
Salt and pepper
¾ pound fish fillets (fresh salmon or whiting)
1¾ teaspoons salt
A pinch of pepper
2 eggs
6 ounces (1½ sticks) softened butter

A pinch of cayenne pepper
A pinch of powdered saffron
1 teaspoon finely chopped fresh tarragon
1 teaspoon finely chopped fresh parsley
1 teaspoon finely chopped fresh chervil
1 teaspoon finely chopped fresh chives

UTENSILS:

Large enameled baking dish
Aluminum foil
Large frying pan
2 bowls
Electric blender
Spatula or wooden spoon
Oval porcelain or earthenware *terrine*, 6 inches long, 4 inches wide, 4 inches deep (*see Note*)

SERVE WITH:

Whipped water-cress sauce (14)

TO MARINATE:

In an enameled baking dish spread out the eel fillets, sprinkle with salt and pepper, and cover with all the ingredients listed above for the marinade. Place in the refrigerator overnight before cooking.

ASSEMBLING THE TERRINE AND BAKING:

Place the dish containing the eel fillets and all the marinade on top of the stove over low heat. Heat the liquid slowly (it should not boil) and simmer, covered with a piece of aluminum foil, for 20 minutes. Remove from the heat, take off the foil, and leave the eel fillets to cool completely in the liquid.

Heat 1½ tablespoons butter in a frying pan and sauté the mushrooms in it for about 5 minutes, or until they begin to brown. Add the shallot, parsley, salt, and pepper to the mushrooms, and continue cooking for 2 minutes more. Then pour the contents of the pan into a bowl and allow to cool completely.

Chill the blender container in the refrigerator for 30 minutes before using it. When cold, place in it the salmon or whiting fillets, 1¾ teaspoons salt, and a little pepper, and blend for 30 seconds or until the mixture forms a homogeneous purée. Continue blending and break in the eggs, one at a time. Blend for 20 seconds, then add the softened butter, cayenne pepper, saffron, tarragon, parsley, chervil, and chives. Blend for another 30 seconds or until the mixture is perfectly smooth; while blending, it is advisable to stop frequently and scrape down the sides of the blender container to make sure all the ingredients are being well mixed. Once it is blended, pour this mixture into a large bowl and stir in the mushrooms and all their seasoning.

Remove the cold eel fillets from their liquid, pat dry with a cloth, and cut each fillet in half lengthwise to make long strips.

Using a spatula or a wooden spoon, cover the bottom and sides of the *terrine* with a layer of the fish-mushroom mixture approximately ½ inch thick. Place a layer of eel fillets on the bottom. Then continue filling the *terrine* with, first, a layer of fish-mushroom mixture, then a layer of eel fillets, until the *terrine* is full. (The last layer should be the fish-mushroom mixture.)

Preheat the oven to 275° F. Place the *terrine* in a high-sided roasting pan and add enough boiling water to the pan to come halfway up the sides of the *terrine*. Cover with a piece of aluminum foil, place in the oven, and bake for 3 hours.

Once baked, remove the *terrine* from the water and allow to cool several hours at room temperature. Then, while it is still slightly warm, place it in the refrigerator and chill overnight before serving. Serve the *terrine* as it is; do not turn it out: Cut ½-inch slices for each person and serve with **Whipped water-cress sauce (14)**.

COMMENTS:

Long, slow cooking is essential if the *terrine* is to be of the desired consistency.

This *terrine* can be made even better if the sides of the mold are first lined with barding fat, then garnished with lemon slices (peel and white membranes removed) before being filled as described above.

CARP OR MACKEREL TERRINE:

I like fish *terrines* made with a variety of good fish, and you could easily make *terrines* following the basic instructions given above with almost any fish of your choice. As alternatives I would suggest carp or mackerel instead of eel, and red wine instead of white in the marinade, for an interesting variant of this recipe. If red wine is used, serve the *terrine* with a **Whipped tomato sauce** (**15**) instead of watercress sauce.

Note: *The size of the* terrine *is important, although the shape is not. Filled to the brim with water, it should hold about 6½ cups. Ed.*

Les feuilletés légers d'entrée

PUFF-PASTRY ENTRÉES

Feuilleté d'asperges au beurre de cerfeuil

43 PUFF PASTRY WITH ASPARAGUS AND CHERVIL

(color picture II)

Ingredients for 4 servings:

4 medium-size fresh asparagus (*see Comments*)
4 cups water
2 teaspoons coarse salt

6⅓ ounces **puff pastry (118)**, fresh or frozen (*see Note, p. 299*)
1 beaten egg

3 tablespoons fresh chervil leaves
4 tablespoons *crème fraîche* (*see p. 352*) or heavy cream
½ pound softened butter, divided into small pieces
Salt and pepper
1 tablespoon lemon juice

UTENSILS:

Vegetable peeler
Saucepan
Rolling pin

Large, very sharp knife
Baking sheet
Pastry brush
Skimmer or slotted spoon
Small *sauteuse* or medium saucepan
Serrated knife
To serve: 4 hot plates, or a long hot serving platter

COOKING THE ASPARAGUS:

Peel the asparagus with a vegetable peeler, starting at the tip and peeling toward the base of the stalk. This is most easily done by holding the asparagus by the tip and pressing it flat (lengthwise) against the table. When the asparagus have been peeled, wash them, then cut them off a little more than 3 inches away from the tip. The rest of the stalks can be saved for making soup; only the tips will be used in this recipe.

In a saucepan, bring the water and salt to a boil, add the asparagus tips, and cook for 7 minutes, then remove from the heat. Leave the asparagus in their cooking liquid to stay warm.

SHAPING AND BAKING THE PUFF PASTRY:

Preheat the oven to 425° F.

While the asparagus are cooking, lightly flour the table, and with a rolling pin, roll out the puff pastry into a rectangle approximately 6½ inches wide, 10 inches long, and ⅛ inch thick. With a large, very sharp knife, cut off the edges of the pastry to form a rectangle 5½ inches wide and 9½ inches long. When cutting, use a quick, straight, downward movement—do not pull the knife along through the pastry. Cut this rectangle again into four bands 5½ inches long and a little more than 2 inches wide (simply divide the length of the large rectangle into four equal parts).

Turn the bands *upside down* on a baking sheet. With a pastry brush, brush the surface of each band with beaten egg, but be very careful not to let any egg drip over onto the edge of the pastry; this would keep it from rising properly. Place in the oven and bake for 12 to 15 minutes, or until a rich golden brown. When done, turn off the oven and keep the pastries warm inside the oven with the door ajar.

MAKING THE SAUCE:

Lift the asparagus tips out of their cooking liquid with a skimmer or slotted spoon and place them in a small *sauteuse* or a saucepan. Add 4 tablespoons of their cooking liquid and 2 tablespoons of the fresh chervil leaves. Bring to a boil and reduce the liquid by half; then add the cream, butter, salt, pepper, and lemon juice, and bring back to a boil. Cook for 1 minute more, shaking the pan with a circular motion to make the sauce spin around the sides. Remove from the heat.

TO SERVE:

With a serrated knife, carefully cut the cooked puff pastries along their centers, forming two halves, top and bottom. Place the bottom halves on the plates or serving platter and lay 10 asparagus tips across each one, five of them facing one way and five facing the other way, alternately. Spoon the sauce over the asparagus, sprinkle with the remaining tablespoon of chervil, then cover with the top half of each pastry and serve immediately.

COMMENTS:

Baby wild asparagus are absolutely delicious in this recipe, if you are lucky enough to find some.

The asparagus season is unfortunately very short, but you can still make this recipe all year if you use canned asparagus. Simply heat them up in a little of their juice before using as you would the fresh asparagus after they have been cooked.

Asparagus may also be replaced by cauliflower. The result is as surprising as it is delicious, and less expensive as well.

Note: *If using cauliflower, count 4 medium flowerets broken into 10 baby flowerets each, measuring a total of 3 cups. Cook them according to the directions given above for asparagus tips.*

Chopped fresh parsley may be used instead of chervil. Ed.

Feuilleté de truffes au vin de Graves
PUFF PASTRY WITH TRUFFLES AND FOIE GRAS 44

Ingredients for 4 servings:

6⅓ ounces **puff pastry** (**118**) (*see Note, p. 299*)
1 beaten egg to brush on pastry

4 ounces canned truffles (4 large truffles)
3½ tablespoons butter
¾ teaspoon salt
A pinch of pepper
4 tablespoons dry white wine (preferably a bordeaux)
4 tablespoons sherry
4 tablespoons truffle juice from the can
2 generous cups heavy cream

4 ounces fresh *foie gras* or canned *foie gras mi-cuit*
1 teaspoon lemon juice

UTENSILS:

Small *sauteuse* or medium saucepan
Wooden spatula
Small sharp knife
Serrated knife
Skimmer or slotted spoon
To serve: 4 hot plates, or a long hot serving platter

SHAPING AND BAKING THE PUFF PASTRY:

Roll out, cut, and bake the puff pastry exactly as described in the recipe for **Puff pastry with asparagus and chervil** (**43**).

COOKING THE TRUFFLES AND THEIR SAUCE:

While the pastries are cooking, cut the truffles into thin *julienne* strips.

In a small *sauteuse* or a saucepan, melt the butter, add the truffles, sprinkle with salt and pepper, and simmer, uncovered, for 3 minutes. Then add the white wine, sherry, and truffle juice. Bring to a boil, and cook, uncovered, over high heat until the liquid has reduced by a third.

Add the cream, bring back to a boil, and boil gently for about 15 minutes, or until the sauce has a rich creamy texture. To check whether it is of the right consistency, dip a wooden spatula into the sauce, lift it out, hold it at a sharp slant, and draw a line in the sauce on the spatula with your finger. If the groove left by your finger does not close up again, the sauce is just the right thickness.

TO SERVE:

Dip a small sharp knife into hot water, then slice the *foie gras* into 8 slices, dipping the knife again for each slice.

With a serrated knife, carefully cut the cooked puff pastries along their centers, forming two halves, top and bottom. Place the bottom halves on the hot plates or serving platter. Lift the truffles out of their sauce with a skimmer or slotted spoon and place them on the pastries. Cover the truffles on each pastry with two slices of *foie gras.* Taste the truffle sauce for seasoning (add salt and pepper if necessary), stir in the lemon juice, and spoon the sauce over the *foie gras.* Cover each pastry with its top and serve immediately.

Feuilleté de Saint-Jacques aux truffes
45 PUFF PASTRY WITH SCALLOPS AND TRUFFLES

Ingredients for 4 servings:

12 large live scallops in their shells (*see Note*)
6⅓ ounces **puff pastry** (**118**), fresh or frozen (*see Note, p. 299*)
1 beaten egg, to brush on dough

1 tablespoon butter
2¾ ounces canned truffles (4 large truffles) cut into *julienne* strips (save the truffle juice)
1⅓ cups heavy cream
Salt and pepper

UTENSILS:

Knife with wide, rigid blade
Kitchen spoon
Bowl

Sieve
Clean thin cloth
Small saucepan with cover
Small *sauteuse* or medium saucepan
Serrated knife
To serve: 4 hot plates, or a long hot serving platter

PREPARING THE SCALLOPS:

Although you can ask your fish dealer to clean the scallops for you, it is preferable to do it yourself. Here's how:

Take a knife with a wide, rigid blade and slip it between the two shells of the scallop. Slide the blade of the knife flat against the inside of the top (flat) shell to detach it. Lift off the flat shell, then, with an ordinary kitchen spoon, detach the scallop and its coral from the curved bottom shell. Hold the shell over a bowl as you do this to catch any juice from the scallop.

With the knife, cut off any black parts, as well as the ribbonlike grayish membrane that surrounds the scallop, then rinse the scallop under cold running water and pat dry on a clean cloth or towel. Strain the juice from the scallops through a sieve lined with a clean thin cloth into a small saucepan.

SHAPING AND BAKING THE PUFF PASTRY:

Roll out, cut, and make the puff pastry exactly as described in the recipe for **Puff pastry with asparagus and chervil** (43).

MAKING THE SAUCE AND COOKING THE SCALLOPS:

In a small *sauteuse* or a saucepan, melt the butter, then add the strips of truffle and simmer, uncovered, for 2 minutes. Add 1 tablespoon of the truffle juice, and the cream, salt, and pepper. Boil gently for 3 to 4 minutes, or until the liquid has reduced by half.

While the sauce is cooking, place the small saucepan containing the juice from the scallops over medium heat and bring barely to a boil. Add the scallops, lower the heat, cover the pan, and simmer for 1 minute, then remove from the heat.

TO SERVE:

With a serrated knife, carefully cut the cooked puff pastries along their centers, forming two halves, top and bottom. Place the bottom halves on the hot plates or serving platter, lift the scallops out of their juice with a skimmer or slotted spoon, and place three of them on each pastry. Add the juice from the scallops to the sauce, then pour the sauce over the scallops. Cover with the top half of each pastry, and serve immediately.

COMMENTS:

A delicious variation of this dish can be made using 8 scallops and 8 large oysters, instead of only scallops. Open the oysters and poach them in their juice for 30 seconds. Add their juice to the sauce as well as that of the scallops.

Another taste which can be added to this recipe is that of little vegetables, cooked as described in the recipe for **Salmon papillotes (61).** After the scallops and sauce have been placed on the pastries, spread 1 tablespoon of vegetables over each portion, then cover with the top of each pastry and serve.

Here is another amusing and original way to serve this dish: Wash, brush clean, and carefully dry 4 of the scallop shells, tops and bottoms. Lightly brush the inside of each top and bottom shell with melted butter, then line each carefully with a very thin layer of puff pastry rolled out approximately 1/16 inch thick. Cut the pastry off around the shells if it goes over the edges. Brush the pastry with beaten egg, then bake in a preheated 425° F oven for 12 to 15 minutes, or until a rich golden brown. When done, the pastries will be exactly the shape of the shells they baked in. Remove the pastries from the shells, fill the bottom (curved) halves with the scallops and sauce, then place the flat-top halves over them, and serve. (The pastry shells are not slit as with the usual *feuilletés*.)

NOTE: *If you buy scallops that have already been shucked, there will not be much juice to poach them in, so it is best to open them yourself. However, if you prefer not to, or if it is impossible to buy scallops still in their shells, poach them in the sauce in the following manner: When you add the truffle juice, cream, salt, and pepper, bring barely to a boil, then add the scallops, lower the heat, cover the pot, and simmer for 1 minute. Lift the cooked scallops out of the sauce with a skimmer or slotted spoon, and keep them warm on a covered plate. Then reduce the sauce as described in the recipe. Ed.*

Feuilleté d'écrevisses à l'oignon croquant PUFF PASTRY WITH CRAYFISH AND SWEET ONIONS 46

Ingredients for 4 servings:

6⅓ ounces **puff pastry** (**118**) (*see Note, p. 299*)
1 beaten egg to brush on dough

32 crayfish tails with 1½ cups **crayfish sauce** (**13**)
6 tablespoons finely chopped sweet onion
1 teaspoon freshly chopped chives

UTENSILS:

Double boiler
Serrated knife
To serve: 4 hot plates, or a long hot serving platter

SHAPING AND BAKING THE PUFF PASTRY:

Roll out, cut, and make the puff pastry exactly as described in the recipe for **Puff pastry with asparagus and chervil** (**43**).

TO SERVE:

Prepare the crayfish sauce several hours, or a day, in advance. Reheat the tails and sauce together in a double boiler.

With a serrated knife, carefully cut the cooked puff pastries along their centers, forming two halves, top and bottom. Place the bottom halves on the hot plates or serving platter, and place equal amounts of crayfish tails and sauce on each one. Sprinkle with the chopped onion and chives, then cover with the top halves of the pastries and serve immediately.

COMMENT:

The raw chopped onion acts a little bit like raw, fresh currants; it communicates a fresh, slightly sweet taste to whatever it is eaten with. You can use it in other recipes in the same way as it is used here.

Millefeuille d'écrevisses
47 CRAYFISH MILLEFEUILLE

Ingredients for 4 servings:

2 cups **crayfish sauce** (**13**) prepared in advance (*for substitution, see Comments*)
1 tablespoon gelatin
3 tablespoons cold water
⅝ cup heavy cream, chilled
1 teaspoon freshly chopped tarragon
1 teaspoon freshly chopped chervil
Salt and pepper

10½ ounces **puff pastry** (**118**), fresh or frozen (*see Note, p. 299*)
32 crayfish tails (left over from making the **crayfish sauce**) (*for substitution, see Note*)
8 crayfish heads (for decoration)

UTENSILS:

Bain-marie or double boiler
Wooden spoon
Mixing bowl, chilled
Wire whisk
Wooden spatula
Rolling pin
Large, very sharp knife
Baking sheet
Fork
Cake rack
Flexible-blade spatula
To serve: Long serving platter

MAKING THE CRAYFISH CREAM:

Heat the crayfish sauce in a *bain-marie* or double boiler. While the sauce is heating up, moisten the gelatin in the water.

When the crayfish sauce is hot, add the gelatin, stirring to help dissolve it and mix it into the sauce. Then remove the sauce from the heat and allow to cool, stirring from time to time with a wooden spoon.

The sauce will cool off faster if you set the pan in a bowl half full of water and ice cubes.

Place the chilled cream in the chilled mixing bowl and whip until stiff with a wire whisk; the cream is ready when it peaks gently and clings to the whisk when it is lifted out of the bowl.

When the crayfish sauce is completely cold and has thickened considerably, add the chopped herbs, then gently fold in the whipped cream with a wooden spatula. The finished cream should be light and airy, rather like a Bavarian cream. Taste for seasoning and add salt and pepper if necessary, then set aside in the refrigerator.

SHAPING AND BAKING THE MILLEFEUILLE:

Preheat the oven to 425° F.

Lightly flour the table and roll out the puff pastry with a rolling pin until it forms a rectangle 8 inches wide, 18 inches long, and 1/16 inch thick.

With a large, very sharp knife, cut this rectangle into thirds, forming three bands each measuring approximately 6 inches by 8 inches.

Lightly sprinkle the baking sheet with water, then lay the pastry bands on it. Prick each band all over with a fork (this will keep the pastry from rising too much), then place in the oven and bake for 20 minutes, or until golden brown. If your oven is not large enough to bake all three bands at the same time, first bake two of them, then, when they are done, bake the third (chill the third band while the others are baking). When the pastries are cooked, lift them off of the baking sheet and onto a cake rack to cool.

TO SERVE:

Place one of the bands of puff pastry on a serving platter and spread half of the crayfish cream over it with a flexible-blade spatula. Arrange 16 of the crayfish tails on the cream, then place another band of pastry on top. Spread three quarters of the remaining cream over this pastry, and place the remaining 16 crayfish tails on top. Cover with the last pastry, and spread the remaining cream in a very thin layer over the top. Decorate with the 8 crayfish heads and carry to the table. Cut into 4 portions and serve.

COMMENTS:

The puff pastry may be rolled out and cut, then placed on the baking sheet and chilled in the refrigerator, for several hours or a day in advance, before being baked. This will keep the pastry from shrinking while baking, something which happens now and then when it is baked right after being rolled out.

A simpler variation of this recipe may be made when you don't have any crayfish sauce prepared in advance. Whip 1⅓ cups heavy cream until stiff, and add to it 2 teaspoons of freshly chopped herbs, 1 teaspoon of lemon juice, 1 tablespoon of tomato paste, and salt, pepper, and cayenne pepper to taste. Instead of using crayfish, poach 32 small *langoustines* for 1½ minutes in salted water and use their tail meat for the decoration.

NOTE: *When rolling the puff pastry out, it is best to roll it into a rectangle slightly larger than the dimensions given, then trim the edges with the knife before cutting it into bands. This not only makes the finished bands more symmetrical, it also permits the pastry to rise more evenly.*

The way in which the pastry is pricked is also very important. The prongs of the fork must go all the way through the pastry—you should feel them hit the baking sheet. If pricked too lightly the pastry will rise too high, as if it had not been pricked at all.

Shrimp may be used instead of crayfish or langoustines. *Ed.*

Les foies gras
FOIE GRAS

Note: *Fresh* foie gras, *with which this chapter is primarily concerned, is a golden substance virtually unobtainable by American cooks. Nevertheless, the techniques with which* foie gras *is handled cannot fail to be of interest, whether one has the opportunity to apply them or not. They are counsels of perfection important to know. The use of substitutes in this chapter, usually chicken livers, is not intended to imitate the original recipe, but rather to suggest especially good ways of treating the ingredients you do have available. Ed.*

Terrine de foie gras des Landes
8 FOIE GRAS TERRINE

Ingredients for one terrine, or 4 to 5 servings:

- 1 uncooked fresh *foie gras* of duck (*see p. 352*), weighing about 1¼ pounds (*for substitution, see Comment*)
- 1 teaspoon salt
- ¾ teaspoon white pepper
- A pinch of nutmeg
- A pinch of allspice

½ teaspoon granulated sugar
2 teaspoons red port
2 teaspoons sherry
2 teaspoons armagnac or cognac

UTENSILS:

Large bowl
Small sharp knife
Deep earthenware platter
Porcelain or earthenware *terrine* with its lid, 6½ inches long, 4½ inches wide, and 2¾ inches deep
Candy thermometer
A thin piece of wood that just fits inside the *terrine*
A 1- to 1½-pound weight

TO PREPARE AND MARINATE:

Place the *foie gras* in a large bowl of lukewarm water for 1 hour. The water will make it whiten somewhat and soften it as well, which will make the *foie gras* easier to devein.

Remove the *foie gras* from the water. Using your hands, separate the two lobes (one is typically larger than the other). With a sharp knife split each lobe in half lengthwise. When it is cut, all the veins that run through the *foie gras* will be visible. Using a small knife and pulling from top to bottom, carefully take out the veins. Inspect the *foie gras* and use the knife to pare off any traces of green that may remain from contact with the gall bladder.

Place the *foie gras* in a deep earthenware platter, season with the salt and pepper, nutmeg, allspice, and sugar, then pour on the port, sherry, and armagnac. Place in the refrigerator and leave to marinate 12 hours or overnight before cooking. Turn the pieces over two or three times while marinating.

TO COOK:

Take the *foie gras* from the refrigerator and leave it at room temperature for 1 hour before cooking. Then remove the *foie gras* from the marinade and place half of the large lobe in the bottom of the *terrine.* Lay the two halves of the small lobe next to each other on top of it, then cover them with the second half of the large lobe, pressing the pieces down gently into the *terrine.*

Preheat the oven to 300° F.

Rinse the earthenware platter used for marinating and place it in the oven. Pour water into it to a depth of about ¾ inch. Let this water heat in the oven to 158° F; check the temperature with a candy thermometer. Place the *terrine*, uncovered, in the water and cook for 40 minutes to 1 hour, or until the melted fat almost covers the *foie gras*. To test whether or not the *foie gras* has cooked enough, place your finger underneath the lobe on the top and down into the center of the *terrine*; the center should be warm, but not hot; the fat on the surface will be considerably warmer than the center.

The water surrounding the *terrine* should be maintained at a constant temperature of 158° F. Check the temperature frequently and add either a little boiling water or a little cold water if necessary to keep it constant.

Remove the *terrine* from the earthenware platter and allow it to cool for about 10 minutes, then place a piece of wood that just fits inside the *terrine* on top of the *foie gras*. Weight the wood down with a small 1- to 1½-pound weight. Leave the *foie gras* to cool at room temperature for 2 to 3 hours, then remove the plank and weight, and chill the *terrine*, covered with its lid, in the refrigerator overnight before serving. This *terrine* is always served cold, and it is, in fact, preferable to chill it for 3 to 4 days before serving.

TO SERVE:

Serve the *foie gras* from the *terrine* it cooked in. Slices of the *foie gras* should be eaten with large slices of toasted, country-style bread (*not* brioche!).

COMMENTS:

Once cooked, the *foie gras* can be kept in the refrigerator for 8 days without spoiling.

After the *foie gras* has been cooked and pressed, a thin coat of fat about ¼ inch thick should cover the surface. If any part of the *foie gras* sticks up above the fat after being pressed, pour a little melted goose fat over it to cover.

There are several tests for recognizing the best quality of uncooked, fresh *foie gras*. Hold the *foie gras* with both hands, a lobe in each hand, and carefully begin to pull the two lobes apart. If the flesh breaks and is stiff (like suet), the *foie gras* is very fatty and will shrink a lot, giving out a lot of fat when cooked. If, on the other hand, the flesh feels very flexible and elastic before tearing, the *foie gras* is probably full of more veins than usual, and, although it will shrink less, it will have less taste and tend to dry out when cooked. The best *foie gras* should be supple when the two lobes are pulled apart, and will stretch before breaking, then break cleanly. This is the best *foie gras* and is ideal for making this *terrine.*

A much less expensive variation of this *terrine* can be made with chicken livers. The method is somewhat different because they don't contain any fat of their own, but the result is surprising and delicious.

For one *terrine*, the same size as in the original recipe, you need:

1¼ pounds chicken livers
2 cups milk (approximately)
1¾ teaspoons salt
1 teaspoon pepper

The other ingredients are the same as for the original recipe, but you will also need 1¼ pounds of fresh lard for cooking the chicken livers.

Remove any greenish parts from the chicken livers, then soak them for 24 hours in the milk; they should be completely covered by the milk.

The next day, drain the livers and pat them dry, then marinate them exactly as described for the *foie gras* (but using the amounts of salt and pepper given here) for 12 hours. It is not necessary to split the chicken livers.

When the livers have finished marinating, remove them from the refrigerator and leave at room temperature for 1 hour. Then drain them and pat them dry with a towel. Melt the lard in a medium-size saucepan, and heat it until it reaches 185° F, then add the chicken livers and simmer them (do not let them boil) for 3 minutes. The livers should be completely covered by the fat; if necessary, cook them in several batches.

When the livers are cooked—they should still be soft and very dark pink inside when done—drain them on a clean cloth for 1 hour. Then lay them in the *terrine* and pour enough of the melted lard over them barely to cover them. Allow to cool for 15 minutes, then place a piece of wood which just fits inside the *terrine* on top of the livers and place a small weight (about 2 pounds) on top. Allow the *terrine* to cool completely, then remove the weight and wood, smooth the lard over the livers, cover the *terrine* with its lid, and place in the refrigerator until the next day. Serve as described in the *foie gras* recipe.

Foie gras frais en gelée de poivre
FOIE GRAS IN PEPPER JELLY 49

Ingredients for 4 servings:

1 uncooked fresh *foie gras* of duck (*see p.* 352), weighing 1¼ pounds (*for substitution, see Comments*)

1 teaspoon salt
1 teaspoon white pepper
2⅔ cups goose fat
1½ tablespoons gelatin
1 cup cold water
2 teaspoons granulated sugar
4 tablespoons wine vinegar
1 teaspoon armagnac
Crushed ice
2 teaspoons peppercorns coarsely crushed in a mortar, or 1 tablespoon very coarsely ground pepper

UTENSILS:

Shallow dish
Medium saucepan
Skimmer or slotted spoon
Plate
2 small saucepans
Bowl and crushed ice
To serve: Chilled serving platter

PRELIMINARY PREPARATIONS:

Do *not* split open or soak the *foie gras* for this recipe. Simply pare off any green spots that may have resulted from contact with the gall bladder. Season the *foie gras* all over with the salt and pepper, then place it in a shallow dish or soup plate, cover it with aluminum foil, and put it in the refrigerator overnight before cooking.

TO COOK:

One hour before cooking, remove the *foie gras* from the refrigerator. Place the goose fat in saucepan and heat it to 185° F. Place the *foie gras* in the goose fat and simmer it for 7½ minutes. Turn the *foie gras* over and continue cooking for another 7½ minutes. Then, using a skimmer or slotted spoon, carefully lift the *foie gras* out of the pot and place it on a plate. Immediately wrap the *foie gras* and plate in aluminum foil, leave to cool at room temperature, then place in the refrigerator to chill overnight.

PREPARING THE JELLY AND SERVING:

Place the gelatin in a saucepan with the cold water. Stir and bring to a boil, remove from the heat, and reserve.

In a second small saucepan place the sugar and vinegar. Stir and bring to a boil, then cook until the sugar caramelizes and the mixture is dark and syrupy. Pour this mixture into the saucepan with the dissolved gelatin, and add the armagnac as well. Then place the pan in a bowl of crushed ice. Stir constantly until the mixture is completely cold and the consistency of olive oil; at this point it will be on the verge of setting. Remove the saucepan from the ice.

Take the *foie gras* from the refrigerator, remove the aluminum foil, and place it on the serving platter. Spoon half of the gelatin over the *foie gras*, sprinkle with the coarsely crushed pepper, then finish spooning the gelatin over the pepper. Return to the refrigerator for at least an hour before serving.

Serve the *foie gras* in its jelly. Cut it at the table into slices a little less than ½ inch thick. Serve some of the jelly with each slice.

Pieces of freshly toasted, country-style bread should be served with the *foie gras*.

COMMENTS:

The *foie gras* can be cooked and refrigerated for up to a month ahead of time if the following instructions are carefully followed:

Once the *foie gras* has finished cooking, remove it from the fat with a skimmer or slotted spoon, and wrap it tightly in a piece of aluminum foil. Place the wrapped *foie gras* back into the fat it cooked in (place the fat in a bowl or *terrine*), allow to cool, and refrigerate in the fat; the *foie gras* should be completely covered by the fat, which will keep it from spoiling.

Once cooked in this way, the *foie gras* can be unwrapped and served as it is, or covered with the pepper jelly as described above.

An equal weight of calf's liver, in one piece, may be substituted for the *foie gras* of duck. In this case do everything as described, but cook the liver for a total of 35 minutes instead of 15 minutes, turning it over once after 17½ minutes. The liver should be pink inside when done.

For a richer texture and flavor, the liver can be larded lengthwise with 4 to 6 long strips of salt pork, but this is not absolutely necessary.

Note: *It is important that the fat not be allowed to boil while cooking the* foie gras *or liver. If it begins to bubble, remove the pot from the heat until the bubbling stops. For best results, use an asbestos pad or other heat-diffusing device.*

If the gelatin catches and solidifies while in the saucepan, place it back over the heat for a few seconds, whisking until the gelatin becomes semiliquid again, then remove the saucepan from the heat.

When spooning the jelly over the foie gras, *it is sometimes helpful to pat it into place with a pastry brush.*

If cooking the foie gras *ahead of time and saving it as described in the Comments, it may be necessary to hold the wrapped* foie gras *under the surface of the fat. To do this, place a small plate or a plank which fits into the bowl or* terrine *on top of the* foie gras *and weight it down with a 1- to 1½-pound weight. Once the fat has cooled to room temperature, remove the plate and weight and refrigerate. Ed.*

Foie gras en habit vert aux blanc de poireaux

50 FOIE GRAS DRESSED IN GREEN WITH LEEKS AND BEANS

Ingredients for 4 servings:

1 fresh uncooked *foie gras* of duck (*see p. 352*) weighing 1¼ pounds (*for substitution, see Comments*)
4 cups water (for *foie gras*)
1½ teaspoons coarse salt (for *foie gras*)
Salt and pepper

4 cups water (for vegetables)
1½ teaspoons coarse salt (for vegetables)
12 large Bibb lettuce leaves, rinsed
16 small leeks (white parts only), tied together
½ pound very small green beans, cut into 2-inch pieces
⅔ cup **chicken stock (2) (3)** (*see Note*)
3 tablespoons port
4 teaspoons truffle juice from canned truffles (optional; *see Note*)
Scant 2 tablespoons butter (for vegetables)
3½ tablespoons butter, broken into small pieces (for the sauce)

UTENSILS:

2 large saucepans
Large bowl
Skimmer or slotted spoon
Small roasting pan
Large frying pan
Small saucepan
To serve: 4 hot dinner plates

PRELIMINARY PREPARATIONS:

Using a sharp knife, pare off any greenish areas from the *foie gras* that may have resulted from its contact with the gall bladder.

Fill a large saucepan with 4½ cups of water and add the coarse salt. Bring to a boil, then drop in the *foie gras* and boil for 1 minute. Remove the pan from the heat and leave the *foie gras* in the water to cool. Keep the pan in a cool place overnight.

TO COOK AND SERVE:

In another large saucepan, bring 4 cups of water to a boil, add the coarse salt, then the lettuce. Boil for 1 minute, then lift the lettuce out with a skimmer or slotted spoon, and place it immediately in a bowl full of cold water to cool for 10 seconds. Remove the lettuce leaves from the water and squeeze out as much of the water as possible, then spread them out on a towel to dry.

Drop the leeks into the same boiling water once the lettuce has been removed. After 4 minutes, drop the beans into the water as well, and boil the two for 6 minutes more. Then drain the vegetables, untie the leeks, and reserve for later use.

Preheat the oven to 350° F.

Carefully lift the *foie gras* out of its water and dry it with a towel. Separate the two lobes, and, using a sharp knife that has been dipped into hot water, cut the *foie gras* into 12 slices about ½ inch thick. Salt and pepper the slices lightly and place a slice on each lettuce leaf. Fold each leaf carefully around the *foie gras*, then place these little packages in a small roasting pan (just large enough to hold them all flat on the bottom) with the central ribs of the lettuce leaves underneath. Add the stock, port, and truffle juice to the roasting pan and place in the oven for 10 minutes.

While the *foie gras* is in the oven, sauté the leeks and green beans in 2 scant tablespoons of butter just long enough to heat them through, then arrange them on the dinner plates; make a semicircle of leeks and beans on each plate. Then, when the *foie gras* is cooked, place three pieces on each plate in a cloverleaf pattern inside the semicircle of vegetables. Keep the plates warm while finishing the sauce.

Pour the cooking liquid from the roasting pan into a small saucepan, boil quickly until it has reduced by half, then start adding the 3½ tablespoons butter, a few pieces at a time. Shake the pan in a circular pattern so that the sauce spins around the sides while the butter is being added. Add salt and pepper if necessary, pour the sauce over the *foie gras*, and serve immediately.

COMMENTS:

Since fresh uncooked *foie gras* is expensive and hard to find, it can be replaced by an equal weight of chicken livers in making this recipe.

Do not prepare or cook them like the *foie gras.* Instead, sauté them for about 2 minutes in a large frying pan in 3½ tablespoons of butter, with 2 finely chopped shallots, a pince of thyme, and salt and pepper. The livers should still be pink inside when cooked. Place one or two livers (depending on size) inside each lettuce leaf and proceed as described above for final cooking and serving.

Note: *If not using truffle juice, use 4 teaspoons madeira when making the sauce. If using chicken livers instead of* foie gras, *the sauce can be made by deglazing the pan the livers cooked in (instead of using stock) as follows:*

When the chicken livers are cooked, lift them out of the pan and add 1 cup water to the pan glaze. Bring to a boil and stir until all the juices from the livers have been dissolved. Then strain the liquid and use instead of stock, following the measurements and method described in the original recipe.

Other vegetables, such as asparagus or peas, may be used instead of leeks and green beans. Ed.

Foie gras de canard aux navets confits

51 FOIE GRAS WITH SWEET BABY TURNIPS

Ingredients for 4 servings:

- 9 cups water
- 1 generous tablespoon coarse salt
- 32 baby turnips the size of small eggs, or 2½ pounds young turnips, peeled and shaped like small eggs
- 2 tablespoons butter
- 2 tablespoons granulated sugar
- 2 tablespoons wine vinegar
- ½ cup sherry
- 4 tablespoons red port
- 4 tablespoons cold water
- 1 ounce truffle (1 very large truffle), cut into thin *julienne* strips (optional)
- 5 tablespoons butter, broken into small pieces

1 fresh uncooked *foie gras* of duck (*see p. 352*) weighing 1¼ pounds (*for substitution, see Comments and Note*)
Salt and pepper
2 tablespoons flour
4 teaspoons cooking oil

UTENSILS:

Large saucepan
Colander
2 large frying pans
Spatula
To serve: 4 hot dinner plates or a hot serving platter

THE TURNIPS AND THEIR SAUCE:

In a large saucepan bring the water and coarse salt to a boil. Add the turnips and boil, uncovered, for 15 minutes, then drain in a colander.

Heat the butter in a large frying pan until it no longer sizzles and is very light brown. Add the turnips and brown quickly on all sides. Sprinkle in the sugar and continue cooking, shaking the pan frequently, until the sugar begins to caramelize and the turnips are a nice brown color. Add the vinegar (it will immediately evaporate), then stir in the sherry, port, and water, and boil for 1 minute. Add the truffle and remaining butter to the bubbling sauce. When the butter has melted, the vegetables are ready to serve. Place the pan over very low heat while preparing the *foie gras.*

PREPARING THE FOIE GRAS:

Use a sharp knife to pare off any green spots from the *foie gras* resulting from its contact with the gall bladder. Dip the knife into hot water and cut the *foie gras* into four equal slices. Salt and pepper the slices lightly, roll them in flour, then pat off all the excess flour before cooking.

Heat the oil in a large frying pan until it begins to smoke, then place the slices of *foie gras* in the pan and cook for 2 to 3 minutes on a side.

TO SERVE:

Remove the *foie gras* from the pan with a spatula and place one slice on each plate. Spoon the turnips and their sauce over the *foie gras* and serve immediately.

COMMENTS:

An equal weight of calf's liver can be used instead of the *foie gras* in this recipe. The combination of flavors is delicious; everyone will want to know the recipe.

Note: *The slices of* foie gras *will be a little more than ½ inch thick. If using calf's liver, the thickness must be taken into consideration, as it affects the cooking time; it is essential that the liver be slightly pink inside when cooked. If overcooked, its delicate taste is ruined. If the liver is ½ inch thick, cook for 2 to 3 minutes on a side as indicated. But if only half as thick (¼ inch), cook only half as long, i.e., 1 to 1½ minutes on a side. Ed.*

Pot-au-feu de foie gras
52 FOIE GRAS POT-AU-FEU

Ingredients for 4 servings:

1 large onion, unpeeled but cut in half
3 quarts **chicken stock (2) (3)**
16 baby carrots
16 baby turnips
8 baby onions
4 very small leeks (white part only)
16 baby cucumbers (fresh gherkins)
24 asparagus tips

Note: If fresh baby vegetables like those listed above are not available, normal-size vegetables cut into pieces 1½ inches long may be used instead.

6½ cups water
1 scant tablespoon coarse salt
4 small potatoes
8 green cabbage leaves
1 fresh uncooked *foie gras* of duck (*see p. 352*) weighing 1¼ pounds (*for substitution, see Comments*)

½ cup red port
½ cup madeira
¼ pound noodles (*fettucini* or *tagliatelli*), preferably homemade
Truffle sauce (11) or **fresh tomato sauce (10)**

UTENSILS:

3 large saucepans
Skimmer or slotted spoon
Cloth and two plates
Colander
To serve: Large hot serving platter

COOKING THE VEGETABLES:

Place the unpeeled onion halves under the broiler, cut side up, and cook until they begin to darken and caramelize, then remove from the heat.

In a large saucepan, place the chicken stock, the darkened onion, the carrots, turnips, baby onions, and leeks. Boil for 5 minutes, then add the cucumbers and asparagus and continue cooking another 5 minutes. Remove the pot from the heat and leave the vegetables in the liquid they cooked in. Remove the caramelized onion halves.

In another saucepan, place the water and coarse salt. Bring to a boil and add the little potatoes. Boil for 10 minutes, then add the cabbage leaves and boil for another 10 minutes. Remove from the heat and keep warm while cooking the *foie gras.*

COOKING THE FOIE GRAS:

Use a sharp knife to pare off any green spots from the *foie gras* resulting from its contact with the gall bladder.

Using a ladle, remove two-thirds of the stock from the pot the vegetables cooked in; leave only enough stock with the vegetables barely to cover them and keep them hot. Ladle the stock into a saucepan large enough to hold the *foie gras.* Add the port and madeira to this stock and bring to a boil; let the liquid boil until it has been reduced by about a third. Lower the heat and place the *foie gras* in the hot liquid and simmer for 15 to 20 minutes. Lift the *foie gras* carefully out of the pan with a skimmer or slotted spoon and wrap it in a clean towel, then place it on a plate. Cover the plate with another plate turned upside down, and keep it warm in a 325° F oven, with the door ajar, while cooking the noodles.

COOKING THE NOODLES AND SERVING:

Bring the *foie gras* cooking liquid to a boil and drop in the noodles. Cook them 6 minutes from the time the liquid comes back to a boil. Pour the noodles into a colander and drain, then keep them warm by placing the colander over the pan containing the vegetables.

Remove the cabbage leaves from the liquid in which they have been kept warm, and arrange them in the middle of the serving platter.

Take the *foie gras* from the oven. Unwrap it and cut it into eight equal slices. Salt and pepper the slices lightly, then place them on the bed of cabbage, arranging them so that the *foie gras* looks whole again. Place the remaining vegetables and the noodles around the *foie gras*. Spoon over them 2 tablespoons of the stock from the vegetable pan and 2 tablespoons of the stock-port mixture that was used to poach the *foie gras* and noodles. Serve immediately, with either **truffle sauce** or **fresh tomato sauce** served in a sauceboat and spooned over the noodles at the table.

COMMENTS:

Depending on its shape, the *foie gras* might need to cook 2 or 3 minutes more than the time given here. A short, round *foie gras* cooks slightly longer, and a long thin one cooks slightly less.

An equal weight of calf's liver, larded lengthwise with about eight strips of salt pork, can be used instead of *foie gras* in this recipe. Cook exactly as described.

The remaining stock-port mixture that was used to poach the *foie gras* is delicious and should not be thrown away. Skim off the fat from the surface, heat it, poach a small egg per person in the hot liquid, and serve this delicious consommé in a bowl with the poached egg floating in it as a first course. Salt and pepper to taste at the table.

NOTE: *Although a cooking time for the noodles is given, it is best to test them for doneness, since some noodles take more than 6 minutes to cook, others less. Homemade noodles can take as little as 20 seconds to cook from the time the liquid comes back to a boil. Noodles should always be cooked* al dente*—i.e., firm, but not crunchy, and never soft and mushy. Ed.*

Coquillages, crustacés & poissons

SHELLFISH & FISH

Huîtres chaudes en feuilles vertes

OYSTERS WRAPPED IN LETTUCE LEAVES 53

Ingredients for 4 servings:

1½ tablespoons butter (for the vegetables)
1 medium carrot, cut into thin *julienne* strips
1 large leek (white part only), cut into thin *julienne* strips
Salt and pepper
4 cups water
1 generous teaspoon coarse salt
24 Bibb lettuce leaves

24 large oysters in their shells (*see Note*)
¼ pound plus 2 tablespoons softened butter, broken into small pieces (for the sauce)
A pinch of pepper
1 tablespoon lemon juice

UTENSILS:

Medium *sauteuse* or saucepan
Large saucepan
Clean cloth or towel
Sieve

Clean thin cloth
Small saucepan
Slotted spoon
Wire whisk (optional)
To serve: 4 oyster plates, or 4 dinner plates covered with a layer of coarse salt

PREPARING THE VEGETABLES:

In a *sauteuse* or saucepan, melt the butter, add the *julienne* of carrots and leeks, sprinkle with salt and pepper, and brown over high heat for 2 minutes, stirring frequently. When done, place in a 350° F oven to keep warm, leaving the oven door ajar.

In a large saucepan, bring the water and coarse salt to a boil, add the lettuce leaves and boil for 1 minute, then drain and cool under running water, and spread on a clean cloth to dry.

PREPARING THE OYSTERS:

Have the fish seller open the oysters for you. When ready to prepare them, line a sieve with a thin cloth, place it over the small saucepan, and hold an oyster over it. Lift off the loosened top shell, then, with a teaspoon, remove the oyster from the bottom shell, pouring its juice through the sieve as you do so. Place the oyster on a plate.

When all the oysters have been removed from their shells, wash the curved bottom shells and place them in the depressions in the oyster plates, or press them into the coarse salt on ordinary plates to keep them from tipping over. Place the plates in the oven with the cooked vegetables.

Bring the strained oyster juice just to a boil, then add the oysters and simmer for 30 seconds. Lift the oysters out of the pan with a slotted spoon.

Remove the plates containing the oyster shells from the oven. Wrap each oyster in a lettuce leaf and place in a shell. When done, replace the plates in the half-closed oven.

TO SERVE:

Place the oyster juice back over high heat, bring to a boil, and reduce by half. Lower the heat and add the butter, a few pieces at a time, shaking the saucepan in a circular pattern to make the sauce spin around the sides. A wire whisk may be used to stir in the butter rather than shaking the pot. When all the butter has been swirled in, add the pepper and lemon juice (do *not* add salt!).

Pour a spoonful of sauce over each oyster, sprinkle with a little of the *julienne* of carrots and leeks, and serve immediately.

COMMENTS:

The oysters may be cooked and wrapped in the lettuce leaves several hours to a day in advance. Keep them in the refrigerator, placed in their shells. Remove them from the refrigerator an hour before serving, and preheat the oven to 475° F. Heat the oysters for 5 minutes in the oven, then garnish as described. The sauce should be made at the last minute.

For special occasions, the *julienne* of vegetables can be replaced by ½ teaspoon of chilled caviar per oyster.

NOTE: *If you have the oysters opened for you, be sure the fish seller is very careful not to lose any of the juice, which is essential to this recipe. It is best to open them yourself. You must use an oyster knife with a very short, thick blade and a shield, and it's best to hold the oyster in a cloth, since the edges of the shells are very sharp.*

In wrapping the oysters in the lettuce leaves, half a leaf may be sufficient for each oyster. The leaf should wrap around the oyster just once, not several times, since the delicate taste of the oyster will be lost if surrounded by too thick a layer of lettuce.

If using a wire whisk in making the sauce, be sure to lift the saucepan off of the heat frequently as you whisk. If left on the heat, the sauce will become too hot, and the butter will simply melt, rather than thicken the sauce. Ed.

Coquilles Saint-Jacques à l'effilochée d'endives
SCALLOPS WITH ENDIVE SAUCE 54

Ingredients for 4 servings:

- 4 medium endives (½ pound)
- 2½ tablespoons butter
- Salt and pepper

1 teaspoon granulated sugar
2 cups heavy cream

16 to 24 scallops (depending on size)
Salt and pepper
Flour to roll scallops in
4 tablespoons butter
1 generous tablespoon freshly chopped chervil or parsley

UTENSILS:

Medium-size saucepan with cover
Frying pan
Skimmer or slotted spoon
To serve: 4 hot dinner plates, or a hot serving platter

MAKING THE ENDIVE SAUCE:

Remove any wilted leaves from the endives and rinse them off under cold running water. Cut them into 1½-inch lengths, then turn each piece sideways and cut the endive into *julienne* strips.

In a saucepan, over medium heat, melt the 2½ tablespoons of butter. When it stops sizzling and begins to turn light brown, add the endive. Sprinkle with salt, pepper, and the sugar, and brown the endive lightly, stirring frequently with a fork, then cover the pot and cook over low heat for 15 minutes.

At the end of this time add the cream and boil gently, uncovered, for 10 minutes or until the sauce is rich and creamy.

COOKING THE SCALLOPS:

If possible, have the fish seller clean the scallops for you. If not, open and clean them according to the directions given in the recipe for **Puff pastry with scallops and truffles (45)**. It is not necessary to save the juice for this recipe.

Before cooking the scallops, prick the orange coral of each one gently with a fork to keep it from splitting open while cooking. Season the scallops and their coral with salt and pepper, then roll them in flour. Tap them gently with your fingers to remove any excess flour.

In a frying pan, melt the 4 tablespoons of butter over high heat until it stops sizzling and begins to turn brown. Add the scallops and sauté rapidly, 1 to 1½ minutes on each side, depending on their size. They should be lightly browned when cooked.

TO SERVE:

Divide the endive sauce evenly among the plates or pour it onto the serving platter. Lift the scallops out of the frying pan with a skimmer or slotted spoon and set them down gently on the sauce. Sprinkle with freshly chopped chervil or parsley and serve.

COMMENTS:

To save time when making the sauce, you may simply cut the endives into very thin rounds, rather than in *julienne* strips.

This sauce is also delicious served with sautéed scallops of veal or with poached poultry.

Les coquilles à la coque de Didier Oudill
DIDIER OUDILL'S SHELL-BAKED SCALLOPS 55

(color picture III)

Ingredients for 4 servings:

12 large scallops in their shells (*see Note*)
1½ medium carrots, peeled
1 medium onion, peeled
4 medium mushrooms, washed
3½ tablespoons butter
Salt and pepper
1 teaspoon freshly chopped tarragon

4½ pounds coarse salt
1 generous tablespoon chopped shallots
8 tablespoons butter
4 ounces **puff pastry** (**118**), rolled out and cut into strips 1¼ inches wide and 10 inches long
½ beaten egg

UTENSILS:

Bowl
Saucepan with cover
Oven broiler pan
Pastry brush
Fork
To serve: 4 hot dinner plates

PREPARING THE SCALLOPS:

Open and clean the scallops according to the directions given in the recipe for **puff pastry with scallops and truffles (45).** Save the juice in a bowl, filtering it as indicated in that recipe. When all the scallops have been removed from their shells, cut them and their corals in half horizontally, forming 24 circles and 24 pieces of coral. Clean 8 of the scallop shells, tops and bottoms, by brushing them off under running water. Dry and set aside.

PREPARING THE VEGETABLES:

Grate the carrots, and cut the onion and mushrooms into thin *julienne* strips.

In a saucepan, melt the butter and add the carrots and onion. Cook 5 minutes, uncovered, then add the mushrooms and cook 3 minutes more. Salt, pepper, add the freshly chopped tarragon, cover the pot, and simmer for 2 minutes, then remove from the heat.

COOKING THE SCALLOPS:

Preheat the oven to 500° F.

Spread the coarse salt in an even layer over the broiler pan that comes with your stove. Set the 8 curved scallop shells in the salt, pressing them down so they won't tip over (see Note). Divide half of the cooked vegetables evenly among the shells, and sprinkle with chopped shallots. Place 3 scallop circles and 3 pieces of coral in each shell, and sprinkle with salt and pepper. Sprinkle the remaining vegetables over the scallops, divide the reserved scallop juice evenly among the shells, and place 1 teaspoon of butter in each one.

Cover each garnished shell with the flat shell that belongs to it. Seal the shells closed with the puff-pastry strips: Brush each strip with beaten egg to make it stick, fold it lengthwise over the crack between the top and bottom shells, surrounding the shells entirely (see color picture III), and press the pastry against both top and bottom shells to make it stick firmly.

Slide the broiler pan carefully into the hot oven and bake for 10 to 12 minutes.

TO SERVE:

When the scallops are cooked, remove some of the salt from the roasting pan (you will have to break it apart with a fork, as it sticks together), and place it on the dinner plates. Set the shells in it as you did before cooking them, two to a plate, and serve as they are so each guest can have the fun of opening the shells himself.

COMMENTS:

Since the quality of the puff pastry is not essential to this recipe, commercially sold frozen puff pastry may be used to make the pastry strips. Or for that matter, you can even use wooden clothespins to hold the shells closed!

NOTE: *Unless the scallop shells are very small, all eight probably will not fit on an ordinary broiler pan. This poses no problem if you are doing only half the recipe, but otherwise, two smaller roasting pans (2¼ pounds coarse salt per pan is sufficient) will have to be used. If you don't have two roasting pans, a very large ovenproof platter, or a baking sheet lined with a sheet of aluminum foil turned up at the edges to keep the salt from spilling, can be used instead.*

Aluminum foil may be used to cover and seal the shells if you don't have any top shells, or are using porcelain shells instead of scallop shells. If you are using puff pastry, it is a nice idea to brush the outside with beaten egg after it is placed on the shells, since it browns better and looks prettier when cooked.

You can have the fish seller open the scallops if you wish, but too much of their juice will inevitably be lost. You can still make the recipe, but the scallops will be less tasty than if their juice had been included. Ed.

56 *Mousseline de Saint-Jacques au coulis d'écrevisses* SCALLOP MOUSSE WITH CRAYFISH SAUCE

Ingredients for 6 servings:

¾ pound fresh scallops (meat and coral only)
1¼ teaspoons salt
¼ teaspoon pepper
1 whole egg
1 egg white
2 cups *crème fraîche* (*see p. 352*)
2 tablespoons melted butter

1⅔ cups **crayfish sauce** (**13**) (*for substitution, see Comments*)
6 crayfish heads and 6 peeled tails, reserved when making **crayfish sauce** (*for substitution, see Note*)
6 slices of truffle, optional (*for substitution, see Comments*)

UTENSILS:

Electric blender
Pastry brush
6 ramekins (inside diameter, 3½ inches; depth, 1½ inches)
Large deep platter
To serve: 6 hot dinner plates, or a hot serving platter

MAKING THE SCALLOP MOUSSE:

In a blender, place the scallops, salt, and pepper, and blend for 3 to 4 minutes. When the mixture is completely smooth, add the whole egg and the egg white, then blend for 1 minute more. Place the blender container with its contents in the refrigerator for 30 minutes or until the mixture is completely cold and very thick.

Remove the blender container from the refrigerator, add the cold *crème fraîche*, and blend for about 10 seconds, or until the mixture is smooth and creamy.

With a pastry brush, brush the inside of the ramekins with the melted butter. Fill the ramekins with the scallop mousse, then place them on a large, deep platter. Add enough boiling water to come half-way up the sides of the ramekins, then place them in a preheated 350° F oven. Lay a sheet of aluminum foil over the top of the ramekins to prevent a crust from forming on the mousses, and bake for 20 minutes.

TO SERVE:

When the mousses are half done, begin heating up the **crayfish sauce** over low heat. Two minutes before serving, add the crayfish tails (if added earlier, they will shrink and become tough).

When the mousses are cooked, turn them out onto individual dinner plates or a serving platter. Remove the crayfish tails from the sauce and set aside. Pour the sauce over the mousses and place a slice of truffle in the center of each one. On the side, arrange the crayfish heads and tails so that they look like 6 whole crayfish, and serve.

COMMENTS:

Mousses of this type can be made with any kind of fish, although the weight of the fish varies depending on its type.

For the same amount of *crème fraîche* and egg use:

¾ pound raw lobster or rock lobster meat

½ pound raw pike, turbot, bream or porgy, whiting, sole, hake, or squid.

Another, simpler method for making this recipe may also be used. Blend 8 ounces of raw fish or shellfish until smooth, then add 2 generous cups of milk, 4 egg yolks, and 2 whole eggs. Blend until smooth and creamy, salt and pepper to taste. Cook and serve as described in the above recipe. The result (more like a custard than a mousse) will melt in your mouth.

If you have a few extra crayfish tails set aside when you made the crayfish sauce, you can place one or several of them inside each mousse before baking; it adds a nice touch to this dish.

Each slice of truffle may be replaced by half a pitted black olive.

The crayfish sauce may also be replaced by **fresh tomato sauce (10)** flavored with a little freshly chopped basil or tarragon.

NOTE: *To test when the mousses are done, stick the blade of a knife into the center of one of them; if the knife comes out clean, they are done. Ed.*

57 *Homard aux truffes à la tomate fraîche et au basilic*
LOBSTER WITH TRUFFLE, TOMATO, AND BASIL SAUCE

Ingredients for 4 servings:

4 small live lobsters weighing just under 1 pound (14 ounces) each (*see p. 165*)

FOR THE COURT-BOUILLON:

4 quarts water
4 tablespoons coarse salt
1⅓ cups white vinegar
Bouquet garni
2 teaspoons coarsely crushed peppercorns

FOR THE SAUCE:

¼ teaspoon finely chopped fresh basil leaves
½ teaspoon olive oil
2 teaspoons butter
1 large truffle weighing ⅝ ounce, cut into *julienne* strips (*for substitution, see Comments*)

Salt and pepper
1⅔ cups heavy cream
2 heaping tablespoons **raw diced tomatoes (96)**

UTENSILS:

Large pot
Large heavy knife or cleaver
Small saucepan
Double boiler (optional)
Scissors
To serve: 4 hot dinner plates, or a hot serving platter

COOKING THE LOBSTER:

Combine the ingredients for the *court-bouillon* in a large pot and bring to a boil.

Crack the large claws of the lobsters by hitting them with the blunt edge of a large heavy knife or cleaver. This makes it easier to remove the meat after cooking. Drop the lobsters into the boiling *court-bouillon* and boil for 5 minutes. Remove the pot from the heat; the lobsters will finish cooking in the hot liquid while you prepare the sauce.

MAKING THE SAUCE:

Chop the basil leaves with a knife and pound them in a mortar with the olive oil until a paste is formed.

In a small saucepan, melt the butter over high heat, and in it sauté the strips of truffle for 30 seconds. Sprinkle with salt and pepper, add the cream, and boil over medium heat for 10 minutes, or until the mixture is thick and creamy. Then add the diced tomatoes and the basil paste, taste for seasoning, and add salt and pepper if necessary. Keep the sauce hot, without boiling, over very low heat or in a double boiler, for 15 minutes. During this time the flavors in the sauce will ripen and blend together.

TO SERVE:

Lift the lobsters out of the *court-bouillon.* Detach the tails and, with a pair of scissors, cut the rings on the underside of the tails and remove the meat. Detach the 8 large claws and remove the meat from them as well.

Remove all the meat from the inside of the lobster heads. Discard the gritty pouch at the back of the heads, but reserve the tomalley and any coral for use in other recipes (sauces, soups, etc.).

With a pair of scissors, cut out a rectangle in the middle of the top of each head and set the claw meat, whole, from each lobster, points sticking up, into the openings.

Place a garnished lobster head on each plate, or place them all on a serving platter. Slice each tail into slices ¼ inch thick, then line the slices up behind the lobster head, giving the presentation the shape of a whole lobster. Pour the sauce over the lobster tails only, and serve.

COMMENTS:

Since it takes a certain amount of time for the flavors of the truffle, tomato, and basil to blend together, this sauce may be prepared a day in advance and reheated, without boiling, when ready to use.

This dish can be enriched by adding 12 oysters (3 per person), poached for 20 seconds in their strained juice. Add this juice to the sauce at the same time as the cream, and place the oysters here and there on the finished plates.

If you don't have truffles, they may be replaced by 1 medium ordinary mushroom, cut into *julienne* strips and cooked like the truffle.

58 *Paupiettes d'écrevisses au thym et aux choux de Bruxelles*
PAUPIETTES OF STRIPED BASS WITH CRAYFISH TAILS AND BRUSSELS SPROUTS

Ingredients for 4 servings:

2 tablespoons olive oil
20 live crayfish, approximately 1½ pounds (*for substitution, see Note*)
½ medium carrot, peeled and diced
¼ medium onion, peeled and diced
1 shallot, peeled and diced
1 small *bouquet garni*
1 clove garlic, crushed but unpeeled
Salt and pepper
A pinch of cayenne pepper
4 teaspoons armagnac
2 tablespoons red port
1 cup dry white wine
2 tomatoes, seeded and quartered
1 generous teaspoon tomato paste

1 cup **cooked diced tomatoes** (**97**)
¼ teaspoon thyme
½ teaspoon freshly chopped tarragon
2 cups water
1 generous teaspoon coarse salt
24 large green Brussels sprout leaves
1 striped bass fillet weighing just over 1 pound
5 tablespoons softened butter

UTENSILS:

Large *sauteuse* or high-sided frying pan, with cover
Skimmer or slotted spoon
Mortar and pestle, electric blender, or food processor
Sieve
Baking dish (*see Note*)
Wooden spoon or small ladle
2 small saucepans
Long flexible filleting knife
Aluminum foil (optional)
Cleaver (optional)
To serve: 4 hot dinner plates, or a hot serving platter

COOKING THE CRAYFISH:

Heat the olive oil in a *sauteuse* or high-sided frying pan over high heat. When the oil is very hot, put all the live crayfish into the pan at once, cover immediately, lower the heat to moderate, and cook for 6 minutes. Then remove the pan from the heat, lift the crayfish out with a skimmer or slotted spoon, and place them on a plate. Detach and peel the crayfish tails and set them aside, as well as 4 crayfish heads, for later use.

Pound the remaining 16 crayfish heads in a mortar or grind them in a blender or food processor. Put them back in the same pan they cooked in, and add the chopped carrot, onion, and shallot, the *bouquet garni*, garlic, salt, pepper, and cayenne pepper. Sauté over low heat, uncovered, for 5 minutes; the vegetables should not color.

Add the armagnac and port, half cover the pan, and boil for about 10 seconds (the liquid should reduce by half), then add the white wine, seeded tomatoes, and tomato paste. Boil, uncovered, for 5 to 10 minutes, or until the liquid has again reduced by half, then strain the sauce through a sieve into the baking dish. Press the solid ingredients with a wooden spoon or small ladle to extract as much juice from them as possible.

MAKING THE PAUPIETTES:

In a small saucepan over low heat, heat together the **cooked diced tomatoes,** the thyme and tarragon, and the crayfish tails. Stir gently, then keep hot but do not boil.

In a second small saucepan, bring the water and coarse salt to a boil, add the Brussels sprout leaves, boil for 15 seconds, then remove the pot from the heat; leave the leaves in their liquid to keep warm.

With a long flexible filleting knife, cut the bass fillet at a sharp slant into 4 thin slices, measuring approximately 6 inches on a side. If you have trouble making the slices thin and regular enough, place them between two sheets of aluminum foil and flatten them gently with the side of a cleaver until they are the right size.

In the center of each slice of bass, place a heaping tablespoon of the tomato sauce prepared earlier, dividing the crayfish tails evenly so that there will be 5 of them in each *paupiette*. Then fold the 4 sides of the slices of fish over the filling, and place them, folded side down, in the baking dish with the crayfish sauce.

TO SERVE:

Preheat the oven to 500° F.

Place the baking dish in the oven and bake for 4 minutes, then lift the *paupiettes* out of the sauce with a skimmer or slotted spoon and place them on the dinner plates or serving platter.

Place the baking dish over high heat and bring the sauce to a fast boil (see Note). Add the butter; as it melts in the rapidly boiling sauce, the sauce will thicken slightly.

As soon as the butter has completely melted, pour the sauce over the *paupiettes*, decorate with the reserved crayfish heads, place the Brussels sprout leaves around the *paupiettes* like the petals of a flower, and serve.

COMMENTS:

The crayfish may be replaced by mussels which have been cooked with a little dry white wine, chopped shallot, and cream, then removed from their shells. After baking, the mussels' cooking liquid is then slightly reduced, a mixture of freshly chopped herbs is added, and this sauce is poured over the *paupiettes* instead of the crayfish sauce in the original recipe.

NOTE: *If using an earthenware or glass baking dish, do not place it over direct heat, as it will crack. Use an asbestos pad or other heat-diffusing device. For this reason it may be preferable to use an enam-*

eled-iron baking dish, or simply to pour the sauce into a small saucepan before heating it and adding the butter.

The baking dish used should be only just large enough to contain the paupiettes *and their sauce. If too large a dish is used, the sauce will evaporate. Ed.*

Homard rôti au four
ROAST LOBSTER 59

Ingredients for 2 servings:

FOR THE HERB BUTTER:

⅔ cup dry white wine
1 teaspoon freshly chopped chervil or parsley
¼ teaspoon freshly chopped tarragon
¼ teaspoon thyme flowers (or chopped leaves)
½ pound softened butter
Salt and pepper

FOR THE ANCHOVY BUTTER:

1 anchovy fillet in oil
1 tablespoon soft butter

FOR THE LOBSTER:

1 live lobster weighing about 2 pounds (*see Comments and Note*)
2 cups **court-bouillon** (8), or 2 cups water plus 2 teaspoons coarse salt
2 tablespoons olive oil

UTENSILS:

2 small saucepans
Fork or wire whisk
Roasting pan (preferably enameled cast-iron) for cooking and serving
Heavy knife or cleaver
Sharp knife or large nail
Cutting board
Large knife

MAKING THE HERB BUTTER:

In a small saucepan, bring to a boil the white wine, chopped herbs, and thyme flowers (or leaves). Reduce the mixture until there are about 3 tablespoons of liquid left.

Allow to cool until barely lukewarm, then add the butter, salt, and pepper. Mix together with a fork, or better yet, beat with a wire whisk, until a smooth cream about the consistency of a mayonnaise is formed. Set aside in the saucepan for later use.

MAKING THE ANCHOVY BUTTER:

Chop the anchovy fillet with a knife, then place it in a small bowl, add the tablespoon of butter, and beat until smooth.

COOKING THE LOBSTER:

Preheat the oven to 500° F.

Place the roasting pan over high heat and add the olive oil. Using your hands, detach the large claws from the lobster with a quick, sharp, twisting movement. Immediately place the lobster itself in the hot oil and roll it over several times to coat the outside of its shell.

Crack the lobster claws slightly with the blunt edge of a heavy knife or cleaver in order to remove the meat more easily after cooking. In a small saucepan, bring the *court-bouillon* or salted water to a boil, add the claws, and cook, covered, for 8 minutes, then remove the pot from the heat and set aside, leaving the claws in their cooking liquid.

When the lobster has been completely coated with oil and its shell has begun to redden, place the roasting pan in the preheated oven and roast the lobster for 8 minutes, then remove from the oven and lower the heat to 425° F.

Take a little less than half of the herb butter and mix it with the anchovy butter, using a fork.

With the tip of a knife, or a large nail, punch a round hole the size of your little finger in the back of the body of the lobster, then push one-third of the herb-anchovy butter through this hole to flavor the meat inside.

Place the lobster back in the oven. This time roast it for a total of 15 minutes. Remove it from the oven after 5 minutes to push half of the remaining herb-anchovy butter through the hole. Replace it in the oven, then 5 minutes later season it in the same way with the remaining herb-anchovy butter, cook 5 minutes more, then remove from the oven.

TO SERVE:

When the lobster is cooked, place it on a cutting board and cut it in half lengthwise with a large knife. Remove the gritty pouch, situated at the top of the head, from each half. Place the opened lobster back in the roasting pan. Lift the claws out of their cooking liquid and shell them, then set the claw meat, whole, in each of the cavities of the body shell, next to the small claws. Serve immediately, with the remaining herb butter in a separate dish.

COMMENTS:

The lobster is divided into three parts: the head or body, the claws, and the tail.

The front tip of the body is really the head and contains a gritty pouch (the stomach), which is always discarded. The rest of the body contains the tomalley (liver) and coral (roe). The tomalley turns green and the coral red when they are cooked, and they are used in thickening sauces and soups.

The claws and tail contain all the best meat of the lobster. In females, the eggs of the roe appear on the exterior of the tail, on the underside, before hatching. These eggs redden when they are cooked and are used like the coral and for garnishing a lobster dish.

NOTE: *However, by law in the United States, for reasons of conservation, lobster fishermen are required to put hatching females back into the sea. They are not seen in our markets.*

Most of us are squeamish about cutting up live lobsters, and, without experience, it can even be somewhat unwise; the claws must be very securely pegged. Have your fish dealer cut it up for you as described in whatever lobster recipe you are using. But then, you must be sure to set about cooking the lobster immediately, *as soon as you get it home. Or, better, have the fish dealer show you exactly how to kill the lobster by hitting it at the back of the head, before cutting it up. This is quick and easy if someone shows you how. Whole lobsters to be poached should go into their* court-bouillon *live. Ed.*

When crustaceans are simply cut in half and grilled, the meat inevitably dries out and becomes tough. In this recipe, the flavored butter which is introduced into the body of the lobster through the hole in the shell makes the meat extraordinarily tender and juicy. Spiny lobsters can also be cooked in this way.

My favorite garnish for this dish is a hot salad, made in the following manner: Cut 1 medium carrot, 1 stalk celery, half the white part of 1 medium-small leek, and 2 medium mushrooms all into very thin *julienne* strips. Melt some butter in a saucepan or frying pan, add the vegetables, sprinkle with salt, pepper, and a little lemon juice, and cook over low heat just long enough to make the vegetables tender. They should still be slightly crunchy when served.

Note: *A wooden-handled* lardoir *(larding needle) is ideal for piercing the hole in the lobster's body shell. The easiest way to insert the butter through the hole is to take some of it on a spoon and push it through the hole with a chopstick or other similar implement. Prop the lobster against the side of the roasting pan so that it won't tip over while you fill it with the butter, and keep it that way so that it won't lose the butter while it is roasting during the last 15 minutes.*

When cutting the lobster, use the point of the knife to pierce the top of the shell, moving from the head toward the tail. Ed.

60 *Homard, langouste, ou écrevisses à la nage*
LOBSTER, SPINY LOBSTER, OR CRAYFISH IN COURT-BOUILLON

Ingredients for 2 servings:

1 live lobster or spiny lobster weighing 1¾ pounds, or 20 crayfish, each weighing about 2 ounces (*see Note, p. 351*)

Court-bouillon (8)

1 tablespoon freshly chopped parsley

UTENSILS:

Large heavy knife or cleaver (for lobster)
Large pot
Large sharp knife (for lobster or spiny lobster)
To serve: Deep oval serving platter for lobster or spiny lobster
Vegetable dish for crayfish

COOKING THE SHELLFISH:

If using a lobster, crack the large claws slightly with the blunt edge of a heavy knife or cleaver to remove the meat more easily when cooked.

Drop the shellfish into a large pot of boiling *court-bouillon* and cook for the following times:

Lobster or spiny lobster: 14 minutes
Crayfish: 2 minutes

TO SERVE:

Lobster or spiny lobster: With a large knife, cut the shellfish in half lengthwise. Remove and discard the gritty pouch (situated toward the back of the head) from each half.

Place the two halves in a deep oval serving platter, garnish with the vegetables from the *court-bouillon*, pour 1 cup of the *court-bouillon* over them, sprinkle with freshly chopped parsley, and serve.

Crayfish: Place them in a vegetable dish, in a mound, sprinkle with freshly chopped parsley, and serve.

Serve the shellfish either hot or cold with one of the following sauces:

French tomato and herb sauce (9)
"Rust" sauce (7)
Foamy butter sauce (6)

COMMENTS:

If using just the cooked crayfish tails in a recipe, you can remove the intestine after cooking by simply pinching it at the tail end and pulling it out, as you would for large shrimp.

In cooking shellfish, you should keep in mind that:

Overcooking toughens them.

Slightly undercooking them makes them particularly tender.

Allowing them to sit in their cooking liquid for a few minutes away from the heat before serving them gives the meat time to decontract and also makes it more tender.

Papillotes de saumon à l'étuvée de légumes
61 SALMON PAPILLOTES

Ingredients for 4 servings:

FOR THE VEGETABLES:

3½ tablespoons butter
1½ medium carrots, peeled and grated
1 medium onion, peeled and cut into *julienne* strips
4 medium mushrooms, cut into *julienne* strips
Salt and pepper
1 teaspoon freshly chopped tarragon (*for substitution, see Comments*)

FOR THE PAPILLOTES:

1¼ pounds fresh salmon fillets (*for substitution, see Comments*)
4 tablespoons cooking oil
Salt and pepper
1 generous teaspoon chopped shallot
12 fresh tarragon leaves
8 tablespoons dry white wine
4 tablespoons **chicken stock** (2) (3)
2 tablespoons soft butter, approximately

UTENSILS:

Saucepan
Tweezers
Flexible filleting knife
Basting brush
4 circles of parchment paper, about 14 inches in diameter (*see Note*)
Large roasting pan
To serve: 4 hot dinner plates

COOKING THE VEGETABLES:

In a saucepan, melt the butter, add the strips of carrot and onion, and sauté over low heat for 5 minutes, then add the strips of mushroom and cook for 3 minutes more. While the vegetables are cooking, stir them from time to time to prevent them from sticking or browning; they should not color.

When the time is up, sprinkle with salt and pepper, add the tarragon, cover the pot and simmer over very low heat for 2 minutes, then remove from the heat and set aside to cool.

MAKING THE PAPILLOTES:

With a pair of tweezers, remove any little bones still left in the salmon fillets. You will feel them by running your fingers lightly in all directions over the surface of the fillets.

When all the bones have been removed, cut the fillets into a total of 12 slices, each a little less than ½ inch thick, using a very sharp, flexible filleting knife.

With a basting brush, brush the surface of the circles of parchment paper with half of the cooking oil. Fold each circle in half, then open it up again. Divide the cooked vegetables into four equal parts; place one part in the center of one of the halves of each circle. On top of each little pile of vegetables place three slices of salmon, then sprinkle with salt, pepper, and chopped shallot. Place a tarragon leaf on top of each slice of salmon, then add 2 tablespoons of white wine and 1 tablespoon of stock to each serving. Add a few dabs of butter (approximately 2 tablespoons in all), then fold the second half of each circle of paper over the garnished half.

To seal the *papillotes*, first make sure the edge of the top half of each circle is in line with the bottom half. Then, starting at one corner, roll a small section of the edge of the semicircle over on itself, then press it down flat. Continue in this way, a small section at a time, around to the opposite corner. When you press the edges of the paper flat, little pleats will form which not only seal the *papillote*, but look pretty as well.

TO COOK AND SERVE:

Preheat the oven to 500° F.

When the *papillotes* have all been sealed, pour the remaining cooking oil into the roasting pan and spread it around with a basting brush. Place the pan in the preheated oven for 5 minutes to heat up. Then remove it from the oven to arrange the *papillotes* in it; they should not touch each other. Quickly place the roasting pan back in the oven and bake the *papillotes* for 2 minutes.

Remove the *papillotes* from the oven, place them on the dinner plates, and serve immediately, just as they are. Each guest can then have the pleasure of opening his own (which will have puffed up and turned golden brown while cooking) and finding out what's inside.

COMMENTS:

These *papillotes* are delicious with lime-flavored **Foamy butter sauce (6)** served on the side in a sauceboat.

If you don't have any fresh tarragon, you may use tarragon which has been preserved in vinegar; in this case, reduce the amount by half.

Aluminum foil may be used instead of parchment paper.

Frozen salmon may be used instead of fresh salmon, and hake or cod may be used instead of salmon. (If using frozen fish, cook the *papillotes* only 1½ minutes.)

NOTE: *Although the utensil list calls for 4 circles of parchment paper 14 inches in diameter, commercially sold parchment paper is often only 12 inches wide. You can cut circles 12 inches in diameter; or, if you prefer to have a larger edge to fold over when making the* papillotes, *cut the paper into an oval 12 inches wide and 14 inches long.*

Before adding the wine and stock, place each papillote *on a plate so that the liquid will stay in the center, rather than running off over the edges of the paper. It is best to seal the* papillotes *while they are still on the plate and to tie off the last fold with a piece of string to prevent the edge from unfolding.*

A little cooking oil brushed over the outside of the papillote *before cooking seals the paper and gives it a nice shine and more golden color when cooked. And although aluminum foil may be used, it is not as pretty as parchment paper, and the fish tends to steam, rather than bake, when cooked in it.*

Depending on the size of the fish fillets, it will be necessary to slice them differently. One large, thick fillet can be cut straight down like roast beef, but long, thin fillets have to be cut at a sharp angle—almost horizontal to the table—to get slices of the proper size and thickness. Ed.

Bar aux algues
BASS COOKED IN SEAWEED 62

Ingredients for 3 or 4 servings:

1 striped bass weighing 2 to 2½ pounds (*for substitution, see Comments*)
3 large handfuls of seaweed (*see Comments*)
1¼ cups water
3 or 4 crayfish (optional)
1½ cups **fresh tomato and herb sauce (9)**
¾ cup **water-cress purée II (103)**

UTENSILS:

Scissors
Oval cast-iron pot with cover
Bain-marie or double boiler
Long sharp knife
To serve: Hot dinner plates, or a hot oval serving platter
Sauceboat

COOKING THE FISH:

Clean the bass and cut the large dorsal fin off with a pair of scissors, or have the fish seller do this for you. Do not scale the fish. In this recipe the scales will help flavor the fish and make it easier to remove the skin after cooking.

Line the bottom of a pot with half the seaweed, then add the water. Sprinkle the inside of the bass with salt and pepper, lay the fish on top of the bed of seaweed, then add the crayfish. Cover the fish with the remaining seaweed, cover the pot, place over high heat, and cook at a rapid boil for 20 to 30 minutes depending on the weight of the fish.

While the fish is cooking, heat the **fresh tomato and herb sauce** in a *bain-marie* or double boiler.

TO SERVE:

First show your guests the fish in the pot, so they can see how it was cooked and smell its wonderful aroma, then take it back to the kitchen to serve.

Remove the bass from the pot and lift off the skin and scales (it will come off very easily). Detach the fillets with a long sharp knife, place them on the dinner plates or serving platter, and sprinkle lightly with salt and pepper.

Spread 4 tablespoons of the tomato sauce over each portion of the fish (the rest should be served in a sauceboat) and surround the fillets with the **water-cress purée.** Place the crayfish, reddened by cooking, on top of the purée for a nice contrast of color, and serve.

COMMENTS:

This method of cooking saltwater fish is excellent; the taste of the fish is heightened and complemented by a variety of other fresh and interesting tastes. To add to its unusual flavor, you might try using freshly ground, freeze-dried green peppercorns instead of black pepper when making this recipe.

Seaweed is not as hard to find as you might think; oysters, lobsters, and other shellfish are often packed in it for shipping. Ask your fish seller to put some aside for you.

But if you are unable to find seaweed, you can use large bunches of parsley instead. In this case, however, you should add a little salt to the water the fish is cooked with.

Many types of saltwater fish may be used instead of bass, such as sole, porgy, red snapper, haddock, and the recipe can be adapted for freshwater fish such as trout, perch, or pike by using a mixture of wild herbs (if you live in the country) such as nettle leaves, sorrel, clover leaves, and thyme to cook the fish in.

Dorade en croûte de sel
SEA BREAM OR PORGY BAKED IN SALT 63

(color picture V)

Ingredients for 2 servings:

1 sea bream or a porgy weighing 1¾ pounds (*for substitution, see Comments*)

3¼ pounds coarse salt

½ cup **fresh tomato and herb sauce (9)**, or **chive sauce (12)**

6 generous tablespoons **water-cress purée I (102)**

UTENSILS:

Scissors

Deep oval earthenware or enameled cast-iron baking dish

Long sharp knife

To serve: 2 hot dinner plates, or a hot oval serving platter

COOKING THE FISH:

Preheat the oven to 475° F.

Clean the fish and cut the large dorsal fin off with a pair of scissors, or have the fish seller do this for you. Do not scale the fish.

Spread a third of the coarse salt evenly over the bottom of a deep baking dish which is just large enough to hold the fish. Lay the fish on top of this bed of salt, then cover it with the remaining salt.

Place the fish in the oven and bake for 30 minutes.

TO SERVE:

Remove the fish from the oven and show it to your guest as it is in the baking dish, then take it back to the kitchen to serve.

Break the hardened crust of salt and lift it off of the fish. Remove the skin; because of the scales, it will lift off easily.

With a long sharp knife, lift off the fillets from the fish and place them either on individual dinner plates or on a serving platter. Salt the fillets very lightly if you think it necessary, then sprinkle them with pepper.

Spoon the chosen sauce over the fillets, then place the **water-cress purée** around the fillets and serve immediately.

COMMENTS:

As it cooks and hardens, the salt forms a hermetic "second oven" around the fish. The presentation of the fish in the salt always impresses and surprises people. Almost any saltwater fish can be cooked in this way—hake, haddock, cod, to name only a few. It is also an excellent way to cook fresh sardines and has a particular advantage in their case; the thick layer of salt keeps their strong smell from invading your kitchen.

Saint-Pierre en sabayon de poivre

64 JOHN DORY WITH A SABAYON PEPPER SAUCE

Ingredients for 2 servings:

1 John Dory weighing 1¾ pounds (*for substitution, see Comments*)
2 teaspoons butter
1 generous teaspoon chopped shallot
Salt and pepper
⅜ cup **chicken stock** (**2**) (**3**)
1 tablespoon dry white wine
6 tablespoons *crème fraîche* (*see p. 352*) or heavy cream
½ teaspoon peppercorns
1 egg yolk
1½ tablespoons cold water

UTENSILS:

Scissors
Oval earthenware baking dish
Aluminum foil
Mortar and pestle, or heavy pot
Sieve
Small saucepan
Long sharp knife
Mixing bowl
Wire whisk
To serve: 2 hot dinner plates or a hot oval serving platter

COOKING THE FISH:

Preheat the oven to 425° F.

Scale and clean the fish, then cut off its fins with a pair of scissors, or have the fish seller do this for you.

Butter an earthenware baking dish with the butter. Sprinkle the chopped shallot over the bottom of the dish, place the fish on top of the shallot, sprinkle with salt and pepper, then add the stock and white wine.

Cover the dish with aluminum foil and place in the oven. Cook for 20 minutes, basting the fish frequently. At the end of this time, add the cream, pouring it all around the fish, then continue cooking for 5 minutes more.

MAKING THE SAUCE:

Coarsely crush the peppercorns in a mortar and pestle, or place them on a cutting board and crush them by hitting them a few times with the bottom of a heavy pot.

When the fish is done, remove it from the baking dish and set it aside on a hot plate. Cover it with a second hot plate turned upside down. Turn the oven down to 325° F.

Strain the cooking liquid through a sieve into a small saucepan. Add the crushed pepper, and boil rapidly, uncovered, until the liquid has reduced by a third.

While the sauce is boiling, remove the skin from the fish and lift off the fillets with a long sharp knife. Place them on hot dinner plates or a serving platter, and keep warm in the oven with the door ajar.

When the sauce is sufficiently reduced, lower the heat to bring it to a gentle simmer.

Place the egg yolk and water in a mixing bowl and beat with a wire whisk for 45 seconds, or until the mixture has increased considerably in volume and is very foamy. Pour the egg mixture into the gently boiling sauce, whisking rapidly as you do so (see Note). Continue whisking the sauce for a few seconds after all the egg has been added—the sauce will become light and foamy—then pour over the fish fillets and serve immediately.

COMMENTS:

The John Dory may be replaced by almost any saltwater fish of your choice—sole, flounder, porgy, snapper, whiting, etc.

Instead of using pepper to season the sauce, you may use other spices or herbs, such as saffron, dill, or chopped tarragon or basil.

Note: *Although you might think that the egg yolk would curdle when added to a boiling liquid, this is not the case if it is first beaten with water, as it is here. The resulting sauce, a* sabayon, *is very different from sauces thickened with egg yolk in the ordinary way. Rather than becoming rich and creamy, it becomes light and foamy, as described.*

Two small fish may be used instead of one large one. In this case, cook for only 15 minutes before adding the cream. If you are using other types of fish (the John Dory is a flatfish), the cooking time may vary greatly, depending on their thickness. To test whether or not the fish is done, run the blade of a knife along the backbone (or along the middle of the side for flatfish). If the meat lifts easily off the bone, the fish is done. Ed.

Merlan à la julienne de légumes
65 WHITING STUFFED WITH VEGETABLES

Ingredients for 4 servings:

4 whiting weighing approximately 8 ounces each

FOR THE VEGETABLES:

3½ tablespoons butter
1⅔ cups grated carrots
1 cup grated celeriac (celery root)
1⅓ cups *julienne* strips of mushrooms
Salt and pepper
¼ cup red port
1 cup *crème fraîche* (*see p.* 352) or heavy cream
½ teaspoon freshly chopped tarragon
1 egg yolk

FOR THE FISH:

Salt and pepper
1½ tablespoons butter
1 tablespoon chopped shallots
2 tablespoons dry white wine
⅜ cup *crème fraîche* (*see p.* 352) or heavy cream
2 tablespoons red port
4 teaspoons white vermouth
1 generous teaspoon freshly chopped parsley

UTENSILS:

Scissors
Filleting knife
Saucepan with cover
Small bowl
Fork
Baking dish
To serve: 4 hot dinner plates

PREPARING THE WHITING:

You can either do this yourself or have the fish seller do it for you: Cut off all the fins with a pair of scissors, then clean the fish by removing their intestines, etc., through the gills. Do not cut their stomachs open to clean them.

Then remove the bones in the following manner: With a filleting knife, make a slit along the entire length of the back, on each side of the bones where the fins were. Slide the knife down along each side to lift the fillets entirely off the bone. When all the meat has been detached from the bone in this way, cut the backbone of the fish with a pair of scissors at both ends, i.e., near the tail and near the head. Remove the backbone in one piece from the inside of the fish; the fish will now form a pocket.

MAKING THE STUFFING:

Melt the butter in a saucepan, then add the grated carrots. Cover the pot and cook for 3 minutes, then add the grated celeriac, cook for 3 minutes more, then add the strips of mushroom. Cook for a final 3 minutes. Stir the vegetables from time to time to keep them from coloring; otherwise, keep the pan covered.

Sprinkle with salt and pepper, then add the port, cream, and chopped tarragon, and cook at a moderate boil for 5 minutes, with the saucepan half covered. At the end of this time, remove from the heat. Beat the egg yolk in a small bowl with a fork, then stir it into the hot vegetables. Allow to cool.

COOKING THE FISH:

Preheat the oven to 500° F.

Season the inside of the whiting with salt and pepper, then stuff them, using two-thirds of the vegetable mixture. Grease a baking dish with the butter, then sprinkle the bottom of the dish with the chopped shallots.

Lay the stuffed whiting on top of the shallots, spread the remaining vegetables around the fish, then spoon the white wine and the ⅜ cup of cream around the fish as well. Place in the preheated oven and cook for 9 minutes, then remove the dish from the oven and add the vermouth and red port. Place the fish back in the oven and cook for 3 minutes more; they should begin to brown slightly.

TO SERVE:

You can either serve the fish in the baking dish or lift them out of the sauce and place them on dinner plates. Pour the sauce over them and sprinkle with chopped parsley.

COMMENTS:

You can cook the vegetables and stuff the whiting up to a day in advance. Then, at mealtime, simply cook the fish in the oven as described.

A number of freshwater fish can also be prepared in this way—trout, perch, etc.

The vegetable sauce is also excellent with poached poultry or fricasseed meats with cream sauces such as *blanquette* of veal, etc.

Bouillabaisse de morue
BOUILLABAISSE OF SALT COD 66

Ingredients for 4 to 6 servings:

1½ pounds very white dry salt cod
⅜ cup olive oil
1 medium onion, peeled and finely chopped
1 medium leek, white part only, finely chopped
1 large clove garlic, peeled and finely chopped
2 medium tomatoes, peeled, seeded, and coarsely chopped
2 medium potatoes, peeled and cut into slices about ½ inch thick
A generous pinch of powdered saffron
Pepper
Bouquet garni
4 cups water
⅜ cup dry white wine

20 thin slices French bread (*see Comments*)
⅜ cup olive oil
1 generous teaspoon freshly chopped parsley

SERVE WITH:

"Rust" sauce (7)

UTENSILS:

Large bowl
Large cast-iron pot
Clean cloth
Basting brush
To serve: Sauceboat
Hot dinner plates

PREPARING THE SALT COD AND COOKING THE VEGETABLES:

With a large knife, cut the salt cod into 4 pieces, then put them into a large bowl of cold water to soak for 24 hours. If possible, leave the bowl under a small stream of cold running water; if not, change the water 4 to 5 times.

The next day, prepare the vegetables. In a cast-iron pot, heat the olive oil, then add the chopped onion, leek, and garlic. Sauté the vegetables over low heat, uncovered, for 15 minutes, stirring occasionally to keep them from sticking or coloring. Add the chopped tomatoes and continue cooking, uncovered, for an additional 5 minutes.

At the end of this time, lay the sliced potatoes on top of the other vegetables.

Drain the salt cod and pat the pieces dry in a clean cloth, then cut the fish into squares approximately 1¼ inches on each side. Lay the pieces of cod on top of the potatoes, season with the saffron and a little pepper—do *not* add salt!—then add the *bouquet garni*, water, and wine.

TO COOK AND SERVE:

Place the pot over high heat and cook at a rapid boil, uncovered, for 25 minutes, then taste for seasoning. The liquid in the pot should be thick and syrupy at this point. This is due not only to this method of cooking at a fast boil, but also to the starch given out by the potatoes, which helps bind the water and white wine with the olive oil. The result is a very thick, rich bouillon, full of the mixed flavors of the vegetables, seasonings, and fish.

When the *bouillabaisse* has finished cooking, cover it and keep it warm over very low heat. Brush both sides of each slice of bread with the olive oil, and brown them under the broiler on both sides.

Remove the *bouquet garni* from the *bouillabaisse*, sprinkle with freshly chopped parsley, and serve as it is, from the pot. Serve the **"rust" sauce** in a sauceboat and the toasted bread on a hot dinner plate.

COMMENTS:

This dish can be entirely prepared from several hours to a day in advance, with the exception of the final cooking. The wine and water may be added to the pot either at the same time as the fish and seasonings, or at the last minute, just before cooking.

Instead of using small pieces of toasted bread, large slices of country-style bread may be brushed with olive oil and toasted as described, then rubbed with garlic and spread with either a mixture of **Raw diced tomatoes (96)** and chopped anchovies or with **"rust" sauce.**

Sole grillée aux huîtres et à la ciboulette
BROILED SOLE WITH OYSTERS AND CHIVE SAUCE 67

Ingredients for 2 servings:

1 large Dover sole weighing 1½ pounds (*for substitution, see Note*)
Salt and pepper
1 tablespoon cooking oil
1 cup **chive sauce (12)** (*see Comment*)

8 large fresh oysters
4 cups water
1¼ teaspoons coarse salt
8 Bibb lettuce leaves
1 teaspoon freshly chopped chives

UTENSILS:

Scissors
3 large plates
Sieve
3 clean cloths
Small saucepan
Slotted spoon
Medium-size saucepan
Basting brush
Filleting knife
Grill for broiling
To serve: 2 hot dinner plates, or a hot oval serving platter

PREPARING THE SOLE:

You may either do this yourself or have the fish seller do it for you: With a large knife, cut the head of the sole off, just behind the gills. Clean the fish. Starting at the tail end, pull off the gray skin; leave the white skin on, scale it, and crisscross it with little slits, using the point of the knife. With the scissors, cut off all the fins, then rinse the sole under cold running water, both inside and out.

Season the fish with salt and pepper, brush it all over with the cooking oil, and set it aside on a plate while you preheat the broiler grill and make the **chive sauce.**

PREPARING THE OYSTERS:

Have the fish seller open the oysters for you.

Line a sieve with a clean cloth and place it over a small saucepan. With an ordinary teaspoon, scoop each oyster out of its shell, holding it over the sieve as you do so to catch all the juice. When all the oysters have been removed from their shells, place them in the saucepan with their strained juice, bring almost to a boil, and simmer for 30 seconds. Then lift them out of the liquid with a slotted spoon and drain them on a clean cloth.

In a medium saucepan, bring the water and coarse salt to a boil, add the lettuce leaves, and boil, uncovered, for 1 minute, then drain. Spread the lettuce leaves on a clean cloth to absorb any excess liquid.

Wrap each oyster in a lettuce leaf, then place them all on a plate, cover with a second plate turned upside down, and keep them warm on the bottom rack of the oven while the sole is being broiled.

TO COOK AND SERVE:

With a basting brush, brush the hot broiler grill with a little cooking oil, then place the sole, skin side down, diagonally across the bars of the grill. Broil for 2 minutes, then shift the sole, with the skin side still down, so that it lies diagonally across the grill in the opposite direction; this will make a crisscross design on the skin. Broil for 2 minutes more on this side, then turn the fish over and grill for a total of 4 minutes on the other side.

When the fish is cooked, lift the four fillets off of the bone with a filleting knife: Make a slit down the center of one side, then slide the blade of the knife between the meat and the bone to detach the two fillets on that side. Turn the fish over and do the same with the other side.

Generously cover the bottom of each dinner plate, or the serving platter, with the chive sauce, then lay the fillets of sole (with the crisscross design facing up) on top of the sauce. Decorate with the oysters, sprinkle with freshly chopped chives, and serve immediately.

COMMENTS:

In this recipe, the chive sauce may be replaced by a **Foamy butter sauce (6)** modified in the following way:

Parboil 1 tablespoon of lemon zest that has been cut into thin *julienne* strips for 1 minute in unsalted boiling water, then drain and add it to the sauce. At the last minute, add to the sauce 2 egg yolks beaten with 3 tablespoons of cold water, to make a kind of *sabayon* (see "The Principles of Binding Sauces [*Liaisons*]," p. 50).

In my opinion, the only way to cook fillets of Dover sole is to leave them on the bone. This not only prevents the flesh from shrinking and twisting like a corkscrew but also from acquiring a horrible rubbery texture.

Whole fish are also excellent breaded and broiled. To cook them, don't roll them in egg and flour; instead, roll them first in melted butter, then in very fine fresh bread crumbs before broiling them. The butter not only keeps the meat tender and juicy, it keeps the fish from sticking to the grill.

Note: *Any flatfish (flounder, turbot, etc.) may be used in making this recipe.*

Breading and broiling as described under "Comments" is a method which works with fish fillets as well as with whole fish, and it may be used very successfully in this recipe. Almost any fish fillets may be used, but it is especially good with those of lemon or gray sole, flounder, and other flatfish. For 2 servings, use ¾ pound fish fillets. Roll the fillets in melted butter and breadcrumbs (ordinary dry bread crumbs may be used instead of fresh ones), then broil the fillets for 2 minutes on each side.

Although directions are given for making a crisscross design on the fish, this is useful only if the fish are being grilled over hot coals or some other source of heat placed under *the grill itself. Since in an oven broiler the heat comes from the top, the grill is not hot enough, once the fish is on it, to make this design. So simply cook the fish for 4 minutes on each side without changing its direction on the grill.*

Depending on the size of the oysters, the amount of lettuce needed to wrap them will vary. If the oysters are small, half a leaf is sufficient for each one. The important thing to remember is that the lettuce leaf should go around the oyster only once; if it is wrapped in too much lettuce, the delicate taste of the oyster is completely lost. Ed.

Le marché du pêcheur en cocotte à la vapeur d'algues
68 MIXED SEAFOOD STEAMED WITH SEAWEED

Ingredients for 4 servings:

1 sea bass weighing 14 ounces
4 large scallops (*see Note*)
4 small red mullets (goatfish) weighing approximately 2 ounces each
24 periwinkles
2 cups water
1¼ teaspoons coarse salt
4 Bibb lettuce leaves
4 large oysters
4 large mussels (*see Note*)
1 fillet of sole weighing 4 ounces

4 large handfuls of seaweed (*see Comments*)
1⅔ cups water
4 large *langoustines* weighing 2½ to 3 ounces each (*for substitution, see Note*)

Scant ½ cup *julienne* strips of carrot
¼ medium onion, thinly sliced
⅔ cup *julienne* strips of leek, white part only
½ cup minced chives
Salt and pepper

SERVE WITH:

Foamy butter sauce (6) and/or
Fresh tomato and herb sauce (9)

UTENSILS:

Small saucepan
Slotted spoon
2 clean cloths
Pin or needle
Oyster knife
Sieve

Small bowl
Ordinary teaspoon
4 round cast-iron pots 8 inches in diameter, with covers (*see Note*)
4 round pastry grills, or circles of aluminum foil, 8 inches in diameter
To serve: 4 hot dinner plates
1 or 2 sauceboats

PREPARING THE FISH:

Ask your fish seller to fillet the bass and to remove the scallops from their shells for you, or do it yourself (do not remove the skin from the fish). For directions on cleaning scallops, see the recipe for **Puff pastry with scallops and truffles (45).**

Wipe off the red mullets and remove their gills, but do not clean (gut) them. Their insides are composed largely of a delicious liver, which is why they are often nicknamed the "woodcocks of the sea."

Wash the periwinkles. In a small saucepan, bring the water and coarse salt to a boil, add the little snails, and poach them gently for 2 minutes. Lift them out of the water with a slotted spoon, then place them on a clean cloth to absorb any excess moisture. With a pin or needle, remove the little corkscrew of meat from the shell. Cut off the black part at the end of each periwinkle's tail.

In the same water the snails cooked in, boil the lettuce leaves for 1 minute, then drain them.

Open the oysters with an oyster knife. Line a sieve with a clean cloth and place it over a small bowl. With an ordinary teaspoon, remove each oyster from its shell, holding it over the sieve as you do so to catch all its juice. Wash the oyster shells, line each one with a lettuce leaf, then place an oyster in each one, pour their strained juice over them, and sprinkle the periwinkles on top. Set them aside.

Wash the mussels carefully, scrape their shells with a knife to clean them, and pull out the "beard" that protrudes from between their shells.

Cut each bass fillet in half, and cut the fillet of sole into four pieces.

COOKING THE FISH:

Cover the bottom of each little pot with a layer of seaweed. Add ⅜ cup of water to each pot, then place a round grill on top of the seaweed. If you don't have grills, use circles of aluminum foil punched full of holes with a trussing needle. Carefully lay the fish and shellfish, including the *langoustines*, on top of the grills. The bass fillets should be placed skin side up.

Sprinkle the strips of vegetables and the chives over the fish, season with salt and pepper, cover the pots, bring the water to a boil, then cook for 3 minutes.

TO SERVE:

Bring the pots to the table and uncover them so that everyone can smell the wonderful aroma of seaweed, then take them back into the kitchen for the final preparations. With a sharp knife, cut the *langoustines* in half lengthwise. Remove the top shell of each mussel, then arrange the fish and shellfish on the dinner plates, as they were arranged in the pots, and serve.

Serve one or both of the suggested sauces at the same time, in sauceboats.

COMMENTS:

Ask the fish seller for the seaweed (kelp) when you buy the oysters, since oysters and other shellfish are often packed in it for shipping.

The fish and shellfish can be prepared up to a day in advance, and placed, as described, in the pots with the seaweed, vegetables, and seasonings. Keep the pots, covered, in the refrigerator until ready to cook.

Toasted slices of French bread spread with **"Rust" sauce** (7) are delicious served with this dish.

NOTE: *Since the fish are not served in the pots they are cooked in, 2 large pots may be used for cooking the fish instead of 4 smaller ones.*

Large shrimp may be used instead of langoustines.

Clams may be used instead of scallops or mussels. Ed.

Le pot-au-feu de la mer
SEAFOOD POT-AU-FEU 69

Ingredients for 4 servings:

FOR THE VEGETABLES:

4 cups water
2 teaspoons coarse salt
4 small leeks, cut into 2-inch lengths
8 baby carrots, peeled (*see Comment concerning baby vegetables*)
8 baby turnips, peeled
8 baby cucumbers (fresh gherkins), peeled
12 fresh asparagus tips, or ¼ pound green beans

FOR THE FISH:

2 sea bass, weighing 10 to 12 ounces each
4 red mullets (goatfish) weighing 3½ to 4 ounces each
1 tablespoon chopped shallot
1 bunch fresh parsley
Salt and pepper
½ cup water

1 scant cup red wine
Bouquet garni, including a branch of fresh tarragon
6 peppercorns
1 teaspoon granulated sugar
4 fillets of sole
1 cup **court-bouillon** (8)
8 *langoustines* (*for substitution, see Note*)

½ cup dry white wine
1 tablespoon chopped shallots
16 medium mussels, cleaned and bearded
Pepper

4 large oysters in their shells
4 large scallops removed from their shells

½ pound softened butter, broken into pieces

1 generous teaspoon butter (to sauté red-mullet livers)
4 slices French bread
1 tablespoon olive oil
4 anchovy fillets in oil
Juice of ½ lemon

UTENSILS:

Large saucepan
Scissors
3 oval cast-iron pans, 2 with covers (*or 1 roasting pan and 2 frying pans with covers. Ed.*)
Skimmer or slotted spoon
2 small saucepans, 1 with cover
Sieve
Clean cloth
Wire whisk
Small frying pan
To serve: 4 hot dinner plates
Sauceboat

COOKING THE VEGETABLES:

In a saucepan, bring the water and coarse salt to a boil. Add the leeks, carrots, and turnips and boil, uncovered, for 10 minutes. Then add the cucumbers and the asparagus tips or green beans, and cook for 5 minutes more. At the end of this time, remove the pan from the heat but leave the vegetables in their cooking liquid to keep hot.

PREPARING AND COOKING THE FISH:

Cut off the fins of the sea bass and red mullets with a pair of scissors, then scale, clean, and wash them. Save the livers of the red mullets and set them aside on a plate.

Preheat the oven to 425° F.

Sprinkle 1 tablespoon of chopped shallot over the bottom of the first oval pan (or roasting pan), then cover the shallots with half of the parsley. Lay the bass on top of the bed of parsley, sprinkle with salt and pepper, then cover the fish with the remaining parsley. Add ½ cup water, cover the pan, and cook in the oven for 8 minutes. At the end of this time, turn the oven down to 350° F, and open the oven door halfway to keep the fish warm without cooking it any longer.

In the second oval pan, place the red wine, *bouquet garni*, peppercorns, and sugar, and boil rapidly, uncovered, for 5 minutes, then lower the heat and poach the fillets of sole in this liquid for 3 minutes. Remove from the heat and cover the pan to keep the fillets warm.

In the third oval pan, bring the *court-bouillon* to a boil, then lower the heat, add the *langoustines*, and poach for 1½ minutes. Lift the *langoustines* out of the pan with a skimmer or slotted spoon, then poach the red mullets in the same pan for 2 minutes. Remove from the heat, and put the *langoustines* back into this pan, as well as the red mullets, and cover to keep warm.

In a small saucepan, bring the white wine and shallots to a boil. Add the mussels and sprinkle with pepper, then cover the pan and cook over high heat for about 6 minutes, or until all the mussels are open. Remove from the heat and take the mussels out of their shells.

Line a sieve with a clean cloth and place it over a second small saucepan. Remove the oysters from their shells, holding them over the sieve to catch their juice. When all the oysters have been shelled, place them in the saucepan with their filtered juice and add the scallops. Poach gently over low heat for 1 minute; the liquid should be hot, but you should be able to touch it with the back of your finger without being burned. Lift the shellfish out of the saucepan with a slotted spoon onto a plate, and keep warm in the oven with the bass.

MAKING THE SAUCE:

With a skimmer or slotted spoon, lift the fillets of sole, the *langoustines*, red mullets, and mussels out of their cooking liquids, and keep them warm in the oven with the other fish. Mix all their liquids together in the saucepan containing the liquid from the oysters, and bring to a boil. Reduce by three-quarters over high heat; there should be about ⅜ cup of liquid left after reduction.

Over high heat, add the butter, whisking at first, then shaking the pan to make the sauce spin around the sides. Once all the butter has been added, remove from the heat.

TO SERVE:

In a small frying pan, quickly sauté the red-mullet livers in a generous teaspoon of butter.

Brush the slices of bread with olive oil and brown them on both sides under the broiler.

With a sharp, flexible knife, lift the bass fillets off the bone.

Distribute half of the sauce evenly among the dinner plates; serve the rest of the sauce in a sauceboat. On top of the sauce in the plates, arrange the fish in a circle in the following order:

1 red mullet
1 fillet of sole
4 mussels
1 sea bass fillet
2 *langoustines*
1 oyster
1 scallop

Leave a space between the different kinds of fish as you arrange them, then fill the spaces with the assorted vegetables.

Place a sautéed liver on each slice of toasted bread, top with an anchovy fillet, and sprinkle with a few drops of lemon juice. Place one garnished piece of toast in the center of each plate, and serve immediately.

COMMENTS:

Instead of using baby vegetables, a large leek, carrot, turnip, and cucumber may be quartered and cut into 2-inch pieces.

If you don't have enough time to make the sauce described above, you may serve this dish with **Fresh tomato and herb sauce** (**9**) prepared in advance, even the day before.

The sauce may also be made more quickly than described. After reducing the mixed cooking liquids, place everything in the blender with the butter and blend until smooth. The vegetables in the *court-bouillon* help thicken the sauce when it is made this way.

Of course, other fish that are less expensive but just as flavorful may be used in making this dish; for example, conger eel, mackerel, whiting.

Note: *Shrimp may be used instead of* langoustines. *Ed.*

Les volailles

POULTRY

Ailerons de volaille au Meursault et aux concombres 70
CHICKEN WINGS WITH CUCUMBERS AND WHITE-WINE SAUCE

Ingredients for 4 servings:

- 28 to 32 chicken wings, weighing a total of 5½ pounds
- ¾ pound cucumber, peeled, seeded, and cut into rectangles 1 inch long or into olive-shaped pieces
- 2 teaspoons coarse salt
- 3 tablespoons butter
- Salt and pepper
- 1 teaspoon finely chopped shallot
- ¾ cup finely chopped fresh mushrooms
- ¼ cup dry vermouth
- ⅔ cup Meursault (or other dry white wine)

- 1⅓ cups heavy cream
- **2 tablespoons raw diced tomatoes (96)**
- ½ teaspoon finely chopped fresh tarragon
- 1 teaspoon finely chopped fresh chervil
- Salt and pepper
- 2 tablespoons butter
- 1 teaspoon granulated sugar
- 1 teaspoon finely chopped fresh chervil (to garnish)

UTENSILS:

Sharp knife
Meat cleaver
Large pot
Towel
Saucepan
Large *sauteuse* or high-sided frying pan, with cover
Skimmer or slotted spoon
Colander
Medium-size frying pan
To serve: 4 hot dinner plates, or a hot serving platter

BONING THE WINGS:

Using a sharp knife, cut off and discard the thin triangular tip of each wing (see Note). Cut the remaining V-shaped piece of each wing in two at the joint. With a meat cleaver, cut off the knobby ends of the bones. It is important to cut off both knobby extremities from each piece of wing so that the remainder of the bones can be removed easily later.

Drop the pieces of wing into a large pot of unsalted boiling water and boil for 3 minutes, then drain and dry the wings on a towel. Leave the wings to cool almost completely, then remove their bones by pushing in the smallest end of each bone with your thumb and pulling it out at the other end of the wing meat.

PREPARING THE CUCUMBERS:

In a saucepan, bring the water and coarse salt to a boil, then add the pieces of cucumber. Boil for 3 minutes, drain in a colander, and reserve for later use.

COOKING THE WINGS AND MAKING THE SAUCE:

In a large *sauteuse* or high-sided frying pan, heat 3 tablespoons of butter, then add the boned wings and a little salt and pepper. Cook them slowly for 5 minutes, then turn them over and cook another 5 minutes. Lift the wings out of the pan with a skimmer or slotted spoon and reserve.

Add the shallots and mushrooms to the pan and sauté for 3 minutes over medium heat. Pour off any excess fat but do not let any of the shallots and mushrooms fall out of the pan. Put back on the heat and add the vermouth and white wine. Scrape the bottom of the pan to dissolve the pan juices, then boil for 2 to 3 minutes or until the liquid has been reduced by three-quarters. Add the cream, tomatoes, tarragon, chervil, and a little salt and pepper. Continue boiling another 2 to 3 minutes or until the sauce reduces again by half. Lower the heat and add the wings to the sauce. Keep warm over low heat but do not boil the sauce again.

TO SERVE:

Place 2 tablespoons of butter in another frying pan. When it has melted, add the pieces of cucumber and sauté until they are golden on all sides. Then sprinkle with the sugar and continue browning for 2 minutes more.

Present the chicken wings and their sauce either on individual dinner plates or on one large serving platter. Surround the wings with the sautéed cucumbers, sprinkle with freshly chopped chervil, and serve immediately.

NOTE: *The ends of the chicken wings not used in this recipe, as well as the bones removed from the meat, can be combined with the water used to parboil the wings, some vegetables, and additional water to make stock—see* **Chicken stock (2).**

It may be necessary to brown the wings in two batches. Use half of the butter for the first batch, the rest for the second. It is important that the pieces be side by side, not overlapping, on the bottom of the pan when browning.

For a more substantial vegetable garnish, the amount of cucumber may be doubled. Ed.

71 *Blancs de volaille au sabayon de poireau*
STUFFED CHICKEN BREASTS WITH LEEK SAUCE

Ingredients for 4 servings:

2½ tablespoons butter
1 medium carrot, peeled and finely chopped
½ medium onion, peeled and finely chopped
2 medium mushrooms, finely chopped
1 large (¾-ounce) truffle, finely chopped (optional)
Salt and pepper
A pinch of thyme flowers or leaves

4 whole boned chicken breasts
Salt and pepper
2 teaspoons butter
1 small leek, white part only, finely sliced
1 teaspoon finely chopped shallot
½ cup tightly packed fresh water cress, stems removed
2 tablespoons port
1 cup **chicken stock** (**2**) (**3**)
1 cup *crème fraîche* (*see p.* 352) or heavy cream

2 egg yolks
3 tablespoons cold water

UTENSILS:

2 small saucepans
Spoon
Sauteuse or frying pan just large enough to hold chicken breasts
Skimmer or slotted spoon
Electric blender
Small bowl
Wire whisk
To serve: 4 hot dinner plates, or a hot serving platter

PREPARING THE VEGETABLE GARNISH:

Heat 2½ tablespoons of butter in a small saucepan. Add the carrot and cook over medium heat for 3 minutes, then add the onion, stir, and cook for 3 minutes more. Finally add the mushrooms and truffle and continue cooking 3 minutes longer. Stir the vegetables frequently during this time to keep them from sticking to the pan. Salt and pepper lightly and sprinkle with a pinch of thyme. Let the vegetables cool so you can handle them easily when stuffing the chicken breasts.

STUFFING THE CHICKEN BREASTS AND COOKING:

Remove the skin from the chicken breasts. Using a sharp knife, slice open each breast so that it will form a pocket (do not cut all the way through). Salt and pepper the inside of each pocket lightly, then place equal amounts of the vegetable garnish inside of each one.

Heat 2 teaspoons of butter in a large frying pan and add the leek and shallot. Cook over medium heat for 10 minutes. Stir frequently and do not let the leek brown. Add the water cress, port, stock, and cream to the pot and boil slowly for another 10 minutes. Gently place the stuffed chicken breasts into the simmering liquid and cook slowly for 10 minutes, turning them over once. Remove the chicken from the pan with a skimmer or slotted spoon to a plate, cover, and place in a 350° F oven with the door ajar while finishing the sauce.

FINISHING THE SAUCE AND SERVING:

Pour all the ingredients remaining in the pan into the blender. Blend until smooth, then pour the sauce into a small saucepan, bring almost to a boil, then keep hot over low heat.

Beat the egg yolks and cold water in a small bowl with a wire whisk for about 40 seconds, or until very foamy and greatly increased in volume, then pour directly into the very hot (but not boiling) sauce, whisking constantly.

Place the stuffed chicken breasts either on one large serving platter or on individual dinner plates and spoon the sauce over them. Serve immediately.

COMMENTS:

Only the white of the leek is used since the green leaves would give a bitter taste to the sauce. The beautiful green color of the sauce is due to the water cress, not to the leeks.

Ask for the best-quality chicken when preparing this recipe; the breast meat should be white, soft, and tender. If you skin the breast yourself, save the skin and sprinkle it into salads after cutting it into little squares and browning it in olive oil until crisp.

The only thing that could improve this recipe is one more, very large, 1-ounce truffle cut into very fine *julienne* strips and added with the egg yolks when finishing the sauce.

Note: *The sauce may be blended before, rather than after, cooking the chicken in it. This not only avoids the problem of removing any water-cress leaves from the chicken breasts, but also means that the chicken breasts may be placed directly on the hot dinner plates and the beaten egg yolks added to the sauce immediately and poured over the chicken, without having to keep the chicken warm in the oven. Ed.*

Volaille en gelée aux grains de poivre

72 PRESERVED CHICKEN IN GELATIN WITH PEPPERCORNS

Ingredients for 4 servings:

4 chicken legs (drumstick and thigh) weighing ½ pound each
Salt
4 slices of bacon
12 white peppercorns
1 tablespoon fresh chervil leaves
1 teaspoon fresh tarragon leaves
1 cup dry vermouth

1½ teaspoons gelatin moistened with 1½ tablespoons water
2 generous cups **chicken stock** (**2**) (**3**)

UTENSILS:

Large earthenware platter
Saucepan
Wide-mouthed preserving jar (1½-quart capacity; *see Note*)
Large pot for processing (*see Comments*)
To serve: Chilled serving platter

TO MARINATE THE CHICKEN:

Salt each piece of chicken lightly all over, rubbing the salt in with your fingers. Wrap a slice of bacon around each chicken leg. Place the legs in an earthenware platter and add the peppercorns, chervil, tarragon, and vermouth. Cover the platter with aluminum foil and place in the refrigerator overnight before cooking. Turn the pieces of chicken over once while they are marinating.

TO COOK:

Heat the chicken stock in a saucepan until it is just lukewarm, then stir in the moistened gelatin.

Place the chicken legs in a large preserving jar, then pour in all of the ingredients used in the marinade as well as the chicken stock. Seal the jar and place it in a large pot of boiling water. Boil (process) for 2 hours, then allow the jar to cool in the water. When cool, remove the jar from the water and refrigerate until the jelly has set.

TO SERVE:

Dip the jar into hot water for a few seconds, then turn the chicken out onto a serving platter and serve immediately.

COMMENTS:

This is the perfect thing to take on a picnic. Once the chicken has finished cooking it has been sterilized and can be kept a long time without spoiling.

When preserving any food, certain rules should be kept in mind:
1) The jar and the rubber ring that seals the top should be cleaned in boiling water and left to dry before using.
2) The jar should never be completely filled to the brim. Most jars have a level indicator that indicates the maximum they can hold.
3) A very large pot must be used when processing. The pot has to be taller than the jar itself; the sides of the jar should be at least an inch from the sides of the pot. Specially made pots are available; they usually have a perforated metal plate that sits on the bottom of the pot. If you do not have such a piece of metal, place a thick cloth or a perforated board on the bottom of the pot so the jar will be protected from the direct heat.
4) The boiling water should cover the jar by about 1 inch.

5) Leave the jar in the pot in which it was processed until the temperature of the water has cooled to lukewarm or has cooled completely.

Note: *It is essential that the mouth of the jar be wider than the bottom when preserving pieces of meat, as in this recipe.*

After an hour, add enough boiling water so that the top of the jar is again covered by as much water as in the beginning.

The jar should always stand upright in the boiling water. To keep it from tipping over, place a 2-pound weight on top. Ed.

Poulet au vinaigre de vin
73 CHICKEN WITH WINE-VINEGAR SAUCE

Ingredients for 4 servings:

1 chicken weighing approximately 3 pounds
Salt and pepper
2 tablespoons butter
6 whole cloves garlic, unpeeled
⅓ cup red-wine vinegar

2½ tablespoons armagnac or cognac
2 teaspoons Dijon mustard
1 teaspoon tomato paste
⅔ cup *crème fraîche* (*see p. 352*) or heavy cream
2 tablespoons butter, broken into six pieces
2 raw diced tomatoes (96)
1 teaspoon fresh chervil leaves

UTENSILS:

Large sharp knife
Large pot with cover
Wooden spoon
Skimmer or slotted spoon
Small bowl
Wire whisk
Strainer
To serve: 4 hot dinner plates, or a hot serving platter

PREPARING THE CHICKEN:

Using a large sharp knife, cut off both legs of the chicken. Cut in such a way that you not only remove the leg and thigh in one piece but the part of the back (about 2 inches in from the end of the tail) where a tender, oyster-shaped piece of meat is lodged.

Cut off all the breast meat with the wings attached. Season the pieces of chicken all over with salt and pepper.

Heat 2 tablespoons of butter in a large pot. Place the chicken, skin side down, into the pot and brown for 5 minutes, then turn over the pieces and brown on the other side for 5 minutes more. Add the cloves of garlic, cover the pot, and cook for 20 minutes over low heat. Remove the breasts and continue cooking the legs 5 minutes more. (The breasts will dry out if cooked too long.) Once the chicken is cooked, pour off half of the fat and liquid that has accumulated in the pot. To do this, hold the lid of the pot in place, but leave a small opening for the fat to pour through, and tilt the pot. The lid will keep the chicken and garlic from falling out of the pot.

Put the legs back into the pot, place over medium heat, and pour in the vinegar. Stir constantly so that all the juices that have caramelized on the bottom of the pot will mix into the sauce as the vinegar boils. Cover the pot halfway and boil the vinegar until it has reduced by three-quarters; as it evaporates, its flavor will penetrate the pieces of chicken. Once the vinegar has been reduced, lift out the chicken with a skimmer or slotted spoon, put it on a plate, cover, and place in a 350° F oven with the door ajar while preparing the sauce.

MAKING THE SAUCE:

In a small bowl, beat together the armagnac, mustard, and tomato paste with a wire whisk, then pour this mixture into the pot the chicken cooked in. Boil for 5 minutes, then, beating with a wire whisk, add the cream. Remove the pot from the heat and add the pieces of butter; continue to beat the mixture constantly as the butter is added. Check the sauce for salt and pepper, then pour it through a strainer, pressing the pieces of garlic with a wooden spoon or small ladle. (The garlic not only flavors the sauce but thickens it slightly.)

TO SERVE:

Place the pieces of chicken on individual dinner plates or one large serving platter and spoon the strained sauce over them. Sprinkle fresh chervil and a little freshly diced tomato over the chicken and serve immediately.

Note: *The back and neck of the chicken are not used in this recipe, so use them to make stock; see* **Chicken stock** (**2**) (**3**).

The pot should be large enough so that all the pieces of chicken fit on the bottom with as little space around them as possible. Ed.

74 *Le poulet "truffé" au persil et sa sauce au malvoisie* CHICKEN WITH PARSLEY "STUFFING" AND MALMSEY VINEGAR SAUCE

Ingredients for 4 servings:

FOR THE STUFFING:

3 1/3 tablespoons softened butter
1 tablespoon whole fresh parsley leaves
Juice of 1 lemon
1 tablespoon cold water
1 teaspoon salt
A pinch of pepper
3 tablespoons farmer's cheese
3 tablespoons finely chopped fresh parsley
1 tablespoon finely chopped fresh chives
1 teaspoon finely chopped fresh tarragon
2 tablespoons finely chopped shallot
2 medium mushrooms, finely chopped
1 slice (1 3/4 ounces) fresh or salted pork belly, finely chopped (*for substitution, see Note*)

FOR THE SAUCE:

1 tablespoon butter
1½ tablespoons finely chopped shallots
3 tablespoons Malmsey wine vinegar (*for substitution, see Note*)
⅓ cup **chicken stock (2) (3)**
3 tablespoons *crème fraîche* (*see p. 352*) or heavy cream
2 tablespoons butter, softened and broken into four pieces
1½ tablespoons **raw diced tomatoes (96)**
1½ teaspoons fresh chervil leaves

UTENSILS:

Electric blender
2 bowls
Fork
Roasting pan
Aluminum foil
Wooden spoon
Sieve
To serve: 4 hot dinner plates, or a hot serving platter

PREPARING THE STUFFING:

Place the 3½ tablespoons of butter, the whole parsley leaves, lemon juice, water, salt, and pepper in the blender. Blend until a homogeneous mixture is achieved. Place this mixture in a bowl and use a fork to mix in the farmer's cheese, chopped parsley, chives, tarragon, shallot, mushrooms, and chopped pork. Mix all well together with the prongs of the fork before "stuffing" the chicken.

"STUFFING" THE CHICKEN:

Cut off the chicken's neck. Use the tips of your fingers to loosen the skin on one breast of the chicken, starting at the base of the neck. Carefully work your fingers in underneath the skin; it will loosen and detach from the breast meat. Continue working your hand in, moving your fingers just enough to distend the skin all the way to the drumstick. The skin should be loose and detached, but not torn, on the entire breast and thigh. Repeat the procedure on the other side of the bird. Once this has been done, take a little of the stuffing and push it with your fingers into the space that has been created between the skin and the meat. Push the stuffing as far back as it will go (to the top of each thigh), then add more stuffing until both breasts have been "stuffed" as well. All the stuffing should be used.

COOKING THE CHICKEN:

Preheat the oven to 450° F.

Season the inside of the chicken with salt and pepper, then place it in a roasting pan, stuffed side up. Prick the skin in several places with a trussing needle, then roast the chicken for 45 minutes. Baste it frequently as it cooks. There is no need to add any grease to the roasting pan; the fat from the stuffing will be enough to keep the chicken from drying out.

Once it is cooked, turn off the oven, put the chicken on a plate, cover it with aluminum foil, and return it to the oven while making the sauce.

MAKING THE SAUCE:

Pour off the fat from the roasting pan. Place the pan on top of the stove and add 1 tablespoon of butter. When the butter has melted, add the shallots, and cook over medium heat for about 2 minutes; the shallots should soften but not brown. Pour in the vinegar, stirring constantly. The vinegar will evaporate quickly; stir to mix in the juices that have caramelized on the bottom of the pan, then reduce the vinegar by three-quarters. Stir in the stock and cream and bring to a boil, reduce this sauce by one-third, then stir in the remaining butter. Pour the sauce through a sieve into a bowl, and add the tomato and chervil. The sauce can be reheated over low heat or kept warm in a double boiler if not served immediately.

TO SERVE:

Remove the chicken from the oven. Cut it into four pieces (two breasts with wings, and two legs). Spoon a quarter of the hot sauce onto each of the plates, or pour all of the sauce onto the serving platter. Place the pieces of chicken on top of the sauce and serve immediately.

COMMENTS:

Generally when roasting chicken, it's best to place the bird in the oven lying on its side, then, a third of the way through the cooking time, to turn it over onto the other side. Finally, finish roasting with the chicken breast up on its back. Turning the chicken this way ensures even browning. However, in this particular recipe the chicken is simply roasted on its back because turning it may puncture the skin and let out some of the stuffing. Normally, allow 15 to 18 minutes a pound in a 450° F oven when roasting chicken.

NOTE: *Malmsey is a sweet wine made in Madeira, Cyprus, and the Canary Islands. Vinegars are made from Malmsey, but if unavailable, sherry vinegar may be used instead.*

Bacon that has been placed in cold water, brought to a boil, and immediately drained and cooled under running water may be used instead of the pork belly.

After loosening the skin, but before "stuffing," sew the skin closed at the tail end. Once stuffed, sew it closed at the neck, then loosely tie the legs together and run a string around the wings to hold them in place while roasting.

The stuffing may be made in the blender. In this case, the ingredients can be coarsely rather than finely chopped, and the mushrooms and pork should be added at the very end, after all the other ingredients are blended together. Ed.

Pintade au vin de Margaux et au lard fumé
GUINEA HEN STEWED IN RED-WINE SAUCE 75

Ingredients for 4 servings:

FOR MARINATING:

1 guinea hen weighing 1¾ pounds (*for substitution, see Note*)
Pepper
8 thin strips of bacon
2 generous cups red wine from Margaux (*for substitution, see Note*)
1 medium carrot, peeled and diced
½ onion, peeled and diced
1 small *bouquet garni*
1 clove
1 clove garlic, unpeeled

FOR COOKING:

3 tablespoons cooking oil
2 tablespoons butter
1 tablespoon flour
2 generous cups **chicken stock** (2) (3)
16 baby onions, peeled
⅓ cup *crème fraîche* (*see p. 352*) or heavy cream
2 tablespoons *crème de cassis*

UTENSILS:

Large knife
Toothpicks
Large bowl
Aluminum foil
Cloth
Large frying pan
Slotted spoon
Large stewing pot
Sieve
To serve: 4 hot dinner plates, or a hot serving platter

TO MARINATE:

Use a large knife to cut the guinea hen into eight pieces; this will mean cutting the thigh from the drumstick and cutting each breast in half just behind the wing. Sprinkle the pieces of guinea hen with pepper and wrap each piece with a thin slice of bacon (do not salt, because of the bacon); use a toothpick to attach the bacon to the meat. Place the pieces of guinea hen in a large bowl and add all the ingredients for marinating listed above. Cover the bowl with aluminum foil and place in the refrigerator overnight before cooking.

TO COOK:

Lift the pieces of guinea hen, still wrapped in the bacon, out of the marinade and dry them with a clean cloth.

Heat the oil in a frying pan, add the pieces of guinea hen, skin side down, and brown for 4 minutes, then turn over all the pieces and brown another 4 minutes. Just before the time is up, melt the butter in a pot, then lift the pieces of guinea hen out of the frying pan with a slotted spoon and add them to the pot. Remove the carrots and onions from the wine marinade and add them to the pot as well. Sauté the vegetables and meat over medium heat until the vegetables begin to brown, then sprinkle them with the flour and continue cooking 4 minutes, stirring occasionally with a wooden spoon. Pour the rest of the marinade ingredients into the pot and add the stock and baby onions. Bring the liquid to a boil, then lower the heat and simmer slowly, uncovered, for 20 minutes.

TO SERVE:

Lift the pieces of guinea hen and the baby onions out of the pot and place them on a plate. Remove the toothpicks, then cover the plate with aluminum foil, and place in a 350° F oven with the door ajar while finishing the sauce.

Add the cream and *crème de cassis* to the pot the guinea hen was cooked in; check for salt and pepper, then boil rapidly for 8 to 10 minutes or until the sauce has reduced by about half.

Place the pieces of guinea hen and bacon on individual plates or one large serving platter and arrange the baby onions around them. Pour the sauce through a sieve over the meat and serve immediately.

COMMENTS:

The *crème de cassis* not only gives a nice taste to the sauce but a beautiful color as well.

The sauce can be enriched and turned into a *civet* by adding 2½ tablespoons of pig's blood, away from the heat, just before serving (the blood should not boil).

The baby onions can be cooked separately and glazed as in **Glazed mixed vegetables (99)**.

Note: *A small chicken or a Rock Cornish hen may be used instead of a guinea hen.*

Although a wine from Margaux is preferable, any bordeaux of good quality could be used. Ed.

76 *Pigeonneau en bécasse*
SQUAB WITH GARLIC

Ingredients for 4 servings:

FOR THE SQUAB:

24 cloves of garlic, peeled

4 squab weighing 1 pound each
2½ tablespoons butter
Salt and pepper
2 tablespoons red port

2 teaspoons butter
1 tablespoon chopped shallot
1½ ounces *foie gras au naturel* (optional; *for substitution, see Note*)
1 tablespoon butter, softened
1 tablespoon *crème fraîche* (*see p. 352*) or heavy cream
Salt and pepper
1 tablespoon softened butter, for the toast
4 thin slices French bread or sandwich bread

FOR THE SAUCE:

1 generous tablespoon finely chopped shallot
2 tablespoons armagnac or cognac
2 tablespoons red port
2 generous cups red wine

UTENSILS:

2 small saucepans
Strainer
Trussing needle and string
Roasting pan
Slotted spoon
Large plate
Aluminum foil
Small frying pan
Electric blender
Sieve
To serve: 4 hot dinner plates

PREPARING THE GARLIC:

Drop the cloves of garlic into a saucepan of boiling water. Boil for 1 minute and drain. Fill the pot with water once again and bring to a boil, add the garlic and boil for another minute, and drain again. Repeat this procedure one last time; thus the garlic will have boiled for a total of 3 minutes in three different waters. Changing the water and boiling in this manner will keep the garlic from being too pungent or bitter after being cooked. Once it is prepared in this way, garlic can be eaten as a delicious vegetable garnish.

PREPARING THE SQUAB AND COOKING:

Clean the birds, save the livers for use in the sauce, and leave the neck and head attached to the body, but take out the eyes.

Use a trussing needle to run a string through both legs and secure them firmly to the body of the bird for cooking. The wings should also be firmly attached to the body with string, and the neck twisted back under one wing and attached to the side of the back. The poultry man can do all this for you.

Preheat the oven to 450° F.

On top of the stove, melt 2½ tablespoons of butter in the roasting pan. Salt and pepper the inside of each bird, then brown them on all sides in the hot butter. Add the blanched garlic to the roasting pan, then place in the oven and cook the squab for 12 minutes. Baste the birds two or three times while they are cooking. Once the birds are done, lift them out of the roasting pan and cut off the legs and the breast meat and wings. Reserve the carcasses for making the sauce.

Place the pieces of squab on a large plate and spoon 2 tablespoons of port over them. Lift the garlic out of the roasting pan with a slotted spoon and place on the plate with the squab. Cover the plate with aluminum foil and place in a warm (350° F) oven with the door ajar. The birds will finish cooking while the sauce is being prepared.

THE FOIE GRAS GARNISH:

Heat 2 teaspoons of butter in a small frying pan. When the butter is hot, add the squab livers reserved earlier and 1 tablespoon of chopped shallot. Brown the livers quickly on all sides; they should cook only about 2 minutes and still be pink inside when finished browning. Lift the livers and shallots out of the pan with a slotted spoon to drain them, and leave to cool before blending with the *foie gras*.

When the livers have cooled, place them in a blender with the *foie gras,* 1 tablespoon of butter, the cream, salt, and pepper. Blend until all the ingredients form a smooth mixture, then pour into a bowl.

With the tablespoon of butter remaining, butter the pieces of bread and toast them under the broiler. Spread the pieces of toast with half of the *foie gras* mixture and place them on the plate with the pieces of squab and garlic while making the sauce.

THE SAUCE:

Using a cleaver, cut each of the carcasses reserved earlier into six pieces. Place them in the roasting pan the birds were cooking in with 1 generous tablespoon of chopped shallot, and brown over medium heat for 4 minutes. Add the armagnac and 2 tablespoons of port, stirring constantly to mix in the juices that have caramelized on the bottom of the pan. Boil the liquid for a few seconds or until it has reduced by three-quarters, then add the red wine and continue rapidly boiling 3 to 4 minutes or until it too has reduced by three-quarters. Once it is reduced, pour the sauce through a sieve into a small saucepan. Heat the sauce but do not let it boil; add the remaining *foie gras* mixture to the sauce, beating constantly with a wire whisk as it is being added. The sauce will become rich and thick. Keep it warm by placing it in a shallow pan of hot water or in the warm oven.

TO SERVE:

Remove the squab from the oven. Take the skin off of each piece of squab and arrange four pieces on each dinner plate, the wings and legs opposite each other in a geometrical pattern. Split open the head and place it at one end of the plate. Place the garlic in between the pieces of squab, spoon the sauce over the birds, then place the pieces of garnished toast on one side of each plate, and serve immediately.

COMMENTS:

Squab is delicious cooked this way with or without the garlic. The birds are also very pretty if served on a few fresh spinach leaves that have been dropped into boiling water for just 30 seconds and drained.

Note: *If you do not have the squab livers, half as many chicken livers can be used instead.*

Chicken livers may also be used instead of the foie gras. *For this recipe, use 2 chicken livers and sauté them with the squab livers and shallot along with a very small sprig of thyme and ½ bay leaf. Sauté and drain as indicated (remove the thyme and bay leaf), then blend with the other ingredients for the sauce. Ed.*

Aiguillettes de caneton au poivre vert
DUCK FILLETS WITH APPLES AND GREEN-PEPPERCORN SAUCE 77

Ingredients for 2 ducks, or 4 servings:

2 ducks weighing approximately 3¼ pounds each
Salt and pepper
1 tablespoon cooking oil

½ cup dry white wine
2½ tablespoons armagnac or cognac
2½ tablespoons liquid from the jar of green peppercorns
¼ cup **chicken stock (2) (3)**
1⅓ cups *crème fraîche* (*see p. 352*) or heavy cream
Salt and pepper

1 tablespoon red-wine vinegar
½ teaspoon granulated sugar

4 teaspoons red port
4 teaspoons green peppercorns
1½ tablespoons finely chopped canned pimientos

2½ tablespoons butter
4 medium apples, peeled, cored, and cut into 8 wedges each

UTENSILS:

Large sharp knife
Large roasting pan
Aluminum foil
2 small saucepans
Wooden spoon
Frying pan with cover
Flexible-blade knife
To serve: 4 hot dinner plates, or a large hot serving platter

PREPARING AND COOKING THE DUCKS:

Slide a large sharp knife between the thighs and the breast and cut off the legs of each duck at the point where they are attached to the body. The legs can be used to prepare **Confit of duck legs preserved in goose fat (79)**; they are not used in this recipe.

Preheat the oven to 500° F. Season the inside of each duck with salt and pepper, and place the ducks in a roasting pan. Baste them with the cooking oil, then place in the oven and cook for 20 minutes. Remove from the oven and cover the roasting pan with a large piece of aluminum foil. Lower the oven setting to 350° F, leave the oven door ajar, and put the roasting pan back in the oven. The ducks will stay hot and finish cooking at the lower temperature while the sauce is being prepared. Letting the ducks sit for a short time in the warm oven also ensures even cooking of the meat, which should be pink when served.

MAKING THE SAUCE:

In a small saucepan place the white wine and armagnac, and bring to a boil. Boil slowly, uncovered, for 6 minutes or until the liquid has reduced by two-thirds. Add the liquid from the green peppercorns as well as the stock, and continue boiling slowly for 5 minutes. Then add the cream, a little salt and pepper, and boil gently for another 15 minutes or until the liquid has reduced by one-third. Stir occasionally and make sure the sauce doesn't boil too quickly.

While the sauce is reducing, boil the sugar and vinegar for 30 seconds in another small saucepan, or until the mixture is a dark-caramel color and the consistency of a light syrup. Pour this vinegar-sugar mixture into the sauce once it has been reduced, then stir in the port, green peppercorns, and pimientos, stirring constantly. Check the seasoning and keep the sauce warm in a *bain-marie* or double boiler if not serving immediately.

THE APPLE GARNISH:

Heat the butter in a frying pan and add the apples. Cook the pieces over low heat for 10 minutes on each side, then cover the pan and keep warm until served.

TO SERVE:

Take the ducks from the oven and use a sharp flexible-blade knife to cut each breast off in one piece. Remove the skin. Cut the breast meat into very thin slices crosswise, holding the knife at about a 20-degree angle to the meat. Arrange the slices of duck in a fan on the plates, spoon the sauce over them, and place the slices of apple around the edges of the plates. Serve immediately.

COMMENTS:

The best and most tender duck meat comes from birds that are not bled when killed. All the blood is left in the body and gives the meat a beautiful pink color, an almost musky flavor, and makes it extremely tender.

All ducks are best if cooked half an hour ahead and then left to rest in the warm oven, as described earlier, before being served.

Instead of slicing the duck breasts before serving, they may be sliced at the table. The breasts are easier to remove if the wishbone has been taken out before the meat is sliced. It's easy to remove; simply cut around it with a pointed knife and pull it out.

The green-peppercorn sauce served with the ducks is also excellent with numerous other dishes: Veal, poultry, beef, and fish, broiled or fried, can all be served with this sauce.

78 *Grillade de canard de Chalosse au beurre d'herbes fines*
DUCK FILLETS WITH SHALLOT BUTTER SAUCE

Ingredients for 4 servings:

2 large duck breasts (*magrets de canard*), skin still attached, but all bones removed, weighing approximately ¾ pound each
3 tablespoons olive oil
3 tablespoons cooking oil
3 tablespoons red wine

⅜ cup finely chopped shallots
½ cup red-wine vinegar
½ teaspoon sherry vinegar
4 tablespoons softened butter, broken into 12 pieces
1 generous teaspoon finely chopped fresh chives
1 generous teaspoon finely chopped fresh chervil
1 generous teaspoon finely chopped fresh tarragon
1 generous teaspoon finely chopped fresh parsley
Salt and pepper

SERVE WITH:

Sautéed potatoes with coarse salt (110) (*see Comments*)

UTENSILS:

Earthenware platter
Cast-iron frying pan
Spatula
Small saucepan
Wire whisk
To serve: 4 hot dinner plates, or a hot serving platter

MARINATING THE DUCK:

Use a sharp knife to cut off any gristle or large veins from the underside of the duck breasts. Use the tip of the knife to score deeply the skin of each breast in a crisscross pattern. Place the breasts, skin side up, in an earthenware platter and pour the two oils and the wine over them. Roll the breasts in this mixture, then leave to marinate in the refrigerator for at least 24 hours. Turn over once, after 12 hours.

COOKING THE DUCK:

Either cook the duck on a grill over an open fire or in a cast-iron frying pan on the stove. If using a frying pan, heat it, without any butter or fat, then place the pieces of duck in the pan, skin side down. The duck's own fat, which will melt while cooking, as well as the oil still coating it from marinating, will suffice for cooking.

Fry the duck meat for 10 minutes over medium heat, then turn it over and cook for 3 minutes on the other side. Lift the duck out of the pan with a spatula, and keep it warm on a plate, covered, in a 350° F oven with the door ajar while preparing the sauce. The duck needs to rest in the oven after being cooked if the meat is to be as tender as possible.

THE SAUCE:

In a small saucepan, place the shallots and wine vinegar. Boil until three-quarters of the vinegar has evaporated. The shallots should be quite soft and moist; there should be about 5 tablespoons of shallots and vinegar left in all.

Add the sherry vinegar, bring to a boil, then immediately lower the heat and start adding the butter, beating the mixture with a wire whisk as the butter is being added. Shake the pan frequently, lifting it off the heat, to make the sauce spin rapidly around the sides, and continue adding the butter, a few pieces at a time. The sauce will thicken and become smoother as the butter is added.

Add the chives, chervil, tarragon, parsley, and a little salt and pepper to the sauce. It is ready to serve; if not served immediately, keep it warm in a *bain-marie* or double boiler.

TO SERVE:

Take the duck out of the oven and cut the meat into thin (1/8-inch) slices. Hold the knife at a slight angle to the meat and cut crosswise so as to make numerous short pieces. Arrange the slices in a fan on one side of individual dinner plates or on the serving platter, and the fried potatoes in another fan on the other side. Spoon the sauce over the duck and serve.

COMMENTS:

Use the fat left in the frying pan after cooking the duck to fry the potatoes.

The duck can be left to marinate in the refrigerator for up to 8 days (the longer it marinates, the better it tastes), but 8 days is the limit, no longer.

Note: *The duck breasts called for in this recipe are indeed very large. Four smaller duck breasts can be used in this recipe, but in this case, reduce the cooking time accordingly.*

Ideally, the breasts used should come from a duck which has been specially fattened to make foie gras *of duck, hence their large size. They also give off a great deal of fat. If ordinary duck breasts are used, it may be necessary to add a spoonful or two of chicken fat while cooking them. Ed.*

79 *Cuisses de canard confites*
CONFIT OF DUCK LEGS PRESERVED IN GOOSE FAT

Ingredients for 4 servings:

4 duck legs (thigh and drumstick) (*see Comments and Note*)
½ clove garlic, peeled
1¼ teaspoons salt
A pinch of pepper
A pinch of nutmeg
½ bay leaf, crumbled
¼ teaspoon thyme
3⅓ cups goose fat

UTENSILS:

Large earthenware platter
2 pots
Slotted spoon
Frying pan
1 large stoneware or glass jar, with cover (1-quart size)

MARINATING THE DUCK:

Place the duck legs on a cutting board and rub them on all sides with the garlic, then with salt, pepper, and a little nutmeg. Place the duck in an earthenware platter, sprinkle with the bay leaf and thyme, cover, and place the platter in the refrigerator overnight before cooking.

COOKING THE DUCK:

Place the duck and all the ingredients used to marinate it in a pot. In another pot, heat the goose fat just enough to melt it, and pour it over the pieces of duck. Bring the fat almost to a boil, then immediately lower the heat and simmer very slowly, uncovered, for 1½ hours. At the end of this time, the duck should be perfectly cooked, and the meat so soft that you can stick a broom straw into it and not feel the least resistance.

TO SERVE:

The duck can be served either hot or cold. If served hot, first lift it out of the fat with a slotted spoon, then heat some of the fat in a frying pan. Place the duck in the hot fat, skin side down, and brown quickly before serving.

If the duck is to be served cold, brown it as described above, then leave it to cool in the refrigerator before serving. Cold, the duck is a perfect summer dish served with a green salad with a nut-oil dressing.

TO STORE:

Once it is cooked, place the duck and all of the fat it cooked in in a stoneware or glass jar; be sure the meat is completely covered by the fat and cover the jar. The duck will keep for several months in the refrigerator stored this way. Or, you can preserve the duck and its fat as described in the recipe for **Preserved chicken in gelatin with peppercorns (72)**. If you plan to do this, cook it for only 45 minutes in the fat, then process it in the jar for about 1 hour.

COMMENTS:

Duck prepared in this way is used in the recipe for **The Pot-au-Feu Restaurant's pot-au-feu (95)**.

Since several recipes in this book use only the breast meat of duck —**Duck fillets with shallot butter sauce** (78), **Duck fillets with apples and green-peppercorn sauce** (77), etc.—use the legs to make this *confit*, which can be stored and used at a later date.

Chicken or guinea-hen legs can be used instead of the duck to make interesting and unusual *confits.*

Note: Confit *can also be made with the breast and wings of the duck as well as the legs. Use the same ingredients given here for one small duck cut into four pieces, i.e., the two legs and the two breasts with wings attached.*

Save the fat used in this recipe. Use it to preserve other ducks in fat or in recipes that call for goose fat. Remember that it has been seasoned.

If you store the confit, *don't forget to brown the meat before serving it. Ed.*

Les gibiers

GAME

Bécasse au fumet de Pomerol

SNIPE WITH RED-WINE SAUCE 80

Ingredients for 4 servings:

- 4 snipe with innards (*for substitution, see Note*)
- Salt and pepper
- 4 thin slices pork belly (*for substitution, see Note*)
- 3½ tablespoons butter

- 4 rounds of sandwich bread about ½ inch thick, cut out with a 2-inch cookie cutter
- 1¾ ounces fresh or canned *foie gras* (*for substitution, see Note*)
- 2 tablespoons *crème fraîche* (*see p. 352*) or heavy cream
- Salt and pepper
- 1 tablespoon armagnac or cognac

- 1 tablespoon finely chopped shallots
- 4 tablespoons armagnac or cognac
- 4 tablespoons red port
- Scant 1½ cups red wine (preferably a Pomerol or other bordeaux)
- 1 teaspoon lemon juice

UTENSILS:

String
Large roasting pan
Wooden spoon
Large plate
Aluminum foil
Spatula
Electric blender
Meat cleaver
Sieve
Small saucepan
To serve: 4 hot dinner plates

PREPARING AND COOKING THE SNIPE:

Remove the feathers from the birds just before cooking, but do *not* take out the heart, liver, or intestines. Leave the neck and head attached, but take out the eyes with a sharp knife. Do not truss the birds or tie them with string; rather, run the long beak through the body, from leg to leg. This will hold the legs in place for cooking.

Salt and pepper each bird, then wrap it in a slice of pork belly to cover the breast meat. Do tie the pork onto the birds with string; the fat from the pork will keep the breast meat from drying out.

Preheat the oven to 450° F.

On top of the stove, melt the butter in a roasting pan and brown the birds on all sides over moderate heat. Then place the birds in the oven for 18 minutes and baste often with the fat in the roasting pan. They will be slightly "rare" when finished cooking. Remove from the oven and take off the pork and discard it.

Cut the wings, legs, and breast meat from the birds. Save the carcasses for making the sauce. Scoop the intestines, heart, and liver out from inside the snipe; discard the gizzard, but keep the other innards for later use.

Place the wings, legs, and breasts on a plate and cover with aluminum foil. Keep the plate in a warm (350° F) oven with the door ajar while making the sauce and the *foie gras* garnish.

THE FOIE GRAS GARNISH:

In the roasting pan the birds cooked in, fry the pieces of bread until they are evenly colored on both sides, then remove and reserve.

Place the innards of the birds, the *foie gras*, 1 tablespoon of armagnac, and the cream in a blender. Blend until smooth and season with a little salt and pepper. Spread one-third of the *foie gras* garnish on the pieces of toast, and reserve the rest for making the sauce. Place the garnished bread in the oven on the plate with the pieces of snipe to keep them warm.

MAKING THE SAUCE:

Use a cleaver or large knife to cut each snipe carcass into six pieces. Place the carcasses in the roasting pan used to cook the birds, add the shallots, and sauté over medium heat for 4 minutes. Pour 4 tablespoons of armagnac and the port into the pan, and stir well with a wooden spoon to detach the juices that have caramelized on the bottom of the pan. Then add the red wine and boil the liquid until it has reduced by three-quarters. Remove from the heat and add the lemon juice. Pour this sauce through a sieve into a small saucepan. Heat the sauce gently—do *not* let it boil—and add the remaining *foie gras* garnish reserved earlier. Whisk the sauce constantly as the *foie gras* mixture is being added; it will thicken and become creamy. If it is not served immediately, keep the sauce warm in a *bain-marie* or double boiler.

TO SERVE:

Take the plate with the snipe and garnished pieces of toast from the oven. Arrange the pieces of snipe symmetrically, with legs and wings opposite each other, on each plate. Split open each head and place it and the neck at one end. Spoon the sauce over the birds, place the pieces of toast at the side of each plate, and serve immediately.

COMMENTS:

I am absolutely against the old habit of serving poultry and game "on toast"; the bread quickly becomes soaked in the sauce, like a *baba au rhum*! When toast or a *croûton* is served to garnish a dish, it should always be crisp, *never* soggy. The garnished toast should be placed next to or near the sauce but *never* in it.

Snipe are hard to find, even in France, since no one (mercifully) has ever been able to hunt them commercially. When they are available during the hunting season, they should be eaten no later than six days after they are shot. They should be kept refrigerated if they are not prepared immediately. If they are hung too long, they lose their delicate taste.

The bird's intestines—large, white, fat, and delicious—should never be discarded but always be eaten with the bird itself.

Note: *Any one of the numerous varieties of woodcock or snipe could be used in this recipe. Squab or dove could be substituted, although these birds' intestines would have to be discarded before cooking. The livers should be saved for the sauce.*

Two chicken livers, sautéed for 2 to 3 minutes in 1½ tablespoons of butter with a tablespoon of chopped shallot and a pinch of thyme and bay leaf, can be used instead of the foie gras *in this recipe. If using birds other than woodcock or snipe, use 4 chicken livers plus the livers of the birds to replace the entrails that are discarded.*

Thin slices of bacon that have been placed in a pot of cold water, brought to a boil, then immediately drained and cooled under cold running water can be used instead of the pork belly. Ed.

81 *Navarin de faisan aux pieds de cochon*
STEWED PHEASANT WITH VEGETABLES AND PORK TROTTERS

Ingredients for 4 servings:

- 1 pheasant, about 1¾ pounds' dressed weight
- Salt and pepper
- 1 large cooked pig's foot, *not* breaded, as is often done in a French *charcuterie (for substitution, see Note)*
- ¼ pound pork belly, thinly sliced (*for substitution, see Note*)
- 12 baby white onions, peeled
- 12 small button mushrooms, cleaned
- 8 baby carrots, or 2 medium carrots cut into 1-inch pieces
- 8 whole turnips, peeled, or 2 medium turnips, peeled and quartered
- 8 baby potatoes, peeled, or 1 medium potato, peeled, halved, then each half quartered

3/8 cup armagnac or cognac
1 cup **chicken stock** (2) (3)
1 cup red wine
Bouquet garni, including a sprig of tarragon
Salt and pepper
1 quart water
2 teaspoons coarse salt
1/3 cup shelled green peas, fresh or frozen
2 large ripe tomatoes
1 clove garlic, peeled
2 tablespoons olive oil

UTENSILS:

Large, very sharp knife
Large pot with cover
Slotted spoon
Small saucepan
Strainer
Electric blender
To serve: Large hot serving bowl (optional)

CUTTING THE PHEASANT AND THE PIG'S FOOT:

Place the pheasant on its back on a cutting board. Slide a large sharp knife inside the bird and cut it open along one side of the backbone. Cut along the other side of the backbone, remove it, and discard. Cut the bird into four pieces, i.e., two legs with the thighs attached and two breasts with the wings attached. Leave the breast meat attached to the bone, as the bone keeps the meat from shrinking as it cooks. Salt and pepper the pieces lightly.

Cut the pig's foot open lengthwise, remove the bones, then cut each piece of the foot in half lengthwise. (Soaking the foot first in hot water until it softens makes it easier to cut.)

COOKING THE MEAT AND VEGETABLES:

Preheat the oven to 400° F.

Cut the pork into small pieces (*lardons*) 1/4 inch wide and place them in a pot with the little onions. Cook over moderate heat until the pork has rendered some of its fat and both it and the onions have begun to brown. (One tablespoon of lard can be added if the pork is particularly lean.) Lift the pieces of pork and the onions out of the pot with a slotted spoon and reserve. Place the pieces of pheasant in the pot, skin side down, and, still over moderate heat, brown, then turn them over. Now add the mushrooms, carrots, and turnips, and continue cooking for 5 minutes, or until the vegetables have begun to brown.

Cover the pot almost entirely; hold the cover on and tip the pot so that the excess fat will pour out but the other ingredients will be held inside. Discard the fat. Add the armagnac to the pot, cover, and boil for 2 minutes, or until it has been reduced by three-quarters. Then add the stock, red wine, *bouquet garni*, and the strips of pig's foot. Salt and pepper lightly, cover the pot, and place in the oven for 25 minutes. Then add the potatoes and the pork and little onions reserved earlier. Continue cooking in the oven for 20 minutes more.

While the meat is in the oven, bring the water and coarse salt to a boil in a saucepan, then add the peas. Cook fresh, very small peas for 10 to 15 minutes (6 minutes will be long enough for frozen peas), then drain and reserve for use as a garnish.

Cut the 2 tomatoes in half crosswise, and squeeze each half to eliminate most of the seeds and water; do not peel the tomatoes. Place the tomatoes in a blender with the garlic, olive oil, and a little salt and pepper. Blend until a beautiful pink purée is formed.

Once the meat has finished cooking, remove the pot from the oven and pour the tomato mixture into it, stirring carefully. Sprinkle the peas over the other ingredients and serve immediately, either from the pot or from a large serving bowl. If the dish is not served immediately, do not add the tomato mixture or the peas. Just before serving, reheat the pheasant and vegetables on top of the stove (do not allow to boil), then add the tomato mixture and peas, and serve.

COMMENTS:

The gelatinous texture of the pig's foot will complement the flavor of the pheasant and keep it from drying out.

The best pheasant are young birds that are less than a year old. When roasting pheasant or other game bird, blend a little farmer's cheese with the bird's liver, 1 chopped shallot, some freshly chopped herbs, salt, pepper, and a teaspoon of armagnac or cognac in a blender.

Place the mixture inside the bird before roasting; the meat will remain tender and juicy.

Note: *The pig's foot, if not purchased already cooked, has to be cooked for 3 hours with water, white wine, sliced vegetables, and seasoning.*

If necessary, 6 ounces of headcheese of good quality, cut into slices, can be used instead of the pig's foot. Do not overseason.

An equal weight of bacon that has been parboiled by placing it in a pot of cold water, bringing it to a boil, and immediately draining and cooling under cold running water may be used to replace the pork belly. Ed.

Perdreaux sur un lit de chou

PARTRIDGE ON A BED OF CABBAGE LEAVES 82

(color picture VI)

Ingredients for 4 servings:

4 young partridges, cleaned, livers reserved
Salt and pepper
4 slices of bread, 2 inches wide
1 whole clove garlic, peeled
4 thin slices fresh pork belly for barding (*see Note*)

1 head of cabbage, weighing about 4½ pounds
3 quarts water
1 generous tablespoon coarse salt
1 quart water
¼ pound salted or fresh pork belly, cut into small pieces (*lardons*)

5 teaspoons butter
¼ cup water
¼ cup dry white wine

UTENSILS:

Large pot with cover
Colander
Large plate
Aluminum foil
Wooden spoon
To serve: 4 hot dinner plates

PREPARING THE BIRDS:

When cleaning the partridges, be sure to save their livers; cut off any greenish parts that may be the result of contact with the birds' gall bladders. Place the livers on a plate and crush them into a purée with the prongs of a fork. Salt and pepper lightly. Rub the four pieces of bread with the garlic, then spread the bread with the livers. Salt and pepper the birds' insides, then place one garnished piece of bread inside each partridge.

Truss the birds and tie a slice of pork belly across the breast; the fat from the pork will keep the meat from drying out or browning too much while cooking.

PREPARING THE CABBAGE AND PORK:

Cut the head of cabbage into four pieces, then cut out the hard central core. Separate the cabbage leaves, and rinse them in cold water. Place 3 quarts of water and the coarse salt in a large pot, bring to a boil, then add the cabbage. Boil for 10 minutes, then drain in a colander. Rinse out the pot, add 1 quart of water, bring to a boil, then drop in the pieces of pork belly. Boil for 1 minute, drain, and reserve.

COOKING THE PARTRIDGES AND CABBAGE:

Melt the butter in a large pot and brown the partridges on all sides over moderate heat for 15 minutes. Remove the pork that was tied around each bird and reserve. Continue browning the birds for 1 minute longer to color the breast meat, then remove them from the pot. Put the birds on a large plate, cover with another plate or aluminum foil, and place in a 350° F oven with the door ajar to keep warm.

Add ¼ cup of water and the white wine to the pot the birds cooked in; stir to detach the juices that have stuck to the bottom. Add the cabbage leaves and the pieces of pork that have been tied around the partridges, as well as the pork that was parboiled earlier. Stir all these ingredients in the juices, salt and pepper lightly, then cover the pot and simmer slowly for 5 minutes.

TO SERVE:

Remove the birds from the oven, remove the trussing strings, then place them in the pot on top of the cabbage, cover, and serve immediately. The pot should be uncovered at the table; each person will be served a whole partridge as well as a portion of cabbage and pork. Or, the birds may be quartered in the kitchen and arranged on the dinner plates as shown in color picture VI.

COMMENTS:

Squab may be used instead of partridge; it is excellent prepared in this way.

Young partridges are preferable for this recipe. Birds that are only two to four months old are the most tender. The feathers at the tips of their wings are pointed (they become rounded with age) and the claws and beak are flexible. The feet of young partridges are delicate, thin, and yellowish, whereas older birds' feet have a grayish color. Partridges are ready to eat two to three days after being shot. They should never be eaten immediately, since the meat needs to rest before being cooked, but the birds should not be aged like pheasant, because a partridge that has been kept too long acquires an unpleasant, sometimes even revolting, taste.

NOTE: *Bacon, placed in cold water, brought to a boil, and drained, may be used instead of pork belly.*

If the birds have already been cleaned and do not have their livers, half as many chicken livers may be used instead. Ed.

Baron de lapereau mange-tout
83 RABBIT WITH GLAZED TURNIPS AND GREENS

Ingredients for 2 servings:

FOR THE TURNIPS:

12 baby turnips with their greens attached (*for substitution, see Comments*)
1 quart water
2 teaspoons coarse salt

3 tablespoons butter
Salt and pepper
2 teaspoons sugar

FOR THE RABBIT:

Saddle and legs from a 2½-pound rabbit
1½ tablespoons butter
Salt and pepper
1½ cups tightly packed fresh spinach leaves, cleaned and stems removed
⅜ cup **chicken stock** (**2**) (**3**)

FOR THE SAUCE:

2 tablespoons softened butter
Salt and pepper

UTENSILS:

Large pot
Vegetable peeler
Sauteuse or frying pan
Large oval pot with cover
Sharp, flexible-blade knife
To serve: 2 hot dinner plates

COOKING THE TURNIPS:

Cut off all but 1¼ inches of the turnips' greens. Place the water and coarse salt in a pot, bring to a boil, and add the turnip greens. Boil for only 1 minute, then drain. Reserve for later use.

Peel the turnips with a vegetable peeler; do not remove the greens still attached. Place the turnips in a *sauteuse* or frying pan, add enough water barely to cover them (they should not float), 3 tablespoons of butter, salt, pepper, and sugar. Cook, uncovered, at a moderate boil for 18 minutes or until all the water has evaporated. Then shake the pan so that the turnips will roll in the syrupy mixture of sugar and butter and become shiny. If the turnips are not to be served immediately, leave a little liquid in the pan, and finish the evaporation just before serving.

COOKING THE RABBIT:

In an oval pot, heat 1½ tablespoons of butter and brown the rabbit in it on all sides. This should take about 4 minutes over medium heat.

Salt and pepper the rabbit lightly, then add the spinach and turnip greens to the pot. Cover the pot and continue cooking over medium heat for 5 minutes.

Lift the rabbit out of the pot. Using a large sharp knife, cut the rabbit in half at the "waist" (at the end of the back or saddle and beginning of the legs). Place the saddle on a plate and cover with aluminum foil; keep it warm in a 325° F oven with the door ajar while the legs finish cooking. Put the legs back into the pot, add the stock, cover, and cook for another 5 minutes. Using a slotted spoon, lift out the legs, as well as the spinach and turnip greens, and put them all on the plate in the oven to stay warm while preparing the sauce.

MAKING THE SAUCE:

Boil the liquid remaining in the pot the rabbit cooked in until it has reduced by about a third, then add 2 tablespoons of butter, a little at a time. Shake the pot as the butter is being added to make the sauce spin around the sides of the pot. Place the pot back on the heat from time to time, but do not let the sauce boil once the butter has been added.

TO SERVE:

Using a sharp, flexible-blade knife, bone the rabbit completely. Try to keep the leg meat intact when boning, and cut the meat from the saddle lengthwise into thin slices.

Spoon the sauce onto each plate, then place the turnip greens and spinach in the center. Place the leg meat on top of the greens, then place the slices of meat from the saddle on top of this. Salt and pepper the meat lightly, place the glazed turnips to one side on the plates, and serve immediately.

COMMENTS:

Even though the cooking times for the rabbit may seem short, they are perfectly calculated so that the meat does not dry out and is extremely tender and juicy when served.

Turnip greens are not just "rabbit food," but a delicious vegetable too often ignored (especially in France). They have a wonderful taste and can be served with veal, chicken, or broiled fish.

If baby turnips are not available, ½ pound of ordinary turnips can be used if they are peeled and cut into pieces the size of a small egg. Large turnips can also be peeled and sliced very thin and sautéed in a frying pan with a little pepper, a tablespoon of olive oil, 1 whole clove of garlic, and ¼ pound of blanched bacon cut into small pieces (*lardons*). Cook the turnips uncovered (do not salt) for 10 minutes. Turn them over several times so they don't stick, and serve them as a vegetable with the rabbit; they're excellent!

Large turnips can also be peeled and cut into paper-thin slices, then deep-fried to make "turnip chips" that will surprise and please your guest.

Note: *The rabbit can be served with noodles as well as turnips, and the rabbit's kidneys can be sautéed quickly in butter and served on top of the meat.*

The rabbit can be cut in half at the "waist" before cooking. This means that a smaller pot can be used. But in any case, it's important that the pot used be large enough so that all the pieces of rabbit can be placed side by side without overlapping.

The saddle meat may be sliced from the bone while the legs finish cooking, and the legs may be boned while the sauce is reducing. Ed.

Râble de lièvre à la betterave
ROAST SADDLE OF HARE WITH BEET SAUCE 84

Ingredients for 4 servings:

2 saddles (the portion of the back between the top of the legs and the rib cage) of hare, skinned, and weighing a scant pound each

FOR THE MARINADE:

3 cups red wine
1 large carrot, peeled and finely chopped
1 onion, peeled and finely chopped
Small *bouquet garni*
8 peppercorns
8 juniper berries
2 cloves

FOR COOKING THE HARE AND FOR THE SAUCE:

Salt and pepper
2 teaspoons olive oil
1 pound cooked beets, peeled and cut into slices 1/8 inch thick
3 tablespoons finely chopped shallots
3 tablespoons red-wine vinegar
1 1/2 cups *crème fraîche* (*see p. 352*) or heavy cream
1 1/2 teaspoons Dijon mustard
1 1/2 teaspoons finely chopped fresh chives

UTENSILS:

Sharp flexible-blade knife
Earthenware platter
Cloth
Strainer
Bowl
Large roasting pan
Large plate
Aluminum foil
Skimmer or slotted spoon
To serve: Large hot serving platter

MARINATING THE SADDLE OF HARE:

Use a sharp knife with a flexible blade to remove the thin membrane that covers the flesh of the hare. Place the saddles in an earthenware platter and add all the ingredients listed for the marinade. The platter should be small enough so that the pieces of hare are covered by the marinade. Place the platter, covered, in the refrigerator for at least 24 hours before cooking; the hare can be marinated up to three days before cooking. Turn it occasionally.

COOKING THE HARE:

Preheat the oven to 475° F.

Lift the meat out of the marinade and dry with a clean cloth. Season lightly with salt and pepper. Strain out the ingredients used in the marinade, and reserve the liquid for making the sauce.

Heat the olive oil in a roasting pan on top of the stove. Brown the saddles of hare over high heat in the oil, then place the pan in the oven and roast for 12 minutes. Remove from the oven, lift the pieces of hare out of the roasting pan, place them on a large plate, and cover with aluminum foil. Lower the temperature of the oven to 450° F, leave the door ajar, and place the covered plate in the oven while preparing the sauce.

PREPARING THE SAUCE:

Place the roasting pan on top of the stove, add the beets and shallots, and sauté over medium heat for 1 minute. Add the strained liquid from the marinade and the vinegar. Stir, and boil until the liquid has reduced by three-quarters, then add the cream. Continue boiling the sauce until it has reduced by half, then remove from the heat. Stir in the mustard, taste for salt and pepper; the sauce is ready to serve. Once the mustard has been added, the sauce should not be allowed to boil; if it is not served immediately, it can be kept warm or reheated in a *bain-marie* or double boiler.

TO SERVE:

Remove the hare from the oven. Use a sharp knife with a flexible blade to remove the meat that lines both sides of the backbone. Cut each piece of meat lengthwise into thin slices, then lay the slices back on the bone; place on a serving platter. Use a skimmer or slotted spoon to lift the beets out of the sauce and place them in a circle around the meat. Spoon the sauce over the meat, sprinkle with the chives, and serve immediately.

COMMENTS:

Even though the thin membrane that covers the flesh of the hare has been removed before cooking, the hare will sometimes contract and twist up when cooked. To avoid this, puncture the top of the backbone in two or three places with the tip of the knife before cooking the hare.

A beautiful and unusual dish can be made using the sauce described here, but serving it with slices of sautéed calf's liver instead of the hare.

Note: *The meat can be cut from the bone and served directly on to hot dinner plates. Sometimes the meat can be difficult to cut neatly. In this case, cut each saddle in half crosswise, and serve on the bone. Ed.*

Viandes & abats

MEAT AND VARIETY MEATS

La charlotte d'agneau de Jacky

85 JACKY'S EGGPLANT AND LAMB CHARLOTTE

Ingredients for 4 servings:

FOR THE EGGPLANT STUFFING:

1 slice white bread, crust removed
2 teaspoons cold milk
4 teaspoons olive oil
1 small eggplant weighing ½ pound
1 pound boned shoulder of lamb
Salt and pepper
⅜ cup heavy cream

FOR THE MEAT STUFFING:

2 teaspoons butter
⅔ cup chopped carrot
⅔ cup chopped onion
1 tablespoon finely chopped celery
2 cloves garlic, peeled

Bouquet garni
1½ teaspoons flour
3 tablespoons dry white wine
1 cup **chicken stock** (2) (3)
2 large tomatoes, peeled, seeded, and chopped
2 large black olives, pitted and finely chopped
Salt and pepper

FOR THE MOLD AND SAUCE:

2 tablespoons olive oil
1 small eggplant weighing ½ pound, peeled and cut into 20 thin slices
2 teaspoons soft butter, for the mold
2 tablespoons soft butter, for the sauce

UTENSILS:

2 small bowls
Brush
Roasting pan
Electric blender
Spoon
Large bowl
Large frying pan with cover
Colander
Medium-size bowl
Small saucepan
Earthenware bowl 6 inches wide
High-sided roasting pan
Wire whisk
To serve: Hot serving platter

PREPARING THE EGGPLANT STUFFING:

Preheat the oven to 400° F.

Crumble the bread and place it in a bowl with the milk to soak. Stir to make sure all the pieces of bread are moistened.

Use a brush to oil lightly the bottom of a roasting pan with the 4 teaspoons of olive oil. Place the whole, unpeeled eggplant in the pan, roll it in the oil, then place it in the oven and bake for 30 minutes.

While the eggplant is cooking, use a sharp knife to remove all fat and gristle from a small piece of the lamb, then dice it; you should have ¼ cup of diced lamb. Place it in the blender, then squeeze out the bread that was left to soak, and place it in the blender as well. Blend for 10 seconds, then empty this mixture into a bowl. Place the bowl in the refrigerator for 15 minutes. Wash the blender container and place it in the refrigerator as well; it must be cold when used to finish the stuffing.

When the eggplant is cooked, take it from the oven, split it open lengthwise, and use a spoon to scoop out all the pulp. Chop the pulp with a large knife, salt and pepper lightly, then put it into a large bowl and place in the refrigerator to cool completely before finishing the stuffing.

Once all the ingredients are cold, place the cream in the blender, add the meat-bread mixture, and blend for 10 seconds. Salt and pepper lightly, then stir this mixture into the bowl with the chopped eggplant refrigerated earlier. Leave the stuffing in the refrigerator until ready to use.

PREPARING THE MEAT FILLING:

Cut the rest of the lamb into eight pieces. Heat 2 teaspoons of butter in a frying pan, and brown the meat on all sides over high heat for about 8 minutes. Add the carrrot, onion, celery, garlic, and *bouquet garni.* Continue cooking over medium heat for another 8 minutes, or until the vegetables are browned. Sprinkle the flour into the pan and stir to coat the meat and vegetables with it; continue cooking 2 minutes longer. Add the white wine, stir, boil for 20 seconds, then add the stock, tomatoes, olives, and a little salt and pepper. Cover the pan and simmer slowly for 40 minutes.

Place a colander over a medium-size bowl. Once the meat has finished cooking, pour it and all the vegetables into the colander. Reserve the liquid that has strained into the bowl and discard the *bouquet garni.* Separate the meat from the vegetables and chop it coarsely with a sharp knife, then place it in a bowl with the vegetables for later use.

ASSEMBLING THE CHARLOTTE:

Heat 2 tablespoons of olive oil in a large frying pan. When the oil begins to smoke, add the slices of eggplant and sauté them for 3 to 4 minutes on a side over moderate heat, shaking the pan occasionally. Then drain and allow to cool before using them to line the earthenware bowl that is to serve as a mold.

Preheat the oven to 425° F.

Melt 2 teaspoons of butter. Use a brush to coat with melted butter the inside of the mold or bowl being used for the charlotte. Line the sides and bottom of the mold with 12 slices of eggplant.

Spoon about 2 tablespoons of the eggplant stuffing over the bottom of the mold to make a layer about 1/4 inch thick, then add the meat filling and cover the filling with the remaining eggplant stuffing. Cover the top of the charlotte with the remaining 8 slices of sautéed eggplant. Place the charlotte in a high-sided roasting pan, and pour enough boiling water into the pan to come about a quarter of the way up the side of the bowl. Place in the oven and bake for 1 hour.

TO SERVE:

Once the charlotte is cooked, take it from the oven and turn it out onto the serving platter. In a saucepan, heat the liquid strained earlier after cooking the meat filling, but do not let it boil. Add 2 tablespoons of butter to the liquid, and shake the pan so that the sauce spins around the sides of the pot. Or, whisk the sauce constantly, away from the heat, while adding the butter. Pour the sauce around the charlotte and serve immediately.

COMMENTS:

Leftover roast leg of lamb, or even roast beef, may be used to make the meat filling.

NOTE: *Smaller, individual charlottes can be made with 3½- to 4-inch bowls or soufflé molds. They are prepared exactly as described here, but the cooking time should be reduced to 35 to 40 minutes.*

To turn out the charlotte, place a plate or serving platter on top of the mold when it comes from the oven, turn immediately upside down, set the plate on a table, and lift off the mold.

The charlotte may be served with **Sautéed potato slices (108).** *Ed.*

Tournedos de veau à la crème de ciboulette
86 VEAL STEAKS WITH CHIVE SAUCE
(color picture IV)

Ingredients for 4 servings:

FOR THE VEGETABLE FILLING:

1½ tablespoons butter
¼ cup diced carrots
1 tablespoon finely chopped celery
3 tablespoons finely chopped onion
⅓ cup finely chopped fresh mushrooms
Salt and pepper
A pinch of thyme

FOR THE MEAT:

4 veal loin steaks 1¼ inches thick, each weighing 5 to 6 ounces (*see Note*)
Salt and pepper
4 thin slices *foie gras* (optional)
2½ tablespoons butter

Chive sauce (**12**) prepared in advance

4 tablespoons madeira
4 slices truffle (optional)

SERVE WITH:

Glazed mixed vegetables (**99**) or
Homemade noodles

UTENSILS:

Small frying pan
Wooden spoon
Large sharp knife
Medium-size frying pan
To serve: 4 hot dinner plates, or a hot serving platter

THE VEGETABLE FILLING:

Heat 1½ tablespoons of butter in a small frying pan, add the carrots, and brown over medium heat for 3 minutes, then add the celery and onion. Continue browning for 3 minutes, stirring frequently, then add the mushrooms and sauté for a final 3 minutes. Remove the pan from the heat, sprinkle the vegetables with a little salt, pepper, and a pinch of thyme, and leave to cool.

PREPARING AND COOKING THE VEAL:

Holding the blade of a large sharp knife parallel to the cutting board, slit each piece of veal on one side through the middle. Do not cut through the other three sides; the veal should form a pocket.

Season the inside of each pocket of veal with salt and pepper, then stuff each one with the vegetable filling, and top the filling with a slice of *foie gras.* Press the pocket closed with your fingers, then season the outside of the veal with a little salt and pepper.

Melt 2½ tablespoons of butter in a medium-size frying pan and brown the meat over medium heat for 4 to 5 minutes on a side. When finished cooking, the vegetable filling should be hot inside the meat.

TO SERVE:

Spoon the **chive sauce** onto each dinner plate, or the serving platter, and place the veal on top of the sauce. Add the madeira to the pan the meat cooked in, and boil for a few seconds, stirring with a wooden spoon to detach the juices that have caramelized on the bottom of the pan. As soon as the madeira and pan juices have combined into a dark, syrupy glaze, spoon it over the meat. Top each piece of veal with a slice of truffle, and serve immediately, accompanied either with **glazed mixed vegetables** or homemade noodles.

COMMENTS:

The whitest veal is always the best.

The frying pan used to cook the veal should be as small as possible, just large enough for the four pieces to lie flat on the bottom. A well-chosen pan of the right size will mean that the juices from the meat are more concentrated, and the taste of both the veal and the glaze will be improved.

Another important factor is the heat over which the veal is cooked. If the veal is browned over too high a heat, it will dry out, and if the heat is too low, it will soften as though it has been boiled. Perfectly even, moderate heat is essential when sautéing all cuts of veal.

Note: *The veal fillet* (tournedos) *used in this recipe corresponds most closely to loin steaks in the United States, although thick slices from the round or veal chops (if thick enough) can be stuffed and cooked as described here. If you are using chops, the rib bone should be cut off for best results. Ed.*

Ris de veau aux salsifis

87 SWEETBREADS WITH SALSIFY

Ingredients for 5 to 6 servings:

2½ pounds veal sweetbreads
2 quarts cold water for parboiling

2¼ pounds salsify (oyster plant)
Large bowl of water plus 2 tablespoons vinegar for peeling salsify

FOR THE "BLANC":

2 tablespoons flour
2 quarts cold water
Juice of 2 lemons
2 teaspoons salt

FOR THE COOKING:

3½ tablespoons butter
½ pound carrots, peeled and diced
½ pound onions, peeled and diced
White of 1 large leek, cleaned and diced
2 tomatoes, peeled, seeded, and chopped
Salt and pepper
3 tablespoons dry vermouth
1⅔ cups dry white wine
1⅔ cups **chicken stock (2) (3)**
Bouquet garni

Salt and pepper
4 thin slices fresh or canned *foie gras*, approximately 2 ounces (optional)
5 teaspoons softened butter

UTENSILS:

Large bowl
Large pot with cover
Colander
Clean towel
2 plates
2-pound weight
Vegetable peeler
Wooden spoon
Skimmer or slotted spoon
Large hot serving platter
Aluminum foil
Strainer
Small saucepan

PRELIMINARY PREPARATIONS:

The sweetbreads: Place the sweetbreads in a large bowl of cold water and leave them to soak for 3 to 4 hours, changing the water once every hour. Or, place the bowl with the sweetbreads in it in the sink, and leave the faucet running so that a small stream of water constantly circulates around them.

Lift the sweetbreads out of the bowl, place them in a large pot, and cover them with 2 quarts of cold water. Place the pot over high heat, bring to a boil, and skim off any foam that appears. Boil rapidly for 3 minutes, then drain the sweetbreads in a colander, and cool immediately under cold running water. Place the sweetbreads on a cutting board and use a sharp paring knife to remove carefully any pieces of gristle or fat.

Wrap the sweetbreads in a clean towel, place them on a large plate, cover with another plate, then put a weight of about 2 pounds on top to form a press. Leave the sweetbreads in this press overnight in the refrigerator before cooking.

The salsify: Wash the salsify, cut off any greens, and peel with a vegetable peeler, holding them flat against the cutting board by one end to avoid touching the peeled portions. Cut each salsify into pieces 2 inches long. As it is peeled and cut, place it in a bowl of cold water acidulated with 2 tablespoons of vinegar; the vinegar will keep it from discoloring.

In a large pot, make a *blanc*: Measure out 2 quarts of water. Place all but 1 cup of the water in a large pot. In a bowl, place the flour, then stir in the reserved cup of water little by little to make a smooth, creamy liquid. Add to the pot, along with the lemon juice and salt, and bring to a boil, whisking frequently. Drain the salsify and add it to the pot, then simmer, uncovered, for 45 minutes. Remove the pot from the heat and leave the salsify to cool in the liquid. Then pour the salsify and its cooking liquid into a bowl and place in the refrigerator overnight along with the sweetbreads.

COOKING THE SWEETBREADS AND SALSIFY:

Melt 3½ tablespoons of butter in a large pot, add the carrots, onions, leek, and tomatoes. Take the sweetbreads from the refrigerator, remove the weight, and unwrap them. Place the sweetbreads in the pot with the vegetables, and salt and pepper lightly. Brown all these ingredients slowly for 10 minutes, stirring occasionally, so that they will brown on all sides.

Add the vermouth and white wine to the pot, bring to a boil, and boil rapidly for 5 minutes so that most of the alcohol evaporates, then add the chicken stock and *bouquet garni*. Lower the heat, cover the pot, and simmer slowly for 20 minutes. Then remove the *bouquet garni*, strain the salsify from its liquid, and add it to the pot with the sweetbreads and vegetables. Continue cooking, covered, for another 10 minutes.

TO SERVE:

Use a skimmer or slotted spoon to lift the sweetbreads from the pot. Open each sweetbread by slicing through the middle (do not go all the way through), so that each sweetbread opens like a book. Salt and pepper the inside of each sweetbread, place a slice of *foie gras* on one side, then fold the sweetbreads closed so that they form a sort of sandwich around the *foie gras*.

Place the vegetables that cooked with the sweetbreads on a large serving platter, put the sweetbreads on top of them, and arrange the salsify all around the edge of the platter. Cover the platter with aluminum foil and keep warm in a 350° F oven with the door ajar while you prepare the sauce.

Strain the liquid from the pot the sweetbreads and vegetables cooked in. Place this liquid in a small saucepan, bring to a boil over high heat, and add 5 teaspoons of butter, a teaspoon at a time. Boil rapidly until the sauce has reduced by about half and thickened slightly. Pour the sauce over the sweetbreads and serve immediately.

COMMENTS:

The sweetbreads can be cooked, without being parboiled and pressed, a day in advance. They still have to be soaked and pared (gristle and fat removed) as described, but they can be cooked right away—the sauce will in fact be even tastier.

Salsify is available canned and can be used instead of fresh salsify in this recipe. Canned salsify is generally very good and, if you use it, you can dispense with the preliminary steps of cleaning and cooking in the *blanc*.

Steak en campagne
STEAK AND BACON, COUNTRY-STYLE 88

Ingredients for 2 servings:

2 sirloin steaks, weighing about 9 ounces each
Salt and pepper
1 tablespoon olive oil
2 large slices country-style bread
2 slices Canadian bacon, 1¾ ounces each
2 generous tablespoons **herb butter (17)**

UTENSILS:

1 cast-iron or stainless-steel grill
Spatula
Large platter
Towel
To serve: 2 dinner plates

STARTING THE FIRE AND PRELIMINARY "SMOKING":

Outdoors, or in a large fireplace, make a fire with dried branches and leaves. Cover with slightly damp branches, preferably with a little moss on them. The moss will keep the dry branches from burning too quickly.

Place the grill over the fire, put the steaks on the grill, and leave for 7 minutes, then turn the steaks over, and leave for another 7 minutes. This first step is to flavor the meat with the smoke coming through the moss, not really to cook it. Remove the meat from the grill and reserve on a large platter.

TO COOK THE STEAKS AND BACON:

Take the mossy damp branches off the fire, and add more dried leaves and branches so that the fire will blaze away. Leave the fire to burn down for about 20 minutes, or until you have a nice bed of hot coals. Place the grill over them.

Salt and pepper both sides of the steaks and brush them with olive oil. Place the steaks on the grill, as well as the slices of bread. If there is not enough room, toast the bread first, then remove it before cooking the steaks. When the bread has been toasted on one side only, remove it and wrap it in a towel while the steaks cook. Cook the steaks until they are the way you like them: rare, medium-rare, medium. (See "Cooking in a Fireplace or on an Outdoor Grill," page 18.) Two minutes before the steaks are ready, place the bacon on the grill and cook it for 1 minute on a side.

TO SERVE:

Place the pieces of bread, toasted side down, on the plates. Place a steak on each piece of bread, spread the steaks with the **herb butter,** then place a piece of bacon on each steak, and serve immediately.

COMMENTS:

The bread is toasted only on one side so that the juices from the meat will soak into the bread and not *through* it. This makes the bread particularly good.

This recipe was invented while I was dove hunting in the autumn cold, sitting behind cover in a little oak forest not far from Eugénie.

NOTE: *A more prosaic (and unfortunately less delicious) version of this recipe can be made by grilling the steaks, bacon, and bread under the broiler—but it's not the same thing. Ed.*

Côte de boeuf sur le sel au beurre vigneron
SALT-ROASTED RIB STEAK WITH HERB BUTTER 89

Ingredients for 4 servings:

One 2½- to 3-pound rib steak
1 tablespoon olive oil
1½ pounds coarse salt
Salt and pepper

SERVE WITH:

Herb butter (17)

UTENSILS:

Meat cleaver
Basting brush
Roasting pan
To serve: Large hot serving platter

COOKING THE MEAT:

Preheat the oven to 450° F.

The rib steak should be cut from the end of the rib roast closest to the sirloin. Have the butcher cut the large curved bone off of the meat, but leave the shorter straight bone attached. Flatten the meat by slapping it with the side of a cleaver, then brush both sides of the meat with olive oil.

Spread the coarse salt over the bottom of a roasting pan, sprinkle with a little water, and place the pan in the oven. Heat until the salt has hardened into a block and has begun to make a quiet crackling sound; this will take at least a half hour. Place the meat on the hot salt and cook for 12 minutes on a side; see Note and also "Cooking in a Fireplace or on an Outdoor Grill," page 18. Halfway through the cooking time of each side, salt and pepper the meat lightly. Once both sides are cooked, take the roasting pan out of the oven, open the oven door, and place the pan on the open door. The meat needs to rest for 15 minutes before being served; turn it over twice during the 15 minutes. This resting time allows the juices to spread evenly through the meat and make it more tender.

TO SERVE:

Lift the steak off of the bed of salt and lay it on a cutting board. Cut it into 8 slices, holding the knife at about a 30-degree angle to the meat. Salt and pepper the slices, and place them on a hot serving platter; try as much as possible to reconstitute the shape of the steak. Spoon on the **herb butter** (it will start to melt immediately) and serve.

COMMENTS:

I think the best rib steaks for grilling this way come from a young female animal, slightly fat, that has had no more than one calf.

It is impossible for salt and pepper to ever reach the center of a large piece of meat such as a rib steak, leg of lamb, or even a large fish. That is why I only season meat lightly before cooking and why it is always preferable to salt and pepper it after it has been cut and is ready to serve.

NOTE: *The cooking time given here (12 minutes to a side) is for a medium steak. Cook the steak 10 minutes to a side for rare, 14 minutes for well-done.*

90 *Grillade de palette de boeuf à la marinade* GRILLED BEEF WITH STEAK-BUTTER SAUCE

Ingredients for 4 servings:

FOR THE MEAT AND MARINADE:

1¾ pounds blade steak or boneless chuck (*to buy and prepare, see Comments*)
3 tablespoons olive oil
3 tablespoons cooking oil
3 tablespoons red wine

FOR THE SAUCE:

2 teaspoons butter
1 generous tablespoon chopped shallots
5 tablespoons dry white wine

1 teaspoon finely chopped fresh tarragon
3 anchovy fillets in oil
A pinch of finely chopped garlic
Salt and pepper
2 teaspoons Dijon mustard
2 teaspoons lemon juice
2 teaspoons armagnac or cognac
2 teaspoons Worcestershire sauce
¼ pound plus 3 tablespoons soft butter

1 tablespoon cooking oil
Salt and pepper
1 tablespoon finely chopped fresh parsley

UTENSILS:

Earthenware platter
Small saucepan
Electric blender
Small bowl
Cloth or towel
Cutting board
To serve: 4 hot dinner plates, or a hot serving platter

MARINATING THE MEAT:

Place the meat in an earthenware platter with the olive oil, cooking oil, and red wine. Cover the platter with aluminum foil and place in the refrigerator for at least 24 hours before cooking. Turn the meat over once every 12 hours.

MAKING THE SAUCE:

Melt 2 teaspoons of butter in a small saucepan and add the shallots, white wine, and tarragon. Boil slowly for 3 minutes, stirring constantly, until the shallots have softened and there are only about 2 tablespoons of the mixture left in the pan. Remove the pan from the heat and allow to cool. (To speed cooling, place the pan in a bowl of ice water.) Spoon the shallot mixture into the blender and add the anchovies, garlic, salt, pepper, mustard, lemon juice, armagnac, and Worcestershire sauce. Blend until a thick, smooth purée is formed, then add the ¼ pound plus 3 tablespoons of soft butter, and blend for 2 minutes more. Once blended, this steak-butter sauce should be soft enough to spread easily; place it in a bowl and reserve while cooking the meat.

COOKING THE MEAT:

Preheat the broiler, or (even better) heat a grill over hot coals in the fireplace or outdoors. Take the meat from the marinade, dry it with a clean cloth or towel, then brush it with a tablespoon of cooking oil. Place the meat on the hot grill and cook according to your taste (see "Cooking in a Fireplace or on an Outdoor Grill," page 18).

Once the meat is cooked, place it on a cutting board and cut it into four equal slices; slice the meat holding the knife at about a 30-degree angle to the meat and cut across the grain. Salt and pepper the slices, place each one on a plate, and spread with a spoonful of the steak-butter sauce. Sprinkle with the chopped parsley and serve immediately. Serve the remaining sauce in a separate small bowl.

COMMENTS:

The cut of meat used in this recipe is sometimes called *le morceau du boucher* (the butcher's cut) in France, because only a few people realize how good it is. Not quite as tender as a sirloin steak, this cut has more taste, and by marinating, it is made quite tender indeed. The blade or boneless chuck is just above the shoulder blade and at the base of the neck. In France, this cut is usually a long narrow piece of meat with a flat piece of gristle running down the middle. This band of gristle has to be removed; ask the butcher to carefully pare the meat. In order to have 1¾ pounds of gristle-free meat, you may have to buy 2¼ pounds of chuck or blade. Once this cut is completely prepared, you will have two long pieces of meat about 14 inches long, 5 inches wide, and 2 inches thick. These steaks can be grilled whole as described in this recipe, or cut into individual steaks before cooking.

Other cuts of meat can be marinated and cooked this way—bottom round, for instance.

If preferred, the cold steak-butter sauce can easily be made into a hot sauce: Place 1 tablespoon of *crème fraîche* (see page 352) or heavy cream in a small saucepan with 2 teaspoons of cold water and bring to a boil. Add the steak-butter sauce as prepared above, whisking constantly; bring to a boil, then remove immediately from the heat. If not served right away, keep warm in a *bain-marie* or double boiler.

Filet de boeuf en poisson
TENDERLOIN MASQUERADING AS A FINE WHOLE FISH 91

Ingredients for 10 to 12 servings:

1 whole tenderloin roast (beef fillet weighing 5 pounds or a little less once it is pared and trimmed)
7 ounces whole canned truffles, drained (reserve the juice) and cut into very thin slices (*for substitution, see Comments*)
Salt and pepper
⅜ cup cooking oil
3½ tablespoons soft butter (for the meat)
5¼ ounces **puff pastry (118)** (*see Note, p. 299*)
½ beaten egg (for the pastry)

FOR THE SAUCE:

⅜ cup liquid reserved from the can of truffles
½ pound soft butter broken into 15 pieces
3 tablespoons finely chopped fresh chervil
3 tablespoons finely chopped fresh chives
Salt and pepper

UTENSILS:

Cutting board
Tape measure
String
Roasting pan
Aluminum foil
Rolling pin
Baking sheet
Pastry brush
Small saucepan
Wire whisk
To serve: Large hot serving platter

PRELIMINARY PREPARATIONS AND MARINATING:

The fillet should be completely free of fat and gristle. A whole tenderloin roast is long and somewhat oval in shape.

Place the roast on a cutting board and slit it lengthwise with a sharp knife: Open it down the middle, cutting the entire length of the roast, but not cutting all the way through the meat, so that, once out, the two halves of the roast open like a book.

Using a small sharp knife, make small deep cuts (about 1¼ inches long) all over the exposed surface of the roast. These incisions should be at regular intervals from each other, about 1¼ inches apart; make them up to the "hinge" that is holding the two halves of the meat together, on both sides, but do not cut into the fold.

Use a tape measure to measure the width of the open roast at each end and note these measurements for later use.

Slide the slices of truffle into the incisions you have made (2 slices in each incision) until all the truffles have been inserted and the roast looks as if it is covered with "scales" like a fish. Salt and pepper the meat lightly, then fold the meat closed so that the roast once again resumes its original shape. Use kitchen string to tie the meat together (tie several strings around it, like a sausage), but do not tie too tightly. Place the fillet in a roasting pan and pour the cooking oil over it. Cover the pan with aluminum foil and place the roast in the refrigerator overnight before cooking.

COOKING THE ROAST:

Preheat the oven to 475° F.

While the oven is heating up, remove the roast from the refrigerator and remove the aluminum foil. Dot the roast with 3½ tablespoons of butter, then place it in the oven (the roast cooks in the oil and pan in which it was marinated). Cook for 30 minutes; after 15 minutes, sprinkle the roast with salt and pepper and turn it over.

While the roast is cooking, prepare the pastry "fish head" and "tail."

MAKING THE "FISH HEAD" AND "TAIL":

Lightly flour a clean table and roll out the puff pastry in two pieces. Roll one piece out to the width of one end of the open roast, and the other to the width of the other end, according to the measurements you made earlier. Each piece should be about 6 inches long.

Using a sharp knife, cut one piece to give it the slightly rounded, triangular shape of a fish's head. Cut a V into the other piece to give it the shape of a fish's tail. Turn the pieces of dough upside down onto a baking sheet. Brush the dough lightly with the beaten egg; do not spill the egg over the edges of the dough. Decorate the head and tail using the tip of a sharp knife: Make light cuts in the head to simulate a few scales, and to draw in an eye, mouth, and gills; make long slits on the tail to simulate the fin.

BAKING THE PASTRY AND FINISHING THE "FISH" (see Comments): When the pastry is ready to be cooked and the roast is done, take the roast from the oven. Lower the heat to 425° F.

Cover the roast with aluminum foil so that it can rest, preferably in a warm place, for 20 minutes, which will be enough time to bake the pastry. Place the baking sheet in the oven and bake the pastry head and tail for 15 minutes. While the pastry is baking, make the sauce.

MAKING THE SAUCE:

Place the reserved truffle liquid in a small saucepan. Bring to a boil, and, whisking constantly with a wire whisk, add ½ pound of butter, a few pieces at a time. The liquid should be constantly boiling as the butter is being added, and you should never stop whisking. Adding the butter should take about 2 minutes, at the end of which time the sauce will have thickened. Remove the sauce from the heat, stir in the fresh chervil and chives, and add salt and pepper if needed. The sauce is ready to serve.

TO SERVE:

When the pastry has finished baking, remove it from the oven. Untie the fillet and place it on a large hot serving platter. Open the roast so that the side with the truffle scales is facing up and place the pastry fish head at one end and the tail at the other. Salt and pepper the meat lightly, spoon the sauce over it, and serve immediately.

COMMENTS:

The pastry head and tail can be baked before cooking the roast. Some fine pastry shops might even prepare them for you.

Although not nearly as flavorful, large fresh mushrooms can be used instead of the truffles. Replace the truffle juice with madeira.

Les tripes à la mode de Papa Guérard
92 PAPA GUÉRARD'S SPECIAL TRIPE RECIPE

Ingredients for 4 servings:

2¾ pounds beef tripe (*see Comments*)
1 calf's foot, split but not boned
1 heel of beef, split but not boned (*see Note*)
4 medium carrots, peeled and thinly sliced
4 medium onions, peeled and thinly sliced
2 cloves
Bouquet garni
2 cloves garlic, unpeeled
1 teaspoon coarse salt
1½ teaspoons freshly ground pepper
1 cup water

3 heaping tablespoons flour
6 tablespoons cold water

1 generous tablespoon finely chopped shallots
⅜ cup dry white wine
1 teaspoon Calvados

SERVE WITH:

Steamed potatoes with bacon and thyme (109)

UTENSILS:

Large ovenproof pot with cover
Small saucepan
Slotted spoon

COOKING THE TRIPE:

Preheat the oven to its lowest setting.

Cut the tripe into pieces about 1½ inches square. Place the calf's foot and heel of beef in a large pot and cover with a thin layer of equal parts of carrots and onions. Place pieces of tripe on top of the vegetables to make a thin layer, and cover with another layer of carrots and onions. Place 2 cloves, a *bouquet garni,* and the garlic on top of these vegetables, then continue filling the pot with alternate layers of tripe and carrots and onions, ending with a layer of vegetables. Once the pot is filled, sprinkle in the coarse salt, pepper, and add a cup of water. Place the pot over medium heat and bring to a boil.

While the pot is heating, mix together the flour and 6 tablespoons of water to make a rather stiff dough. Roll the dough between the palms of your hands to make it into a long thin sausage shape that will be used to seal the pot before baking.

Once the liquid in the pot has come to a boil, lower the heat, place the strip of dough around the entire rim of the pot, moisten it slightly with a damp pastry brush, and press the top of the pot into place. The pot will be hermetically sealed and ready for baking. Bake the tripe for 8 hours; do not open the pot during this time.

TO SERVE:

Just before the tripe has finished cooking, place the shallots in a small saucepan with the white wine, and boil until the shallots have softened and there are approximately 2 tablespoons of the mixture left.

Remove the pot from the oven; use a knife to pry off the top. Take the dough from around the rim of the pot and discard. Remove the calf's foot and heel of beef from the pot with a slotted spoon. Bone them and cut the meat into 1¼-inch squares, and put these back into the pot. Add the shallot-wine mixture to the pot as well as the Calvados. Boil very slowly, uncovered, for 10 minutes, stirring the tripe carefully with a fork. Cover the pot and serve immediately from this same pot, with **steamed potatoes with bacon and thyme** on the side.

COMMENTS:

The best tripe comes from recently killed animals. The flavor and texture are extraordinary; woo your butcher. . . .

To be sure the tripe is perfectly clean, you may soak it in cold water for 24 hours, changing the water several times. If there is any doubt about the freshness of the tripe (i.e., how recently the animal was killed), the amount of water may be doubled, but do not add any more than that. In no case should the tripe be parboiled, since this removes the natural meat juices that are essential to this recipe.

It is important to add the wine-shallot mixture at the very end of the cooking time. If the wine were to cook with the tripe, it would discolor them, and, more important, the wine-shallot mixture lends a refreshing taste to the dish when added at the last minute.

For me, one of the most exquisite combinations imaginable is to serve the tripe prepared as described here with a salad made of fresh, sliced truffles seasoned only with a little olive oil and lemon juice. Eat a little tripe, then a little truffle—the combination is sublime.

NOTE: *Two calves' feet may be used if heel of beef is unavailable. Ed.*

Jambon à l'os au coulis de champignons
93 HAM WITH MUSHROOM SAUCE

Ingredients for 4 servings:

1½ tablespoons softened butter
4 slices of York ham, weighing 4 ounces each (*see Comments and Notes*)
Pepper
⅜ cup dry white wine

1 cup water
Generous ½ teaspoon coarse salt
3 tablespoons freshly shelled small peas

2 teaspoons butter
½ pound fresh mushrooms, cleaned and coarsely chopped
1 tablespoon finely chopped shallots
⅓ cup dry white wine
⅜ cup white port
1 cup *crème fraîche* (*see p. 352*) or heavy cream
1 cup, tightly packed, fresh sorrel leaves that have been washed and cut into strips (*for substitution, see Note*)

UTENSILS:

Large ovenproof earthenware platter
Aluminum foil
2 small saucepans
Strainer
Electric blender

COOKING THE HAM:

Preheat the oven to 325° F.

Butter the earthenware platter with 1½ tablespoons of butter. Place the slices of ham on the platter and sprinkle with a little pepper. Pour ⅜ cup of white wine into the platter, then cover with a piece of aluminum foil. Place the platter in the oven; the ham should heat through, but the wine should not boil; boiling would make the ham tough.

MAKING THE SAUCE:

In one saucepan boil the water and coarse salt. Drop the peas into the boiling water and cook for 15 minutes, then drain. Pour a little water back into the pan and bring to a boil. Set the strainer with the peas in the pan and keep them warm in the steam.

In another saucepan melt 2 teaspoons of butter and add the mushrooms and shallots. Sauté over medium heat for 2 minutes, then add ⅓ cup of white wine and boil, uncovered, for 4 minutes or until all the liquid has evaporated. Add the port and cream and bring to a boil; continue boiling slowly for 4 minutes, then pour this mixture into the blender. Blend for 2 minutes, then pour the sauce into a saucepan. Bring to a boil, add the sorrel, and boil for 30 seconds more. The sauce is ready to serve.

TO SERVE:

Remove the ham from the oven, pour off the cooking liquid, and discard it. Spoon the sauce over the ham, then sprinkle with the peas, and serve in the platter the ham cooked in.

COMMENTS:

If making this recipe for 8 or 10 people, use a small ham that has been poached and sliced in advance. After cooking the slices as described here, reconstitute the original shape of the ham as much as possible, and present it "whole." You might want to poach a whole ham yourself one day. Hams need to be soaked at least 24 hours in cold water before cooking, and, when poaching a large one weighing about 16 pounds, be sure to cook it slowly for a long time—6 hours.

A truly luxurious version of this dish can be made with wild mushrooms such as fresh morels, fairy-ring mushrooms (*mousserons*), etc., instead of ordinary mushrooms. If wild mushrooms are used, only 2¾ ounces are needed (making about 3/4 cup when chopped), and the chopped shallots should be omitted; otherwise make the sauce as described.

Note: *York ham is sold cooked; other cooked hams may be used in this recipe.*

Fresh spinach and 1/2 teaspoon lemon juice can be used instead of the sorrel. Ed.

Pot-au-feu de langues

94 BOILED TONGUES WITH VEGETABLES AND TOMATO SAUCE

Ingredients for 4 to 6 servings:

1 beef tongue, roots removed, weighing 2 1/4 pounds
1 calf's tongue, roots removed, weighing 1 1/4 pounds
3 quarts cold water, approximately
Salt and pepper
3 quarts **chicken stock** (**2**) (**3**)
1 onion, peeled and sliced
1 carrot, peeled and sliced
Small *bouquet garni*

12 baby carrots, peeled (*see Comments*)
12 baby turnips, peeled (*see Comments*)
6 small leeks, white part only
4 cups water
2 teaspoons coarse salt
6 very small potatoes
6 slices of cucumber 1 1/2 inches thick, seeds scooped out
16 fresh asparagus tips
Salt and pepper

SERVE WITH:

1 cup **fresh tomato sauce** (**10**)
Small bowl of coarse salt
A jar of Dijon mustard
Pickled gherkins (*cornichons*)
Pickled onions

UTENSILS:

Large bowl
Clean cloth
Large pot with cover
Skimmer or slotted spoon
Strainer
2 pieces of cheesecloth
String
Saucepan
To serve: Large hot serving platter

COOKING THE TONGUES:

Place the tongues in a large bowl of cold water and soak them for 3 hours before cooking them. Change the water every hour, or place the bowl in the sink and let a small stream of cold water run into the bowl for the full 3 hours.

Drain the tongues and dry them with a clean cloth. Place them in a large pot and add 3 quarts of cold water; the tongues should be covered. Do not salt. Bring the water to a boil, then boil slowly, uncovered, for 30 minutes. Skim off whatever foam rises to the surface while the tongues are boiling.

Preheat the oven to 400° F.

Drain the tongues (discard the water), cool them, and peel off the rough skin that covers them. Salt and pepper the tongues, place them back in the pot, and add the stock, onion, carrot, and *bouquet garni*. Cover the pot and place in the oven to cook slowly for 2 hours.

Thirty minutes before the tongues have finished cooking, tie the carrots, turnips, and leeks in a piece of cheesecloth and add them to the pot. Ten minutes later, begin boiling the potatoes in a saucepan with 4 cups of water and the coarse salt. Wrap the cucumber and asparagus in another piece of cheesecloth and add them to the pot with the tongues 10 minutes before the 2-hour cooking time is up.

TO SERVE:

Lift the tongues out of their cooking liquid, and cut each one into slices about ¼ inch thick. Place the slices on a hot serving platter, assembling them so that the tongues appear to be whole again, and sprinkle with salt and pepper. Unwrap the two packets of vegetables and arrange them around the edge of the serving platter. Place a small potato inside each of the hollowed-out slices of cucumber. Alternate all the vegetables so that the tongues will be encircled by a mixture of colors. Spoon a little of the cooking liquid onto the serving platter and serve immediately, accompanied by a **fresh tomato sauce,** a bowl of coarse salt, Dijon mustard, *cornichons,* and pickled onions.

COMMENTS:

The liquid the tongues cooked in should not be discarded. Skim the fat off the surface and serve the delicious bouillon as a soup before serving the tongue. The bouillon can be served in hot individual soup bowls as it is, or in one of the following ways:

1) with *croûtons* and grated cheese;
2) with 2 tablespoons of bordeaux wine added to each bowl just before serving;
3) with a teaspoon of *crème fraîche* and a teaspoon of port added, as well as one whole egg, which will poach slowly in the hot soup.

If baby carrots and turnips are unavailable, medium-size ones, peeled and cut into olive-shaped pieces, can be used instead. In this case, use 2 to 3 of each vegetable.

NOTE: *If both kinds of tongue are not available at the same time, a total weight of 3½ pounds of either kind of tongue could be used alone.*

The vegetables are wrapped in cheesecloth to make them easier to remove after cooking.

The **fresh tomato sauce** *should be prepared in advance or while the tongues are cooking.*

The condiments served with the tongues should be used sparingly, but they are essential and should not be omitted; they are eaten alternately, or at the same time, as the meat. Ed.

Le pot-au-feu du Pot-au-Feu
THE POT-AU-FEU RESTAURANT'S POT-AU-FEU 95

Ingredients for 4 servings:

13 cups **chicken stock (2) (3)** (*see Comments*)
1 generous tablespoon coarse salt
4 peppercorns
1 pound oxtail, cut into pieces
1¼ pounds short ribs of beef, cut into 4 pieces
½ onion, unpeeled, stuck with 1 clove
½ onion, unpeeled, browned under the broiler
¼ head of celery
1 whole head of garlic, unpeeled
Small *bouquet garni*

10 ounces lean salt pork
4 cups cold water
4 very small potatoes, peeled
¼ small head of cabbage, leaves detached

8 baby carrots, peeled (*see Comments*)
8 baby turnips, peeled (*see Comments*)
4 very small leeks, cleaned
4 slices cucumber 1½ inches thick, seeds scooped out
¼ pound green beans, strings and tips removed

1 recipe **Confit of duck legs preserved in goose fat (79)**
8 slices of bone marrow ½ inch thick, previously soaked overnight in cold water, then patted dry (*see Note*)
1 cup cold water
½ teaspoon coarse salt
1 tablespoon softened butter
4 slices bread, preferably from a French-style loaf

SERVE WITH:

Fresh tomato sauce (10)
Small bowl of coarse salt
Jar of Dijon mustard

Pickled gherkins (*cornichons*)
Pickled onions
Horseradish sauce (*see Note*)

UTENSILS:

Large pot
Skimmer or slotted spoon
Medium-size pot
2 pieces of cheesecloth
String
2 saucepans
Large plate
To serve: 4 large hot dinner plates

COOKING THE MEAT AND VEGETABLES:

Place the stock in a large pot, add the salt and pepper, and bring to a boil. Drop the oxtail, short ribs, onion halves, celery, garlic, and *bouquet garni* all into the boiling liquid. Carefully skim off any foam that rises to the surface until no more foam appears. Lower the heat and simmer the meat slowly, uncovered, for a total of 3 to 3½ hours. While the meat is cooking, prepare the **fresh tomato sauce** and horseradish sauce (see Note).

An hour and a half after the time the meat begins cooking, place the salt pork in a separate pot with 4 cups of cold water; do not salt. Bring the water to a boil, then lower the heat and simmer the pork for 1½ hours. Add the potatoes and cabbage to the pot with the pork for the last 30 minutes of the cooking time; the pork, cabbage, and potatoes should finish cooking at the same time as the meat.

When the cabbage and potatoes are added to the pot with the pork, wrap and tie the baby carrots, turnips, and leeks in a piece of cheesecloth and add them to the pot with the meat. Ten minutes later, wrap up and tie the cucumber and green beans in another piece of cheesecloth and add them to the pot with the meat as well.

HEATING THE CONFIT AND MARROW:

Ten minutes before the meat has finished cooking, place the *confit* in a saucepan and barely cover with liquid taken from the pot the pork is cooking in. Simmer over low heat until ready to serve.

Place the slices of bone marrow in another saucepan, add 1 cup of cold water and the coarse salt; the marrow should be barely covered by the liquid. Bring slowly to a boil; as soon as the liquid boils, remove the pan from the heat.

TO SERVE:

Butter the bread and place it under the broiler to toast. Lift the marrow out of its liquid with a slotted spoon and place 2 slices on each piece of toast. Place the garnished toast on a plate in a warm (350° F) oven with the door ajar while you are dressing the dinner plates.

Lift the vegetables wrapped in cheesecloth out of the pot and unwrap them. Lift the cabbage and potatoes from the pot with the pork. Place a piece of hollowed-out cucumber in the center of each dinner plate and put a small potato on top. Using a skimmer or slotted spoon, lift the meat, pork, and *confit* from the pots in which they have cooked. Arrange the meats and remaining vegetables on each plate, and add the garnished toast.

Spoon some of the meat's bouillon over everything except the toast. Salt and pepper lightly, and serve immediately. Accompany with bowls of coarse salt, Dijon mustard, **fresh tomato sauce,** horseradish sauce, *cornichons*, and pickled onions.

COMMENTS:

This recipe can be made using water instead of stock for cooking the meat. In this case you'll have to choose between having flavorful beef or flavorful bouillon: The beef is best when the water is brought to a boil before the beef is added; the bouillon is best if the beef is placed in cold water, *then* brought to a boil. Using stock instead of water means that both the bouillon and the meat will be succulent and delicious.

The bouillon resulting from the cooking of the meat should never be discarded. Serve it in individual hot soup bowls before the main course, as it is or garnished in one of the following ways:

1) with *croûtons* and grated cheese;
2) with a tablespoon of bordeaux wine added to each bowl just before serving;
3) with a teaspoon of *crème fraîche* and a teaspoon of port added to each bowl, as well as one whole egg, which will poach slowly in the hot soup.

If baby carrots and turnips are unavailable, medium-size vegetables (2 to 3 of each), peeled and cut into olive-shaped pieces, can be used instead.

NOTE: *For this recipe buy a marrowbone 3 to 4 inches long. To extract the marrow from the bone, see the Note to the recipe for* **Brioche with marrow and red butter sauce (37).**

Horseradish sauce can be made in the following way:

Ingredients for 4 servings:

Generous ½ cup fresh bread crumbs
¼ cup heavy cream
½ cup fresh grated horseradish
A pinch of salt
1 tablespoon granulated sugar
1½ teaspoons cider vinegar or wine vinegar
1½ teaspoons Dijon mustard

Place the fresh bread crumbs in a bowl and add the cream. Stir to make sure all the bread is moistened, then allow to sit for 5 to 10 minutes while you grate the horseradish.

Beat the bread crumbs and cream until smooth with a wire whisk, then stir in the grated horseradish, salt, sugar, vinegar, and mustard. The sauce is ready to serve.

If fresh horseradish is unavailable, commercially sold horseradish grated and preserved in vinegar may be used, though it is vastly inferior to fresh horseradish. If using it, omit the vinegar in the recipe. Ed.

Les légumes
VEGETABLES

Tomate fraîche concassée
RAW DICED TOMATOES 96

Ingredients for 5 cups:

- 2 quarts water
- 3½ pounds ripe tomatoes
- Salt and pepper

UTENSILS:

- Large pot
- Large knife
- Colander
- Cutting board
- Bowl

Bring the water to a boil in a large pot. Cut out the little stem and green core from each tomato, drop the tomatoes into the boiling water, and boil for 15 seconds. Turn out the tomatoes into a colander and place immediately under cold running water, or lift the tomatoes out of the pot with a slotted spoon and drop them into a bowl of ice water. Once the tomatoes have cooled, they can be peeled easily. Split the peeled tomatoes in half crosswise, and squeeze each half to remove the seeds and excess water.

Place the seeded tomatoes on a cutting board and chop them with a large knife; they should be coarsely but evenly chopped into small pieces. Season with a little salt and pepper, place in a bowl, and, if not using the tomatoes immediately, cover the bowl with aluminum foil and store in the refrigerator.

Tomate concassée cuite

97 COOKED DICED TOMATOES

Ingredients for 3 cups or 4 servings:

1 teaspoon olive oil
2 shallots, peeled and finely chopped
5 cups **raw diced tomatoes (96)**
2 cloves garlic, whole and unpeeled
Small *bouquet garni*
Salt and pepper

UTENSILS:

Large saucepan with cover
Bowl
Aluminum foil

Heat the olive oil in a large saucepan, add the shallots, and cook slowly until they begin to soften and color. Add the **raw diced tomatoes,** garlic, and *bouquet garni.* Cover the pan partially with its lid, lower the heat, and simmer slowly for 30 minutes to allow some of the moisture in the tomatoes to evaporate.

Remove the garlic and *bouquet garni* and add salt and pepper if needed. If not used immediately, pour the tomatoes into a bowl, cover the bowl with aluminum foil, and store in the refrigerator.

Confiture d'oignons à la grenadine GRENADINE AND ONION "JAM" 98

Ingredients for 3 cups sauce or 8 servings; or, if served as a vegetable, 4 servings:

¼ pound butter
1½ pounds medium-size white onions, peeled and finely sliced
1 teaspoon salt
1½ teaspoons pepper
⅔ cup granulated sugar
⅜ cup sherry vinegar
2 tablespoons grenadine syrup (*for substitution, see Comments*)
1 cup red wine

UTENSILS:

Large frying pan or *sauteuse* with cover
Wooden spoon

Heat the butter in a large frying pan until it turns light brown and no longer sizzles. Add the onions, salt, pepper, and sugar. Stir well, then cover the pan and lower the heat. Simmer the onions, stirring occasionally, for 30 minutes, then add the sherry vinegar, grenadine syrup, and red wine. Uncover the pan and continue cooking 30 minutes more over low heat; the sauce should bubble very slowly. This dish may either be served hot as a vegetable, or cold as a sauce with pâtés.

COMMENTS:

Crème de cassis may be used instead of grenadine syrup.

Raisins, prunes, or dried apricots (cut into small pieces) may be added (to taste) for the last 30 minutes of cooking.

Les petits légumes glacés

99 GLAZED MIXED VEGETABLES

Ingredients for 2 servings:

4 baby carrots with their tops attached (*see Comments*)
4 baby turnips with their greens attached (*see Comments*)
4 spring onions with their greens attached

FOR THE CARROTS:

1 tablespoon softened butter
¼ teaspoon salt
¾ teaspoon granulated sugar
Pepper

FOR THE TURNIPS AND ONIONS:

2 tablespoons softened butter
½ teaspoon salt
1½ teaspoons granulated sugar
Pepper

UTENSILS:

Vegetable peeler
Colander
2 large frying pans or *sauteuses*
To serve: 2 small hot plates

PREPARING THE VEGETABLES:

Cut off all but about an inch of the greens and tops from the carrots and turnips. Leave a short stem of green about the same length on each of the onions. Peel the carrots and turnips. Cut the little roots from each onion and remove the first outer skin. Wash the carrots and turnips under cold running water, then drain in a colander.

COOKING THE VEGETABLES:

Place the carrots in a frying pan or *sauteuse*. The pan should be just large enough for all the carrots to fit in one layer, with as little extra space around them as possible. Add just enough water to barely cover them, 1 tablespoon butter, ¼ teaspoon of salt, ¾ teaspoon of sugar, and a little pepper. Place the pan on the stove over high heat until the liquid boils, then immediately lower the heat and simmer the carrots slowly, uncovered, for 20 minutes.

Place the turnips and onions in another frying pan or *sauteuse*; like the carrots, these vegetables should all fit in one layer in the pan with as little space around them as possible. Add enough water to barely cover them, 2 tablespoons of butter, ½ teaspoon of salt, 1½ teaspoons of sugar, and a little pepper. Bring the liquid to a boil over high heat, then immediately lower the heat and boil the vegetables slowly, uncovered, for 18 minutes.

The water in both pans will evaporate as the vegetables cook, and the butter and sugar will form a syrup. Toward the end of the cooking time, as the syrup forms, shake the pans frequently so that the vegetables will roll in the syrup and be perfectly coated and shiny when ready to serve.

TO SERVE:

When the vegetables are cooked, arrange them artistically on two small plates and serve at the same time as the main dish they accompany.

COMMENTS:

Baby carrots and turnips with their tops and greens are not always available. Medium-size carrots or turnips can be peeled and cut into olive-shaped pieces and used instead of the baby vegetables.

Other vegetables besides those used in this recipe can be cooked the same way, provided they are either cut into olive-shaped pieces before cooking (celeriac is an example) or are small vegetables to begin with, such as fresh peas, green beans, etc.

The vegetables can be slightly browned by continuing the cooking after all the water has evaporated until the syrup begins to caramelize around the cooked vegetables.

100 *Purée mousse de betteraves au vinaigre*
SWEET AND SOUR BEET PURÉE

Ingredients for 4 servings:

1 teaspoon olive oil
1½ medium onions, peeled and thinly sliced
1 clove garlic, peeled and crushed
3 tablespoons red-wine vinegar
¼ cup **raw diced tomatoes (96)**
¾ pound raw beets (8 small beets), peeled and very thinly sliced
Salt and pepper

1½ tablespoons *crème fraîche* (*see p. 352*) or heavy cream
⅜ cup **chicken stock (2) (3)**

UTENSILS:

Large frying pan or *sauteuse* with cover
Wooden spoon
Electric blender

Heat the olive oil in a large frying pan or *sauteuse*. Add the onions and garlic, and sauté until soft but not colored. All of the moisture should evaporate, which will take about 5 minutes; stir the onions frequently to prevent their sticking to the pan.

Stir in the vinegar, then add the tomatoes and sliced beets. Season with salt and pepper, stir to mix all the ingredients well, then cover the pan, lower the heat, and simmer slowly for 1 hour.

When finished cooking, pour the contents of the pan into an electric blender and add the cream and stock. Blend for 2 minutes; the resulting purée should be smooth and light, almost like a mousse. If not served immediately, keep warm, or reheat in a *bain-marie* or double boiler.

COMMENTS:

Although this combination of ingredients might surprise some people, it is delicious, especially when served with game instead of the traditional (and boring) chestnut purée so common in French restaurants.

Purée mousse de céleri
CELERIAC PURÉE 101

Ingredients for 4 servings:

¾ pound celeriac (celery root)
1 quart milk
Salt and pepper
½ cup rice (*see Comments*)
2 tablespoons *crème fraîche* (*see p. 352*) or heavy cream

UTENSILS:

Vegetable peeler
Large saucepan with cover
Colander
Bowl
Electric blender

Peel the celeriac and cut it into eight pieces. Place the pieces in a saucepan and add the milk, salt, and pepper. Bring the liquid to a boil over high heat, then add the rice and stir for 1 minute. Lower the heat, partially cover the pan, and simmer for 20 minutes.

When the rice and celeriac are cooked, pour them into a colander; save their cooking liquid in a bowl. Place the rice and celeriac in a blender, add 1 tablespoon of cream, and blend for a total of 3 minutes, adding the remaining cream as the vegetables are being blended. To thin the purée, add a little of the cooking liquid reserved earlier (approximately ⅜ cup), and blend for another minute. Taste for salt and pepper. If not served immediately, keep warm in a *bain-marie* or double boiler, or reheat over very low heat before serving.

COMMENTS:

Normally potatoes are mixed with celeriac when making this purée. But using rice instead makes the purée equally creamy and also ensures that none of the flavor of the celeriac is lost.

I have just tried an unusual variant of this recipe made with 2 medium apples, peeled, cored, and quartered (½ pound of peeled apple quarters), instead of rice. They are only added and cooked with the celeriac 10 minutes before the celeriac is done. The combination of the two tastes is very subtle and absolutely delicious.

Note: *When the apples are used, the milk may curdle because of their acidity. This is of no importance at all, because it is unnecessary to add any of the cooking liquid when making the purée with apples. Ed.*

Purée mousse de cresson I

102 WATER-CRESS PURÉE I

Ingredients for 1 cup, to be used in sauces, etc.:

- 4 bunches water cress yielding 5 cups tightly packed leaves, cleaned and stemmed
- 4 cups water
- 2 generous teaspoons coarse salt

UTENSILS:

Large pot
Colander
Electric blender

Remove the stems from the water cress and wash thoroughly before cooking. Fill a large pot with the water, add the coarse salt, and bring to a boil. Drop the water cress into the boiling water and boil rapidly for 3 minutes, then pour immediately into a colander and hold under running water to cool. When cooled this way the water cress will keep its dark-green color.

Drain the water cress, then place it in a blender and blend for 2 minutes. The purée is now ready to use in flavoring and coloring various dishes. If not used immediately, the purée may be frozen.

Note: *It is not absolutely necessary to freeze the purée unless it is to be stored for a very long time. It will keep for up to 2 weeks in the refrigerator if placed in a tightly closed jar. Ed.*

Purée mousse de cresson II
WATER-CRESS PURÉE II 103

Ingredients for 4 servings, as a vegetable:

2 cups **water-cress purée I** (**102**)
2 teaspoons lemon juice
6½ tablespoons butter
½ cup *crème fraîche* (*see p. 352*) or heavy cream
Salt and pepper

UTENSILS:

Saucepan
Wooden spoon

Place the **water-cress purée I** in a saucepan, add the lemon juice, butter, and cream; taste, and add salt, and pepper if needed. Warm the purée slowly over low heat, stirring constantly with a wooden spoon. Serve immediately when hot.

COMMENTS:

Although **water-cress purée I** can be made in advance and stored, this purée can only be made just before serving; it will turn greenish yellow if kept for even a short time. Unlike **water-cress purée I,** it is meant to be served as a vegetable and is *not* combined in other dishes or sauces.

Purée mousse de haricots verts
GREEN BEAN PURÉE 104

Ingredients for 4 servings:

3¼ pounds fresh green beans
3 quarts water
2 generous tablespoons coarse salt
3 tablespoons *crème fraîche* (*see p. 352*) or heavy cream
3 tablespoons butter
Salt and pepper

UTENSILS:

Large pot
Skimmer or slotted spoon
Large bowl
Electric blender
Large frying pan
Wooden spoon

Remove the tips and strings from the beans. Place the water and coarse salt in a large pot and bring to a boil. Drop the beans into the boiling water and continue boiling rapidly for 10 minutes. Remove the beans with a skimmer or slotted spoon and drop them immediately into a large bowl of ice water. Drain the beans completely, then place them in the blender, and blend for 2 minutes to make a smooth purée. Add the cream and blend for 1 minute more.

Just before serving, make a nut-brown butter by heating the butter in a frying pan over medium heat until it no longer sizzles; all of its humidity will have evaporated. Add the purée to the butter, stirring constantly with a wooden spoon, remove from the heat, add salt and pepper as needed, and serve. If not served immediately, keep warm in a *bain-marie* or double boiler, or reheat over very low heat.

COMMENTS:

The beans can be cooked and puréed in the blender in advance, but the cream should not be added until later. Of course the purée should only be added to the brown butter just before serving. The purée without the cream can be stored like **water-cress purée I.** See the Comments (and Note) following that recipe.

The water the beans are boiled in is deliberately oversalted so that they will cook quickly and not lose any of their color. It is essential that the beans be cooled in very cold water immediately after cooking; the cold water both removes the excess salt and prevents the beans from overcooking.

Purée mousse de poireaux
LEEK PURÉE 105

Ingredients for 4 servings:

5¼ pounds leeks
4 tablespoons butter
Salt and pepper

2 generous tablespoons *crème fraîche* (*see p. 352*) or 3 tablespoons heavy cream
3 tablespoons butter

UTENSILS:

Clean cloth or towel
Large frying pan
Electric blender

Cut off the green parts and the roots of the leeks and discard. With the tip of a knife, split open the white part lengthwise, about halfway down to the bulb end, and wash the leeks carefully under running water, separating the "leaves" to remove any dirt that might be lodged among them. Pat the leeks dry in a clean cloth or towel, then slice them.

Melt 4 tablespoons of butter in a frying pan, then add the leeks. Cook over medium heat, stirring frequently, for a couple of minutes; do not allow them to color. Salt and pepper lightly, lower the heat, and continue cooking for 30 minutes. Stir the leeks occasionally to be sure they don't stick to the pan. When they are cooked, pour the leeks into the blender and blend for 4 minutes to make a smooth purée. Add the cream and continue blending for 1 minute longer.

Just before serving, heat 3 tablespoons of butter in a frying pan until it no longer sizzles; all the moisture it contained will have evaporated. When this happens, and the butter begins to turn a light-brown color, add the purée, and stir constantly with a wooden spoon to mix together the purée and butter. Remove from the heat, add salt and pepper as needed, and serve. If not served immediately, keep warm in a *bain-marie* or double boiler, or reheat over very low heat.

COMMENTS:

Leeks need to be blended longer than most vegetables when making a purée since they are a very stringy vegetable. Even after blending, filaments might remain in the purée; in this case it is best to work the purée through a fine sieve to make it perfectly smooth. The total amount of purée will be reduced by about 20 percent.

Leeks are called the "asparagus of the poor"; personally I think this superb vegetable is second to none. Leeks can be prepared in various ways that are all delicious; here are some suggestions:

LEEK SALAD:

Cook the white part of the leeks in boiling salted water for 20 minutes, then drain and cool. Serve with a **Vinaigrette gourmande (16).** (Some thin *julienne* strips of truffle sprinkled over this salad make it unforgettable.)

SAUTÉED LEEKS WITH CREAM:

After cooking the sliced leeks as described for the purée, simply add a little cream and butter and serve. This simple combination is one of the finest vegetable garnishes imaginable.

106 *Petites crêpes de maïs* TINY CORN CRÊPES

Ingredients for 4 servings (5 crêpes per person):

FOR THE BATTER:

¾ cup flour
1 teaspoon salt
A pinch of pepper
1 egg
1 egg yolk
1 cup milk
3½ tablespoons butter

½ cup canned corn kernels, drained
1 tablespoon finely chopped fresh chervil
3 tablespoons cooking oil

UTENSILS:

Large bowl
Wire whisk
Small saucepan
Brush
Large frying pan
Ordinary tablespoon
Spatula
Large plate
To serve: 4 small hot plates

MAKING THE BATTER:

Place the flour in a large bowl. Make a well in the center so that the bottom of the bowl is visible. Sprinkle the salt and pepper over the flour, then break the egg into the middle of the well, add the egg yolk, and begin stirring the eggs with a small wire whisk. Pour the milk very slowly into the center of the well and gradually incorporate the surrounding flour. Beat with the whisk until a smooth, creamy, liquid batter is formed.

Melt the butter in a small saucepan to make a nut-brown butter; when the butter no longer sizzles it has lost all of its moisture and has cooked enough.

Whisking constantly, pour the brown butter into the crêpe batter, then leave it for at least an hour to rest before cooking.

MAKING THE CRÊPES:

Just before cooking the crêpes, stir the corn and fresh chervil into the batter.

Brush the bottom of a large frying pan with a light coating of oil. Heat the oil over high heat, then add batter to the pan a tablespoon at a time. Each tablespoon of batter will make one tiny crêpe. Don't crowd the pan; make as many crêpes as you can at once, but leave enough space between them so that they will not touch when cooking and can be turned over easily. The crêpes will brown quickly on the first side; they can be turned over after several seconds and will be done soon after, when the second side has browned.

If you are cooking large quantities, the first crêpes made will have to be kept warm while the others are cooking. Preheat the oven to

350° F. As soon as the crêpes come from the pan, place them on a large lightly buttered plate, then place them in the oven with the door ajar.

Normally 5 crêpes per person is sufficient. Serve them on small plates next to the main dish they accompany.

COMMENTS:

The batter can be made in an electric blender. Simply place all the ingredients used in the batter in the blender at once and blend until smooth. When the batter is made this way, the corn and chervil should be added to it immediately after blending, then the batter left to rest for an hour before cooking. Although the batter can be made in advance, the crêpes themselves are always best when cooked just before serving.

These crêpes can be served alone as appetizers, or as a vegetable with poultry, and they are especially good with duck and game.

Ragoût d'artichauts aux asperges
107 STEWED ARTICHOKES AND ASPARAGUS

Ingredients for 4 servings:

12 small artichokes (*see Note*)
2¼ pounds large asparagus
½ lemon

1½ tablespoons butter
¼ pound salt pork belly, cut into small cubes (*lardons*)
½ medium onion, peeled and chopped
⅜ cup dry white wine
1 cup **chicken stock (2) (3)**
¾ cup **raw diced tomatoes (96)**

2 tablespoons butter, softened and broken into small pieces
1 tablespoon finely chopped fresh chervil

UTENSILS:

Ordinary teaspoon
Vegetable peeler
Cutting board
Medium saucepan with cover
Wooden spoon

TO PARE THE VEGETABLES:

If the artichokes still have their stems, break them off. Pull off the largest leaves around the base. Use a small knife to pare off all the remaining leaves from the base of each artichoke, then use a large knife to cut off the remaining leaves along the top edge of the hard, meaty base. Once this has been done, use an ordinary teaspoon to scoop out the tiny purple leaves and the choke that remain in the center of each artichoke bottom. To prevent them from blackening from contact with the air, rub each one with half a lemon, then cut them into quarters.

Peel the asparagus with a vegetable peeler to remove the stringy outer skin; peel each asparagus starting from just below the tip and going toward the base of the stem. This is best done by holding the asparagus flat against a cutting board and turning it as necessary as you peel. Cut each asparagus into pieces 2 to 3 inches long.

TO COOK AND SERVE:

Melt 1½ tablespoons of butter in a saucepan, add the pork and onion, and cook over moderate heat, stirring frequently, for about 3 minutes. The onion should soften but not brown. Add the artichoke bottoms and asparagus to the pan, stirring to mix them with the other ingredients. Salt and pepper lightly, then add the white wine and bring to a boil. Boil rapidly for 1 to 2 minutes or until the liquid has reduced by half, then add the stock and tomatoes. Lower the heat, cover the pan partially, and boil slowly for 18 minutes or until the asparagus is tender and all but approximately 4 tablespoons of the liquid has evaporated. Just before serving, add the remaining 2 tablespoons of butter and the chervil. Shake the pan until the butter has melted, and serve immediately.

Note: *The artichokes for this recipe should be small, about 2 inches* *across the base. If larger artichokes are used, 8 are sufficient; their bottoms should be cut into 6 to 8 pieces before cooking.*

Salt pork, depending on its degree of salting, may have to be soaked before cooking; ask advice about this from the person who sells it.

Instead of salt pork belly, cubed bacon that has been parboiled may be used instead: Place the bacon in a pot of cold water, bring to a boil, then immediately drain and cool under cold running water. Ed.

108 *Pommes à la peau*
SAUTÉED POTATO SLICES

Ingredients for 4 servings:

- 4 large potatoes weighing approximately 7 ounces each, or 1¾ pounds in all
- 2 cups cold water
- 1½ tablespoons coarse salt
- Salt and pepper
- ⅓ cup butter

UTENSILS:

- Clean cloth or towel
- Large pot or steamer
- Colander
- Large frying pan
- Spatula
- *To serve*: Large hot vegetable dish, or 4 small hot plates

Wash the potatoes in cold water to remove any dirt. Wipe them dry in a clean cloth or towel but do not pare.

Place the water and coarse salt in a pot and bring to a boil. Add the potatoes and cook for 30 to 35 minutes; the potatoes can be steamed over the same amount of salted water and will be even better. Drain the potatoes in a colander and leave to cool for several minutes. Cut the potatoes into slices a little more than ¼ inch thick and season the slices on both sides with salt and pepper.

Melt the butter in a large frying pan, cook over high heat until the butter begins to foam, then cover the bottom of the pan with the sliced potatoes. Each slice should lie flat in the pan; when you are cooking large quantities, the potatoes will have to be fried in several batches. Fry them about 2 minutes on a side, then lift them out of the pan with a spatula and serve immediately.

The potatoes may be served from one vegetable dish, or individual servings can be arranged on small plates to accompany the main dish.

COMMENTS:

The potato skins brown in the hot butter and give the potatoes a fresh, almost fruity taste.

Pommes de terre vapeur au lard et au thym
STEAMED POTATOES WITH BACON AND THYME 109

Ingredients for 4 servings:

- 4 large potatoes weighing approximately 6½ ounces each, or a total of 1½ pounds
- 4 slices of bacon weighing a total of 6 ounces, each slice cut in half
- ½ teaspoon thyme (or, preferably, thyme flowers)
- Salt and pepper

UTENSILS:

- Clean cloth or towel
- Ordinary teaspoon
- Couscous pot or steamer
- 4 small hot plates

Wash the potatoes under cold running water, wipe them dry with a clean cloth or towel, but do not peel. Split the potatoes in half lengthwise and scoop out enough pulp from each half potato to make a very shallow indentation. Salt the potatoes very lightly, then place a half slice of bacon on each half potato. Sprinkle the bacon with thyme and a little pepper.

Fill the bottom of a couscous pot or steamer with water and bring to a boil. Place the potatoes in the top half of the pot, bacon side up. If necessary, they can be placed on top of each other. Cover the pot and steam the potatoes for 30 minutes.

Serve the potatoes on small plates as soon as they are done and sprinkle lightly with salt and pepper before taking them to the table.

COMMENTS:

While the potatoes are steamed, some of the fat in the bacon will melt into the potatoes and spread its flavor as well as that of the thyme through the pulp.

Potatoes steamed in this way can be turned into a main dish by simply adding a high-quality cooking sausage of your choice to the steamer with the potatoes and cooking them all together; this makes for a hearty, country-style meal.

110 *Pommes frites au gros sel*
SAUTÉED POTATOES WITH COARSE SALT

Ingredients for 4 servings:

- 1½ pounds potatoes
- 4 tablespoons goose fat
- 1 clove garlic, whole and unpeeled
- 2 tablespoons softened butter, broken into 3 pieces
- ½ tablespoon coarse salt
- ½ tablespoon finely chopped fresh parsley

UTENSILS:

Vegetable peeler
Bowl
Colander

Clean cloth or towel
Large frying pan or *sauteuse* with cover
Slotted spoon
To serve: Large hot vegetable platter (optional)

Peel the potatoes, then stand them upright and cut them into large pieces the shape of orange wedges. As each piece is cut, place it into a large bowl of cold water. Wash all the pieces of potato under cold running water, then drain and dry completely in a clean cloth or towel.

Heat the goose fat in a large frying pan or *sauteuse*. When the fat begins to smoke, add the garlic and potatoes. Lower the heat and brown the potatoes slowly on both sides, turning them frequently with a slotted spoon. Once the potatoes have begun to brown, cover the pan and leave them to simmer for 15 minutes.

Lift the potatoes out of the pan with a slotted spoon and place them on a plate. Pour the fat from the pan into a bowl (it can be used in other recipes). Put the potatoes back into the pan and add the butter. Shake the pan gently over low heat until the butter has melted and soaked into the potatoes. Sprinkle with the coarse salt and parsley and serve immediately.

COMMENTS:

In a variant of this recipe, the potatoes can be cooked up to an hour ahead of time and kept warm in the oven. If this is done, once the potatoes have soaked up the butter, allow them to cool to lukewarm in the pan.

Preheat the oven to 350° F.

Beat 2 egg yolks in a bowl and pour them over the warm potatoes. Stir the potatoes around in the beaten egg so that they are all well coated, sprinkle with the coarse salt and parsley, then pour into a baking dish. Place them in the oven until ready to serve. The egg yolk seals the potatoes and keeps them from getting soggy.

Purée de pommes de terre au persil

111 MASHED POTATOES WITH PARSLEY

Ingredients for 4 servings:

1¾ pounds "floury" mashing potatoes
4 cups cold water
2 teaspoons coarse salt
1⅔ cups milk
6 tablespoons softened butter, broken into 8 pieces
¼ cup finely chopped fresh parsley

UTENSILS:

Vegetable peeler
Large pot
Small saucepan
Colander
Fork
Wooden spoon

Peel the potatoes and cut them into quarters. Place them in a pot with the cold water and coarse salt. Bring to a boil over high heat, cover, lower the heat, and boil slowly for 20 minutes. The potatoes should not be overcooked.

Bring the milk to a boil in a small saucepan, then place over very low heat to keep warm.

Drain the potatoes in a colander. Away from the heat, put them back into the pot they were cooked in. Mash the potatoes using the prongs of a fork, adding the butter as you do so. The butter will mix with the potatoes that are deliberately left a bit lumpy; this texture is important. Place the pot over medium heat and add the boiled milk, stirring constantly with a wooden spoon. The milk should be added a little at a time; as it is added, the potatoes will become creamier and lighter. When ready to serve, sprinkle in the parsley, stir well, then serve immediately.

COMMENTS:

These potatoes are always best when made just before serving; if they must be made ahead of time, keep them warm in a *bain-marie* or double boiler. Cover the surface of the potatoes with a thin layer of milk to keep them from drying out.

Never beat or mash the potatoes with a wire whisk; they become gluey and lose some of their flavor.

Poêlée de pommes de terre aux carottes
POTATO AND CARROT PANCAKES 112

Ingredients for 4 servings (4 pancakes):

8 tablespoons butter, in all
Scant 1½ cups grated carrots
2 cups grated potatoes
Salt and pepper

UTENSILS:

Small saucepan
Sieve
Small bowl
2 clean cloths or towels
Colander
Small frying pan
Wooden spoon
4 small crêpe pans or blini pans, 5 inches in diameter
Spatula

PRELIMINARY PREPARATIONS:

Melt 6 tablespoons of butter in a small saucepan; heat it very slowly and do not let it boil. Then pour it through a very fine sieve into a small bowl and reserve. Butter prepared this way is said to be clarified, since all the impurities have been strained out; it should be perfectly clear (see Comments).

Pat the grated carrots dry in a clean cloth or towel and reserve. Place the grated potatoes in a colander, rinse thoroughly under cold running water, then pat dry with another clean towel; rinsing the potatoes eliminates some of their starch.

TO COOK AND SERVE:

Melt 2 tablespoons of butter in a small frying pan. Add the carrots and cook slowly for 9 minutes, stirring frequently. The carrots should begin to soften but not be allowed to brown. Season with salt and pepper, then remove the pan from the heat and reserve.

Generously salt and pepper the grated potatoes. Use half of the clarified butter to grease the four small crêpe pans (approximately 2¼ teaspoons per pan). Place enough grated potato into each of the pans to cover the bottom. Press the potatoes with the prongs of a fork to flatten them into each pan. Divide the cooked carrots among the four pans; use the fork to press the carrots lightly onto the layer of potatoes, then cover the carrots with the remaining grated potatoes. Spoon the remaining clarified butter over the assembled pancakes and flatten each one again gently with the fork. Cook each pancake over high heat for 5 minutes, then turn over using a spatula. The cooked side should be crisp and golden brown. Lower the heat and continue cooking slowly for 10 minutes. Serve the pancakes immediately, either in the crêpe pans or on four saucers placed on the table next to the diners' dinner plates.

COMMENTS:

It is essential that the grated potatoes be washed thoroughly in cold water before cooking, otherwise the starch will make the pancakes stick to the pan.

Clarifying the butter is not absolutely necessary, but it is preferable, since clarified butter will not scorch like ordinary butter and thus prevents little burned spots from spoiling the appearance, as well as the taste, of the pancakes.

NOTE: *The small crêpe pans called for here may be difficult to find, so blini pans or other very small frying pans may be used instead. The pancakes can all be cooked in one very large frying pan, but care must be taken when assembling and turning them so that they do not touch when cooking.*

For a more copious vegetable, this recipe may be doubled. Either make 4 pancakes using pans 6 inches in diameter, or make 8 small ones. The first 4 may be kept warm on a rack in the oven (don't pile them on top of each other) while the rest are cooking in the four pans. Ed.

Mon gratin "dauphinois"
GRATINÉED POTATOES MICHEL GUÉRARD 113

Ingredients for 4 servings:

1¾ pounds potatoes
1 teaspoon salt
A pinch of pepper
1 cup milk
1 cup *crème fraîche* (*see p. 352*) or heavy cream
½ clove garlic, peeled and finely chopped
A pinch of nutmeg
2 tablespoons softened butter

UTENSILS:

Vegetable peeler
Clean cloth or towel
Saucepan with cover
Wooden spoon
Slotted spoon
4 round cast-iron enameled baking dishes, approximately 5 inches in diameter
Large roasting pan

Peel the potatoes and cut them into slices ⅛ inch thick. Do not wash the potatoes, but place them in a clean cloth or towel and pat them to remove any excess moisture. Using your hands, rub the potatoes well with salt and pepper.

Preheat the oven to 450° F.

Pour the milk into a saucepan, add the potatoes, bring the milk to a boil, then immediately lower the heat. Cover the pan and simmer the potatoes over low heat for 10 minutes, then add the cream, garlic, and nutmeg. Continue cooking slowly, covered, for 20 minutes longer.

While the potatoes are cooking, stir them occasionally to prevent them from sticking to the bottom of the pan; be careful not to crush or break them. Once they are cooked, lift the potatoes out of the pot with a slotted spoon. Place an equal number of slices in each of the individual baking dishes, then pour enough of the cooking liquid into each dish to cover the slices. Dot the surface with a little butter (about 2 tablespoons in all). Place the baking dishes in a large roasting pan, then pour enough boiling water into the pan to come about halfway up the sides of the dishes. Place the roasting pan in the oven, and bake for 10 minutes or until the surface of the potatoes begins to brown, then remove from the oven and serve immediately.

COMMENTS:

I don't know why, but potatoes cooked this way always have a pleasant cheeselike taste. Could it come from the starch in the potatoes combining with the taste of the cream? Anyway, it is essential not to wash the potatoes before cooking them. This way the starch on each slice is left intact and helps thicken the cream-milk mixture during the baking. Prepared just this way, the potatoes are delicious, but for those who can't resist the temptation, a little grated cheese can be sprinkled over them just before they go into the oven.

Ragoût de spaghetti aux petits légumes

114 SPAGHETTI WITH MIXED VEGETABLES AND MUSHROOM SAUCE

Ingredients for 4 servings:

- 1 large cucumber, weighing approximately 10 ounces
- 4 cups water
- 2 teaspoons coarse salt
- 1½ tablespoons shelled green peas
- 1 cup small cauliflower flowerets
- 2 tablespoons butter
- 3 tablespoons cooking oil
- 1 cup fresh or canned *cèpes* (*Boletus* mushrooms), diced (*see Note*)
- Scant ½ cup diced button mushrooms
- 1 artichoke bottom, fresh or canned, diced
- Salt and pepper

FOR THE SAUCE:

⅓ cup dried morels (*see Comments*)
1 large (½-ounce) fresh or canned whole truffle (*see Comments*)
1 tablespoon finely chopped fresh chervil
3 tablespoons cold water
2 tablespoons *crème fraîche* (*see p. 352*) or heavy cream
7 ounces (2 sticks less 2 tablespoons) softened butter
2 tablespoons **raw diced tomatoes (96)**
Salt and pepper
1 teaspoon lemon juice

7 ounces very thin spaghetti
3 quarts water
2 tablespoons coarse salt

UTENSILS:

Vegetable peeler
Ordinary teaspoon
2 large pots
Colander
Large frying pan with cover
Small bowl
Clean cloth or towel
Small saucepan
Wooden salad utensils
To serve: Large hot serving platter

COOKING THE VEGETABLES:

Peel the cucumber, split it open, lengthwise, and use an ordinary teaspoon to scoop out all the seeds. Cut the cucumber into quarters, lengthwise, then cut the strips into olive-size pieces. Use a small knife to round the ends and sides of each piece to make them look like approximately 20 "mini-cucumbers."

Fill a pot with 4 cups water, add 2 teaspoons of coarse salt, and bring to a boil. Add the peas and boil for 9 minutes, then add the cucumbers. Continue boiling for 2 minutes more, then add the cauliflower flowerets, and boil all together for a final 4 minutes. Pour the vegetables into a colander and allow to drain thoroughly.

Melt 2 tablespoons of butter in a large frying pan with the cooking oil. When hot, add the diced artichoke, *cèpes*, and mushrooms, and sauté for 3 minutes, then add all the other vegetables that were previously cooked, and sauté quickly over high heat for about 1 minute more. Season with salt and pepper, then lower the heat, cover the pan, and keep the vegetables warm while making the sauce.

MAKING THE SAUCE:

Wash the dried morels to eliminate all dirt, then soak them for about 15 minutes in a bowl of warm water. When the mushrooms have softened, dry them carefully in a clean cloth or towel, then cut each one into 4 strips, lengthwise. Cut the truffle into thin *julienne* strips.

In a small saucepan, place the chopped chervil and 3 tablespoons of cold water, and boil over high heat until half of the water has evaporated. Add the cream to the pan, and then the butter, first broken into nut-size pieces. Now add both the morels and the truffles and then the diced tomatoes. Season with salt and pepper. Bring the sauce to a boil and cook for just 30 seconds, then remove from the heat and add the lemon juice. The sauce is ready to serve; keep it hot.

COOKING THE SPAGHETTI AND SERVING:

Break the spaghetti in half with your hands. Place 3 quarts of water and 2 tablespoons of coarse salt in a large pot. Bring the water to a boil, then add the spaghetti. So that it will not stick together, stir the spaghetti with a fork until the water comes back to a boil. Once the water boils again, stop stirring and cook the spaghetti for 6 minutes, then pour into a colander and drain. Hold the spaghetti under cold running water for a couple of seconds (this will remove a bit of excess starch), then put it back into the hot pot in which it cooked. Pour the sauce into the pot with the spaghetti and mix well, using two wooden salad utensils, then place the spaghetti in the middle of a large serving platter. Place all the sautéed vegetables around the edge of the platter and serve immediately.

COMMENTS:

If you don't have *cèpes*, morels, or truffles, the dish will not be the same, but it will still be good made with ordinary mushrooms to replace them.

For convenience's sake, or if you are making this for a lot of people, many things can be prepared in advance. The vegetables that are boiled together can be cooked up to a day ahead of time, then sautéed with the other vegetables just before serving. Even the spaghetti can be cooked in advance if the following instructions are carefully followed:

Once the spaghetti has been cooked as described earlier, drain it in a colander placed over a large bowl so that all the water can be saved, then hold the spaghetti under cold running water until it has cooled completely. To reheat the spaghetti, just before serving, pour the spaghetti water back into the pot and bring to a boil. Add the spaghetti, boil for exactly 30 seconds, then drain, and finish preparing the spaghetti as described in the recipe. Reheated in this way, the spaghetti will still be cooked *al dente* as it should be.

Note: *Dried* cèpes *may be used instead of fresh or canned ones. For this recipe, use 2/3 cup dried* cèpes *soaked in warm water for 30 minutes or until soft, then dice and cook as described. Ed.*

Les desserts

DESSERTS

115 *La pâte sablée sucrée*
SWEET SHORT PASTRY

Ingredients for approximately 1 pound, 2 ounces of pastry dough; enough for two 9-inch tarts, 4 to 6 servings each:

1¾ cups (9 ounces) flour
⅓ cup (2½ ounces) granulated sugar
¾ teaspoon vanilla sugar (*see p. 355*)
⅓ cup powdered almonds (*see p. 329*; optional)
A pinch of salt
5 ounces (1 stick plus 2 tablespoons) softened butter, cut in 6 pieces
1 egg
1½ teaspoons cold water (optional)

UTENSILS:

Food processor (optional)
Plastic bag for refrigerating

MAKING THE DOUGH:

Method I (by hand): Place the flour on a clean table and use your fingers to make a well in the center; the table should be visible in the middle of a high-sided ring of flour. Sprinkle the flour with the sugar, vanilla sugar, powdered almonds, and salt. Place the butter and egg in the center of the well. Using one hand, start mixing the butter and egg together with the tips of your fingers, while pushing small quantities of the flour into the egg-butter mixture with your other hand. As the flour mixes with the egg and butter, use both hands to work the dough with the tips of your fingers, as lightly and as quickly as possible. By "pinching" the dough between your thumb and index finger, the ingredients will rapidly mix together. As soon as all the ingredients have combined into a dough, form it into a ball; if it is too dry to do this, add the water.

Now the dough should be kneaded (*fraiser*) in the following manner: With the heel of your hand, break off little pieces of the dough by pushing them away from you against the table. Once all the dough has been broken into little pieces and crushed in this manner, form it all into a ball again, flatten it slightly with the palm of your hand, then place it in a plastic bag and refrigerate it overnight before baking.

Method II (with a food processor): Place all the ingredients except the egg and water into the food processor. Turn it on; then, after 15 seconds, add the egg and water. In another 15 seconds, the ingredients should be blended and have formed themselves into a ball. Take the dough out of the machine, flatten it with the palm of your hand, then place it in a plastic bag and refrigerate it overnight before baking.

TO STORE AND USE THE DOUGH:

This dough can be kept in the refrigerator for 8 days in a sealed plastic bag. It can also be frozen, in which case it can be kept for up to 2 months. If the dough is frozen, it must be taken from the freezer and placed in the refrigerator the night before it is needed. Whether first frozen, then refrigerated, or simply refrigerated, the dough should be removed from the refrigerator and left at room temperature for 1 hour before being rolled out to be baked.

This dough can be used in various pie, tart, and cookie recipes (see Comments). Before baking, preheat the oven to 425° F.

COMMENTS:

Pâte sablée can be rolled out, cut into circles, and baked for 10 to 15 minutes to make an ever-popular cookie called a *sablé.*

It is also ideal for making delicious fruit tarts, following the directions in the basic sample recipe given below:

116 *Tarte aux fraises ou aux framboises*
STRAWBERRY OR RASPBERRY TART

Ingredients for one 9-inch tart, 4 to 6 servings:

9 ounces (½ recipe) **sweet short pastry (115)**
1 cup **pastry cream (122)** flavored with 1 teaspoon rum or Kirsch
¾ pint strawberries or raspberries, cleaned and hulled
Strawberry or raspberry sauce (124)

Lightly flour a clean table and roll out the dough until it is about ¼ inch thick and about 9 inches wide. Make the dough any shape you like: round, square, oblong. Place it on a baking sheet and pinch the edges to form a slightly raised border. Prick the dough all over with a fork so that it will not rise and form bubbles while baking, then place it in the preheated (425° F) oven for 15 to 20 minutes, or until golden brown. Remove from the oven and leave to cool completely before filling.

Once cool, spread a thick layer of rum- or Kirsch-flavored **pastry cream** over the baked piecrust, then cover with neat rows of fresh strawberries or raspberries, all set upright, hulled ends down, on the cream. Spoon a little fresh **strawberry or raspberry sauce** over the fruit and serve.

VARIANTS:

French or poached pears may be used instead of strawberries or raspberries. In this case do not spoon any sauce over the fruit. Caramelize the pears as explained in the recipe for **Caramelized pear pastries (142).**

Note: *Almost any fresh or poached fruit can be made into tarts as described here. The method given for making* **strawberry or raspberry sauce** *can be used to make a sauce with whatever fruit you have chosen for the tart. Ed.*

La pâte brisée SHORT PASTRY 117

Ingredients for approximately 1 pound of pastry dough; enough for four 8-inch tarts:

- 1⅔ cups (8 ounces) flour
- ⅓ cup nonfat dry milk
- 2 teaspoons granulated sugar
- 1 teaspoon salt
- 6 ounces (1½ sticks) softened butter, cut into 6 pieces
- 1 egg
- 1 tablespoon cold water

UTENSILS:

- Food processor (optional)
- Plastic bag, for refrigerating

MAKING THE DOUGH:

Method I (by hand): Place the flour on a clean table and use your fingers to make a well in the center; the table should be visible in the middle of a high-sided ring of flour. Sprinkle the flour with the nonfat dry milk, sugar, and salt. Place the butter and egg in the center of the well. Using one hand, start mixing the butter and egg together with the tips of your fingers, pushing in the flour little by little with your other hand. Then use both hands to pinch and mix the ingredients together with the tips of your fingers; work as quickly as possible. Finally, add the water, little by little, until the mixture stiffens and adheres to form a dough. Form it into a ball, then knead it (*fraiser*) by breaking off little pieces of dough with the heel of your hand and pushing them away from you against the table. When all the dough has been broken up into little pieces and crushed in this manner, form it back into a ball. Flatten the dough lightly with the palm of your hand, then place it in a plastic bag and leave it in the refrigerator overnight before baking.

Method II (with a food processor): Place all the ingredients except the egg and water in the processor. Run the machine for 15 seconds, then add the egg and water, and run for another 15 seconds. The ingredients will mix and form into a ball of dough by themselves. Remove the dough from the machine, flatten it lightly with the palm of your hand, then place it in a plastic bag and leave it in the refrigerator overnight before baking.

TO BAKE:

Preheat the oven to 425° F.

Remove the dough from the refrigerator, roll it out into the desired shape, and bake according to the directions in the recipe you are using.

COMMENTS:

In a sealed plastic bag, this dough can be kept in the refrigerator for up to 8 days.

It is important that only a small amount of water be used, just enough to make the ingredients come together into a workable mass. If more water than necessary is added, the pastry will be tough and dry when it is baked.

Thanks to the egg used in it, this pastry can be used instead of puff pastry for various fruit tarts; see **Hot apple tarts (138)** and Comments to that recipe. The egg allows the dough to absorb the fruit juice without becoming soggy.

If the sugar is omitted in this dough, it can be used to make meat pies, *pâtés en croûte*, and to bake various cuts of meat wrapped in pastry.

NOTE: *This pastry dough can be used with or without a mold in making the tart described. If it is simply placed on a baking sheet, with a pastry brush slightly moisten the edges of the dough with water and roll the edges over to form a border. Ed.*

La pâte feuilletée
PUFF PASTRY 118

Ingredients for making 1½ pounds dough (*see Note for measuring*):

1¾ cups (9 ounces) flour (*see Comments*)
½ cup cold water
1 teaspoon salt
3½ tablespoons softened butter

½ pound plus 2 tablespoons butter, refrigerated

UTENSILS:

Large knife
Plastic bag for storing
Food processor (optional)
2 sheets of plastic wrap or parchment paper
Rolling pin

MAKING THE DOUGH, STEP 1:

Method I (by hand): Place the flour on a clean table and use your fingers to make a well in the center. The table should be visible in the middle of a high-sided ring of flour. Place the water, salt, and 3½ tablespoons of butter in the well. Use the tips of your fingers to mix these ingredients together while gradually incorporating the flour. Use one hand to pinch and mix the butter/water/flour mixture and the other to push progressively the remaining flour down into the well. When most of the flour has been incorporated, use both hands to finish mixing all the ingredients. Form the dough into a ball, then flatten it slightly with the palm of your hand. Use a sharp knife to slit the surface of the dough in a checkerboard pattern (see illustration). These slits will make the dough easier to roll out when the time comes. Place the dough in a plastic bag in the refrigerator and leave for 2 hours before rolling out.

Method II (with a food processor): Place the flour, water, salt, and 3½ tablespoons of butter into the food processor. Run the machine for 25 seconds or until the ingredients have mixed and formed themselves into a ball. Remove the ball of dough from the machine, flatten it

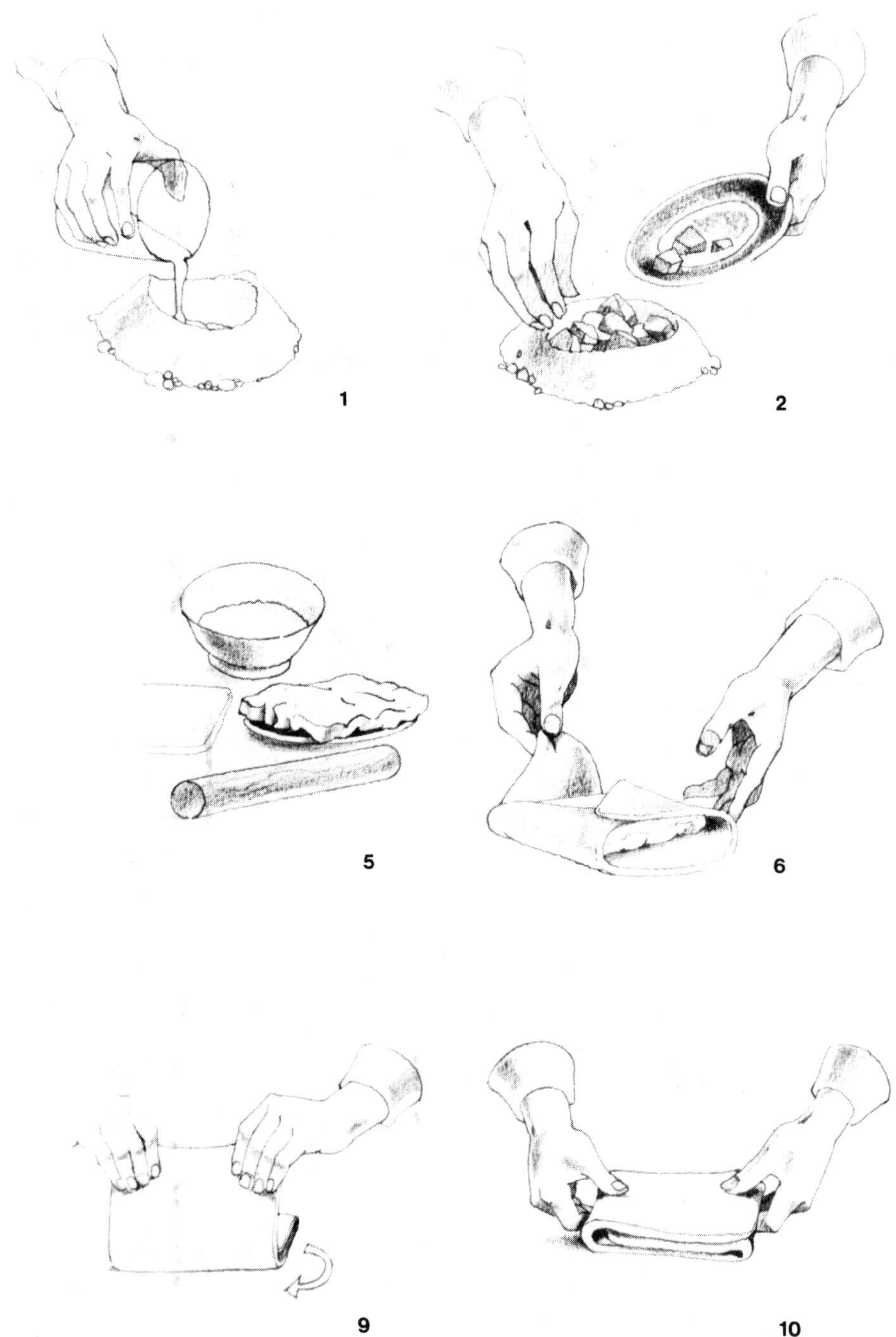
1
2
5
6
9
10

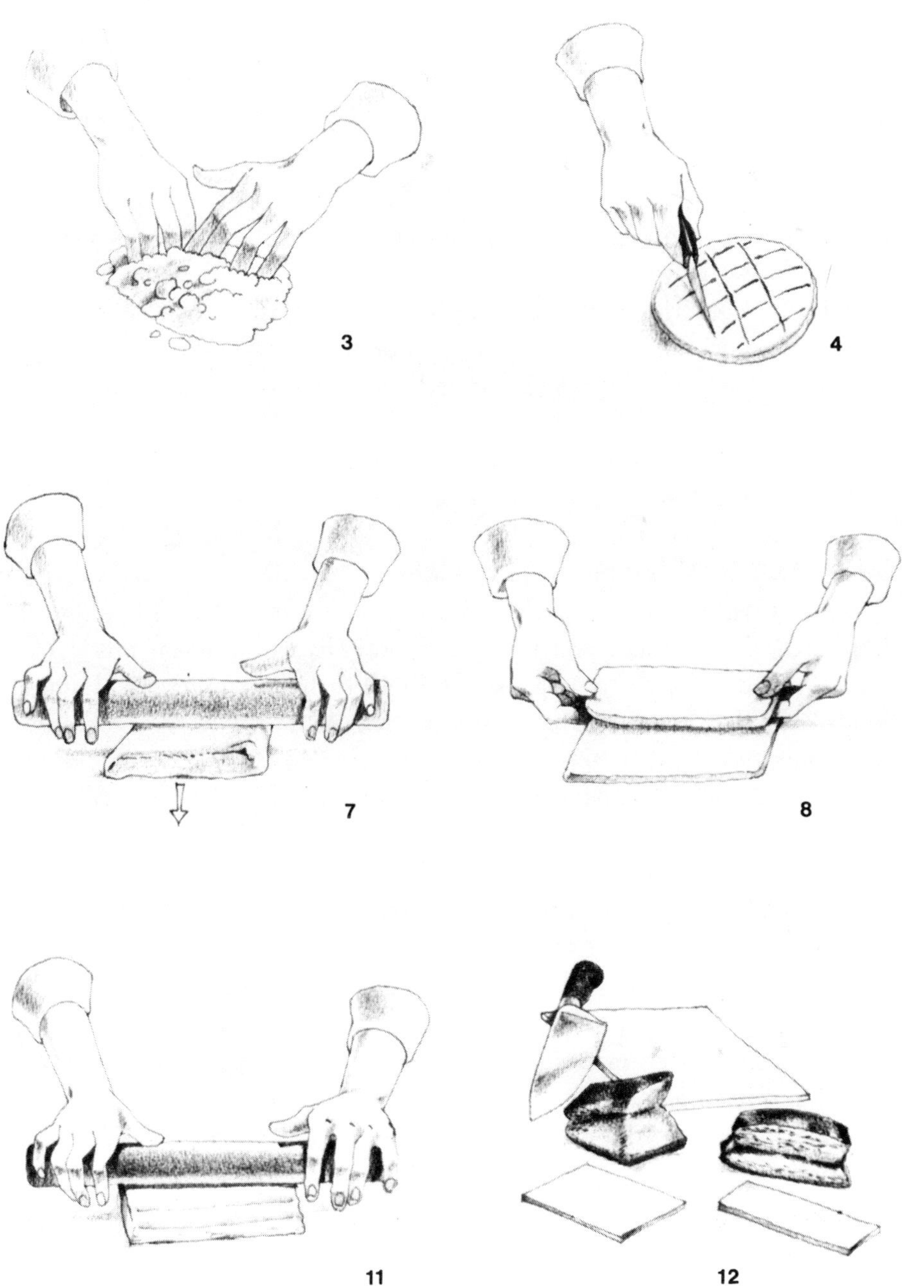
3
4
7
8
11
12

slightly with the palm of your hand, and slit the surface as described above. Place the dough in a plastic bag and refrigerate it for 2 hours before rolling it out.

MAKING THE DOUGH, STEP 2:

Take the remaining butter from the refrigerator, place it on a sheet of plastic wrap or parchment paper, then cover it with another sheet. Using a rolling pin, tap the butter to flatten it until it forms a square approximately 6 inches on a side. Flattening the butter this way makes it much easier to work with.

Lightly flour the table, take the dough from the refrigerator, and roll it out until you have a square of dough approximately 10 inches on a side. Place the flattened butter kitty-corner in the center of the dough: the sides of the butter square should face the corners of the square of dough (see illustration). Fold the corners of the dough inward over the butter. The butter should be completely enclosed by the dough and, after folding, the "package" should look like an envelope in which the butter has been hidden.

On the lightly floured table, roll the dough out. Do not press down too hard when rolling, and roll continually away from you until you have formed a rectangle approximately 10 inches wide and 20 inches long. Fold the dough in thirds, folding first one end of the rectangle until only one-third of the dough is left uncovered, and then folding the second end over the first end (see illustration). The dough will now form three equal layers. The action of rolling the dough out and folding it in this way is called a "turn" (*tour*).

Once the dough has been folded, turn it so that the fold in the dough is perpendicular to you. Roll out the dough until it once again forms a rectangle approximately 10 inches wide and 20 inches long. Fold the dough again into thirds as described before. The dough has now been given two turns. Place the dough in a plastic bag and leave for 30 minutes before rolling it out again.

Remove the dough from the refrigerator and give it two more turns, then return it to the refrigerator for another 30 minutes, or longer. Each time the dough is rolled out, it becomes slightly more elastic. It is essential that it be rolled out as evenly as possible, never pushing the rolling pin too hard at any time.

Remove the dough from the refrigerator and give it two final turns, bringing the total to six turns. The dough is now ready to use (see Note).

USING THE PUFF PASTRY:

Preheat the oven to 425° F.

After the sixth turn, the dough can be rolled out and cut into the shape desired, placed on a baking sheet, and baked according to the directions in the recipe you are following.

FREEZING THE DOUGH:

After the sixth turn, roll the dough out and cut it into the desired shapes, such as small rectangles for making "Puff Pastry Entrées" (page 125), circles or squares for tarts; see **Hot apple tarts (138).** Place sheets of plastic between the pieces of dough if piling them one on top of another, then place them inside plastic bags and freeze. When wanted, preheat the oven to 425° F, take the dough from the freezer, and bake immediately, either garnished or not, according to the recipe you are following.

COMMENTS:

While in New York, I developed a variation of this dough for use in the United States. Although the recipe given above will work very well, a slightly lighter puff pastry was obtained by using a mixture of flours in the proportion of 3 parts all-purpose flour (we used Gold Medal) to 1 part cake flour (we used Very Best). For the measurements given in the above recipe this means:

Generous 1⅓ cups (6½ ounces) all-purpose flour
Generous ⅓ cup (2½ ounces) cake flour

The choice of butter was also very important where we worked; Land O' Lakes was found to be the best available to us at the time.

All the other measurements as well as the method for making the pastry remain the same.

When making puff pastry, both the dough made in step 1 and the butter used when rolling out the dough in step 2 must be cold. Ideally, they should both be of the same consistency when rolled out. In hot weather, or in a warm kitchen, it is best to cool the table used to roll out the dough by placing ice trays on it 30 minutes before rolling out the dough.

When cutting puff pastry, use only a large, very sharp knife with a straight-edge blade. Cut the dough with one, quick clean stroke; do not pull the knife through the dough or squeeze the edges of the dough by pressing down too slowly, or else the edges of the dough will not rise properly.

Why does puff pastry "puff"? Like magic, a piece of dough that is nearly paper-thin suddenly rises as much as 20 times its original height when placed in the oven. This "miracle" has baffled many amateur chefs, when in fact it is easy to explain. When the dough is rolled out, alternating layers of dough (flour and water) and butter are formed. When baked, the butter begins to "fry" and pushes up the layer of dough just above it. Simultaneously, the water in the dough turns to steam, which tries to escape, pushing up the layer above it. The result is the miracle of perfect puff pastry.

NOTE: *When you are rolling the dough out to give a turn, it may be narrower than the 10 inches described. This is not important—do not roll across the dough to make it wider. Simply roll it a little longer; the dough should be between 1/4 inch and 3/8 inch thick before folding. When you are giving the turns to puff pastry, it should be rolled only lengthwise, never crosswise. However, once all six turns have been given, it may be folded or rolled in any direction to form the shape desired.*

If, in the course of giving the dough its turns, the butter breaks through the dough, don't panic. Pat the hole copiously with flour, continue rolling until you can fold it in thirds. Then, chill it before giving it any more turns if you were on the first of two turns. From time to time, check the bottom of the pastry by lifting it up as you are rolling it out to be sure it is not sticking to the table, and flour the table frequently, although very lightly, each time. Anytime the butter breaks through, be sure to clean the table (or rolling pin) to remove any butter sticking to it before continuing.

In order for it to rise correctly, all *the edges of puff pastry must be cut. Roll the dough out slightly larger than the size needed (this is often indicated in the recipes), then cut off the edges. For best results, chill the pastry for 15 to 30 minutes before cutting if working in a warm kitchen.*

Any scraps may be packed into a ball and used like any other pastry dough.

PUFF PASTRY WEIGHTS AND MEASURES: *In various recipes, specific weights of dough are called for. If you are not using a scale, the following information will help when measuring puff pastry.*

Roll out the full amount of dough and cut a rectangle that is 1/3 inch thick, 6 3/4 inches long, and 4 3/4 inches wide. This rectangle weighs 6 1/3 ounces and can be cut as described in the recipes (**43**) *to* (**46**) *to make 4 individual puff-pastry entrées, or left whole to make one 9-inch round tart bottom or one 8-inch square tart bottom. The full amount of dough can thus be used, for instance, to make a total of 12 puff-pastry entrées and one small 7-inch tart.*

Other useful size-weight relationships for the recipes in this book are as follows:

5 1/4 ounces = a rectangle 5/16 inch thick, 6 3/4 inches long, and 4 inches wide

7 ounces = a rectangle 5/16 inch thick, 6 3/4 inches long, and 5 1/4 inches wide

10 1/2 ounces = a rectangle 5/16 inch thick, 6 3/4 inches wide, and 8 inches long

12 2/3 ounces = a rectangle 5/16 inch thick, 6 3/4 inches wide, and 9 1/2 inches long

14 ounces = a rectangle 5/16 inch thick, 6 3/4 inches wide, and 10 1/2 inches long.

For intermediate measures, it should be noted that to add (or subtract) 1/2 inch to the width will add (or subtract) about 3/4 ounce to (from) the total weight of a given rectangle. Ed.

Pâte à chou
CREAM-PUFF PASTRY 119

Ingredients for approximately 1 1/2 cups batter, enough for making 20 to 30 cream puffs or éclairs:

1/2 cup milk
1/2 cup water
3/4 teaspoon salt
1 teaspoon granulated sugar

¼ pound softened butter
1 cup (5 ounces) flour
5 medium-size eggs
Powdered sugar to sprinkle on the pastries before baking

UTENSILS:

Small saucepan
Wooden spoon
Bowl
Wire whisk
Baking sheet
Nonstick parchment paper (optional)
Pastry bag with ⅝-inch nozzle
Sugar sifter for confectioner's sugar
Serrated knife

MAKING THE BATTER:

Place the milk, water, salt, sugar, and butter in a small saucepan. Bring to a boil over high heat; as soon as it boils, remove the pan from the heat and start adding the flour gradually, beating the mixture constantly with a wooden spoon while pouring the flour into the pan. Once all the flour has been added, place the saucepan back over the heat and continue beating vigorously for 1 minute. Part of the water will now evaporate and the batter will become smooth and detach easily from the sides of the pan. Place the batter in a bowl (preferably first warmed with hot water, then emptied). Now add the eggs, one at a time: The secret to making perfectly smooth cream-puff batter is simple and consists of beating the dough energetically while adding each of the first 4 eggs, but beating only just enough to incorporate the last egg when it is added. When all the eggs have been incorporated and the batter is quite smooth, it is ready to bake.

BAKING THE PASTRIES:

Preheat the oven to 425° F.

Lightly grease a baking sheet or cover it with nonstick parchment paper. Spoon the batter into a pastry bag fitted with a ⅝-inch plain nozzle and gently squeeze the batter out onto the baking sheet. If making cream puffs, squeeze the batter out into little mounds; to make éclairs, squeeze the batter into sausagelike strips about 4 inches long. Sprinkle the pastries generously with confectioner's sugar, then place the baking sheet in the oven. Bake for 15 minutes, then lower the temperature of the oven to 400° F, and wedge a wooden spoon between the oven door and the side of the oven to keep the door ajar during the second half of the baking time. Continue baking for another 15 minutes, then remove from the oven and allow to cool before filling and serving.

COMMENTS:

Fillings: Cream-puff pastry can be filled with sweet creams to make desserts, or with savory cheese and meat mixtures to make entrées and appetizers. In either case, split the puffs open with a serrated knife once they have cooled. The filling is placed inside, using either a pastry bag or a small spoon.

To make an interesting appetizer, fill the puff with a mixture of farmer's cheese, grated Swiss cheese, diced ham, and freshly chopped herbs.

A very popular dessert, especially with children, is cream puffs filled with whipped cream.

My own version of the classic *profiterole*, made with cream puffs, is given at the end of the recipe for **Honey ice cream (132)**.

Much of the liquid (milk and water) used in making the batter will evaporate during baking. Since the steam created will be trapped inside the cream puffs, it will make each puff rise and create an air pocket inside the puff or éclair that makes it perfect for filling.

When you are making cream-puff pastry, it is always best to make a large amount of the batter; the amount given here is what I consider the minimum. If the ingredients were halved to make less batter, the cream puffs would not be as light or delicious. Don't be afraid of making more than you need. Once the cream puffs have been baked, they can be placed in a plastic bag and kept in the refrigerator up to a week, or they can be frozen and kept up to a month. In either case, don't crowd them when filling the bags, and make sure the bags are tightly closed. Refrigerated cream puffs can be used directly from the refrigerator to make cold desserts as needed; when frozen, the cream puffs must be placed in the refrigerator to thaw 24 hours before filling and serving.

120 *La pâte à baba ou à savarin*
BABA OR SAVARIN DOUGH

Ingredients for 2 cups of dough; enough for two cakes serving 4 to 5 people each:

FOR THE DOUGH:

1/3 ounce active dry yeast
2 tablespoons lukewarm water
1 3/4 cups (9 ounces) all-purpose flour
3/4 teaspoon salt
3 medium-size eggs
3/8 cup warm milk
2 teaspoons granulated sugar
5 tablespoons melted butter

Ingredients for 1 cup dough; enough for one cake serving 4 to 5 people or two **Ali Baba cakes (144)**:

FOR THE DOUGH:

1/6 ounce active dry yeast
1 tablespoon warm water
1 scant cup (4 1/2 ounces) all-purpose flour
Scant 1/2 teaspoon salt
1 medium-size egg plus 1/2 beaten egg
3 tablespoons warm milk
1 teaspoon granulated sugar
2 1/2 tablespoons melted butter

Ingredients for the rum syrup for one cake; double the measurements for two cakes:

1/2 cup water
6 tablespoons granulated sugar
1 tablespoon rum
5 teaspoons rum to finish each cake

TO GARNISH AND GLAZE EACH CAKE:

Apricot sauce (125)
2 cups **pastry cream (122)**, or

2 cups **whipped cream (121)**, or
Fresh fruit salad

UTENSILS:

Large bowl
Wire whisk
Wooden spoon
1 or 2 ring molds 8 inches in diameter
Pastry brush
Cake rack
Plastic bags for freezing
Saucepan
Small ladle
Bowl or deep dish
Serving platter
Sauceboat

MAKING THE DOUGH:

Place the yeast in a bowl and add the warm water progressively, beating with a wire whisk. Mix the flour and salt together, sprinkle them into the bowl while stirring with a wooden spoon, then add 1 egg if making one cake, 2 eggs for two cakes, beating the mixture constantly. Beat until the ingredients are smooth, then beat in the remaining egg (or ½ beaten egg), and add the warm milk little by little. Beat vigorously for 10 minutes, lifting the spoon into the air to stretch and "air" the dough, which should become smooth and elastic. Once the dough stretches when the spoon is lifted from the bowl, add the sugar and melted butter. Continue beating for 5 minutes more to incorporate perfectly these last two ingredients. The dough should now stretch without breaking. Leave the dough to rise for 30 minutes, covered, in a warm place. At the end of this time, punch it down by beating it with the wooden spoon, then flatten the dough slightly to make a compact mass.

TO BAKE:

Preheat the oven to 400° F.

Butter the mold(s) using a pastry brush and a little melted butter. Fill the mold no more than halfway with the dough, then place in a warm place. Leave the dough to rise, covered, for 1 hour or until it reaches the edge of the mold. Place the mold in the oven and bake for 18 to 20 minutes. To make sure it is cooked, stick the blade of a knife into the cake; if the knife comes out clean and dry, the cake is done. Turn the cake out onto a cake rack immediately when it is taken from the oven. Leave to cool for several minutes, then if freezing a cake for later use, place it while still warm in a plastic bag, seal, and freeze.

TO SERVE:

Place the water and sugar for the rum syrup in a saucepan and bring to a boil. As soon as the liquid boils and the sugar has dissolved, remove from the heat, leave the syrup to cool slightly, then add the rum while the syrup is still warm. Leave the cake on the rack and place the rack over a deep dish or bowl. Using a ladle, pour the rum syrup over the cake; the excess syrup will drip into the bowl and should be ladled back over the cake until it has been thoroughly soaked with the syrup. (Professionals, who make several cakes at once, will dip them into large pots of syrup to soak them thoroughly. This is, however, a tricky operation, since the cakes have to be totally covered by the rum syrup for about a minute, then carefully lifted out of the syrup and placed on the serving platter. The cakes swell when they are soaked with the syrup.)

Place the cake on a serving platter and spoon 5 teaspoons of rum over it. Brush the cake with **apricot sauce,** then fill the center with **pastry cream** (which can be caramelized), or with **whipped cream,** or with a fresh fruit salad of your choice. Serve the cake immediately, with the remaining apricot sauce served in a sauceboat.

COMMENTS:

Sometimes these cakes will stick to the sides of the mold and be difficult to turn out. To avoid this, wrap each cake tightly in aluminum foil as soon as it is taken from the oven. The steam trapped inside the aluminum foil will detach the cake from the mold and it will turn out perfectly.

Doughs that rise, such as this one, are best when made in rather large quantities. When baking cakes that are not to be served immediately, be sure to wrap and freeze them while they are still warm. If simply refrigerated, the cakes will keep for 12 days, whereas frozen cakes can be kept for up to 2 months. If frozen, the cakes should be placed in the refrigerator to thaw for 24 hours before serving.

Note: *If serving a refrigerated cake, or a thawed frozen one, place it for 10 to 15 minutes in a 350° F oven to warm, then spoon the warm syrup over it, and finish as described. Ed.*

La crème Chantilly
WHIPPED CREAM 121

Ingredients for 2 cups whipped cream:

- 1 cup heavy cream, or
- 1 cup *crème fraîche* (*see p. 352*) plus 3 tablespoons cold water and 3 tablespoons finely crushed ice (*see Comments*)
- 2½ tablespoons confectioner's sugar
- ¾ teaspoon vanilla sugar (*see p. 355*)

Ingredients for 4 cups whipped cream:

- 2 generous cups heavy cream, or
- 1⅔ cups *crème fraîche* plus ⅜ cup cold water and 6 tablespoons finely crushed ice (*see Comments*)
- ⅓ cup confectioner's sugar
- 1½ teaspoons vanilla sugar (*see p. 355*)

UTENSILS:

Large bowl, preferably metal
Wire whisk

Place the cream in a large bowl and refrigerate for 1 hour before whipping. Metal bowls are preferable since they chill more quickly. Both the cream and the bowl should be very cold when taken from the refrigerator, otherwise the cream will not whip easily or be light and airy.

Remove the cream from the refrigerator, add the sugar and the vanilla sugar, and start beating the cream slowly with a wire whisk.

Beat with an even motion for 2 minutes; the movement of your wrist should be loose and relaxed. The cream will begin to puff up as it is beaten and will double in volume; when this happens, continue beating, but more energetically, for 30 to 40 seconds more. By this time, the cream will have stiffened almost like beaten egg whites and will hold its shape on the wire whisk. Once the cream has stiffened, stop beating, since too much whisking will make the cream separate. It is now ready to use.

COMMENTS:

Whipped cream can be kept for 6 to 12 hours in the refrigerator; if it loses a little water during this time, beat it quickly for a few seconds just before using.

Either heavy cream or *crème fraîche* can be used to make whipped cream. If *crème fraîche* is used it must be diluted with cold water and crushed ice (added when you add the sugar) before being whipped.

Granulated sugar can be used instead of confectioner's sugar in making whipped cream.

Crème pâtissière
122 PASTRY CREAM

Ingredients for making 1¼ cups pastry cream:

1 cup milk
¼ vanilla bean, split lengthwise
5 teaspoons granulated sugar

3 medium-size egg yolks
3½ tablespoons granulated sugar
1 tablespoon flour
1 tablespoon cornstarch

Ingredients for making 2½ cups pastry cream:

2 generous cups milk
½ vanilla bean, split lengthwise
3½ tablespoons granulated sugar

6 medium-size egg yolks
6 tablespoons granulated sugar
2 tablespoons flour
2 tablespoons cornstarch

UTENSILS:

Saucepan
Bowl
Wire whisk

Place the milk, vanilla bean, and the smaller amount of sugar in a saucepan and bring to a boil.

Place the egg yolks and the larger amount of sugar in a bowl. Beat vigorously for 1 minute, using a wire whisk, or until the mixture begins to lighten in color. Sprinkle the flour and cornstarch into the bowl, carefully stirring them into the egg-sugar mixture with the whisk until the ingredients are well mixed and perfectly smooth.

Remove the vanilla bean from the pan of milk, then pour half of the boiling milk into the bowl with the other ingredients. Beat vigorously with the whisk as the milk is added, then pour the contents of the bowl into the pan with the remaining milk. Continue whisking, place the pan over high heat, and boil for 1 minute. Beat the cream constantly and be sure that none of it sticks to the bottom of the pan; lower the heat if necessary. Remove the pan from the heat and pour the cream into a bowl.

Allow the cream to cool before using. To prevent a skin from forming as it cools, rub the surface of the pastry cream with a piece of butter. Pastry cream can be kept, covered, in the refrigerator for several days.

COMMENTS:

A delicious variant of this recipe can be prepared by using rice flour instead of ordinary flour.

Pastry cream is used in many desserts and can be flavored in various ways. One of my favorites is to mix a few raisins (previously soaked in rum) into the cream, then to use the cream to fill small crêpes which I then heat quickly in the oven and sprinkle with a little brandy or liqueur just before serving.

123 *Crème d'amandes* ALMOND CREAM

Ingredients for making 1 cup almond cream:

3½ tablespoons softened butter
Scant ½ cup confectioner's sugar
½ cup powdered almonds
1 medium-size egg
1 tablespoon cornstarch
1 teaspoon dark rum

UTENSILS:

Bowl
Wooden spoon
Electric blender (optional)

Method I (by hand): Place the butter in a large bowl and beat it with a wooden spoon until it has the consistency of a soft, smooth paste. Mix the sugar and powdered almonds together, then sprinkle the mixture little by little into the butter, stirring constantly. When all the sugar and powdered almonds have been added, beat with the spoon for 2 minutes more, then add the egg and beat until all the ingredients mix to form a smooth, thick cream. Finally stir in the cornstarch and rum. Smooth the surface of the cream. It is now ready to use.

Method II (with a blender): Place the butter, sugar, and powdered almonds in the blender. Blend at the slowest speed for 1 minute, then add the egg, blend 30 seconds more, and finally add the cornstarch and rum and blend for a final 15 seconds. The cream is ready to use.

COMMENTS:

This cream can be kept for up to 8 days if refrigerated in a tightly sealed container. If refrigerated, the cream should be left at room temperature for 30 minutes before using so that it will have time to soften and resume its original texture.

Here's an easy dessert that can be made with almond cream: Slice a brioche or egg bread into slices about an inch thick, spread each slice with a thick layer of almond cream, sprinkle with confectioner's sugar, then place in a hot (450° F) oven for several minutes to color. Serve on hot plates, straight from the oven.

Sauce coulis de framboises, fraises, ou cassis RASPBERRY, STRAWBERRY, OR BLACK-CURRANT SAUCE 124

Ingredients for 6 servings:

1¼ pints fresh or frozen raspberries, strawberries, or black currants
¾ cup granulated sugar, or to taste
Juice of 1 lemon

UTENSILS:

Colander
Clean cloth or towel
Electric blender
Container with cover (for storage)

Remove all stems and leaves from the berries. Place the fruit in a colander and wash quickly under cold running water, then drain and spread on a towel to dry.

Place the berries in the blender with the sugar and lemon juice and blend for 2 minutes. Pour the sauce into a container and keep refrigerated before serving. For those who prefer a perfectly smooth fruit sauce, it should be worked through a fine sieve to eliminate all seeds or filaments before refrigerating.

COMMENTS:

Fruit sauces can be kept for 8 days if refrigerated in a tightly closed container, or for up to 2 months if frozen. If frozen, the sauce should be placed in the refrigerator to thaw for 24 hours before serving. Once thawed, beat the sauce lightly with a whisk so that the ingredients will be well blended.

When you are making black-currant sauce with fresh currants, it is preferable to leave the little stem attached to the fruit and even add several black-currant leaves to the fruit in the blender. When this is done, the resulting sauce must, of course, be worked through a fine sieve before being served.

Note: *If using frozen fruit, allow it to thaw completely before making the sauce, and add sugar, if any, to taste. Ed.*

125 *Sauce coulis d'abricots*
APRICOT SAUCE

Ingredients for 6 servings:

15 large fresh apricots, split in half and pitted
1 cup water
6½ tablespoons granulated sugar
1 vanilla bean, split open lengthwise
1 tablespoon dark rum

UTENSILS:

Medium saucepan
Wire whisk
Electric blender

Place the apricots, water, sugar, and vanilla bean in a saucepan; bring to a boil, then lower the heat and simmer slowly, uncovered, for about 25 minutes. Stir often with a wire whisk while the apricots are cooking to prevent them from sticking to the bottom of the pan. When finished cooking, the liquid should have been reduced by one-third its original volume and the mixture should look somewhat like a thin apricot marmalade.

Take out the vanilla bean and pour the mixture into a blender, add the rum, and blend for 2 minutes. The sauce is now ready to serve.

This sauce can be served either hot or cold. If served cold, it should be refrigerated after being blended.

COMMENTS:

To store in the refrigerator, or to freeze, see the Comments to **Raspberry, strawberry or black-currant sauce (124).**

Almonds can be added to this sauce after it comes from the blender. If blanched almonds are used, simply split 12 of them open with the tip of a small knife and place them in a bowl with a tablespoon of Kirsch or rum for 1 hour. Drain the almonds and stir them into the sauce.

To blanch almonds yourself, drop them into a pot of boiling water, leave for 2 minutes, then drain, and rinse them immediately under cold running water. The thin brown skin that surrounds each almond will now come off easily when you squeeze the almond between your thumb and index finger. Split each almond in half and soak in rum or Kirsch as described above, then stir into the sauce.

Sauce coulis de pêches au caramel
CARAMEL AND PEACH SAUCE 126

Ingredients for 6 servings:

3 cups water
1¾ cups granulated sugar
1 whole vanilla bean
3 peaches weighing approximately 1 pound in all

6½ tablespoons granulated sugar
2 tablespoons cold water
1 teaspoon lemon juice
2 tablespoons cold water

UTENSILS:

Medium saucepan with cover
Slotted spoon
Colander
Small saucepan with cover
Electric blender
Sauceboat

COOKING THE PEACHES:

Place the water, sugar, and vanilla bean in a saucepan. Bring to a boil, then drop in the whole peaches, lower the heat, and simmer slowly, covered, for about 15 minutes. Lift the peaches out of the liquid with a slotted spoon and place them in a colander to drain and cool. (Save the cooking liquid; it can be used to poach other fruit.) Once the peaches have cooled, peel them, split them open, and remove the pits.

MAKING THE CARAMEL:

Place 6½ tablespoons of sugar in a small saucepan and add 2 tablespoons of cold water and a teaspoon of lemon juice. Bring to a boil and continue boiling slowly for 5 minutes or until the syrup is a dark-caramel color; shake the pan occasionally so that the syrup will spin around the sides of the pan, thus making the caramel cook more evenly. To keep the caramel from solidifying when it cools, add 2 more tablespoons of cold water to the pot, away from the heat, after the caramel has finished cooking. Be careful; the cold water will make the hot caramel splatter, so have the cover of the pan at hand, and as soon as the water has been added, cover the pot immediately.

FINISHING THE SAUCE:

Place the peaches in a blender, blend for 30 seconds to make a smooth purée, then pour in the caramel and continue blending for another 15 seconds. Pour the sauce into a bowl or sauceboat and allow to cool before serving. This sauce is always served cold; it can be refrigerated before serving.

COMMENTS:

To store this sauce in the refrigerator, or to freeze it, see the Comments to **Raspberry, strawberry, or black-currant sauce (124)**.

Drained canned peach halves may be used when making this sauce. They do not need to be cooked before blending with the caramel.

An equal weight of fresh pears, or an equal amount of canned pears, can be used to replace the peaches.

NOTE: *If using canned fruit, use 6 halves if the fruit are large, 8 halves if small. Ed.*

Sauce chocolat
CHOCOLATE SAUCE 127

Ingredients for 6 servings:

6½ tablespoons unsweetened Dutch cocoa
¾ cup granulated sugar
1 cup cold water
5 teaspoons softened butter

UTENSILS:

Small saucepan
Wooden spoon
Wire whisk
Bain-marie or double boiler

Place the powdered cocoa, sugar, and water in a saucepan. Stir with a wooden spoon until a smooth liquid is formed, then place the pan over high heat and bring to a boil. Once it boils, lower the heat and continue cooking at a moderate boil for 3 minutes. Stir the sauce constantly with a wire whisk while it is cooking. Add the butter, continue whisking, cook for 4 minutes longer, and make sure none of the sauce sticks to the bottom of the pan. The sauce should now be thick enough to coat a spoon dipped into it; when it reaches this point it is ready to serve.

Chocolate sauce is always served hot. If not served immediately, it can be reheated or kept warm in a double boiler or *bain-marie*.

COMMENTS:

I have tried every recipe imaginable for making chocolate sauce, and this one is not only the best, but the simplest as well!

It can be kept refrigerated in a tightly closed container for 8 to 15 days. When needed, it can be heated in a *bain-marie* or double boiler. After being refrigerated, a teaspoon of cold water should be added, and the sauce should be whisked constantly while being reheated.

A delicious dessert can be made with poached pears, **Honey ice cream (132)** and this chocolate sauce. Simply place the pears on a plate with spoonfuls of ice cream around them, then spoon the hot chocolate sauce over all and serve.

NOTE: *If the sauce seems too thin at the end of the cooking time, continue boiling until it coats the spoon. Ed.*

Sauce aux grains de café
128 COFFEE SAUCE

Ingredients for 5 to 6 servings:

- 1 cup milk
- 2 tablespoons granulated sugar
- 1 tablespoon freshly ground coffee (medium grind; *see Comments*)
- 3 egg yolks
- 3 tablespoons granulated sugar

UTENSILS:

Medium saucepan with cover
Bowl
Wire whisk
Wooden spoon or spatula

Place the milk and 2 tablespoons of sugar in a medium saucepan and bring to a boil. When the milk boils and starts to rise in the pan, add the ground coffee, cover the pan immediately, and remove from the heat. Leave to infuse for 15 minutes.

While the coffee is infusing, place the egg yolks and 3 tablespoons of sugar in a bowl. Beat vigorously with a wire whisk for 1 minute or until the mixture lightens perceptibly and becomes pale yellow.

Pour the coffee-milk mixture into the bowl with the egg yolks, whisking constantly and vigorously as the liquid is being added. Pour the contents of the bowl back into the saucepan and place over low heat to thicken the sauce. Heat the sauce for 6 to 8 minutes, but do not allow it to boil. During this time, stir the sauce gently, but continuously, with a wooden spoon or spatula. To make sure the sauce has been cooked enough, test it in the following manner: Stir with the wooden spoon or spatula, then lift the spoon out of the sauce at a sharp angle (do not hold it flat). Draw a line down the middle of the spoon with your finger tip. If the sauce has finished cooking, the line will remain clean; if not, the top edge will not hold its shape and will cover the line because the sauce is too runny.

This sauce is always served cold. Once it has finished cooking, pour it into a bowl; stir frequently while it cools so that it will remain perfectly smooth. If necessary, the cooling can be speeded up by placing the bowl of sauce in a larger bowl half full of ice cubes and cold water.

COMMENTS:

The coffee must not be ground too fine, since the specks of coffee in the sauce are one of its essential features.

It is important that the sauce not be allowed to boil when it is heated to thicken; if it is heated too much, the egg yolks will cook and cause the sauce to separate. If this happens, all is not lost, however; the sauce can be rescued by pouring it immediately into an electric blender and blending for 15 seconds to make it smooth again. In the absence of a blender, the sauce can be poured into a bottle and shaken energetically as if you were making a cocktail.

Coffee sauce can be kept refrigerated in a tightly closed container for up to 3 days.

Melon en sorbet
129 MELON SHERBET WITH STRAWBERRIES

Ingredients for 6 servings:

¾ cup wild strawberries, stems removed *(for substitution, see Note)*
1 tablespoon granulated sugar
1 tablespoon rum
⅔ cup milk
⅔ cup confectioner's sugar
6 small canteloupes or muskmelons, weighing approximately 10 ounces each
2 tablespoons rum

Mint leaves (optional)
Strawberry or other leaves to decorate
Strawberry sauce (124)

UTENSILS:

2 small bowls
Small saucepan
Spoon
Electric blender
Electric ice-cream freezer

To serve: Serving platter
Sauceboat

PRELIMINARY PREPARATIONS:

Place the strawberries in a bowl with a tablespoon of sugar and a tablespoon of rum. Refrigerate for at least 30 minutes.

Place the milk and confectioner's sugar in a saucepan, bring to a boil, then remove from the heat and allow to cool completely.

Cut off the top of each melon about ½ inch under the stem. Lift off the tops. Using a small spoon, scoop the seeds out of each melon and discard, then scoop out all the pulp from inside each melon. Scoop off whatever pulp is attached to the melon tops. Place all of the pulp in a bowl and place the emptied melons and their tops in the refrigerator.

MAKING THE SHERBET:

Place the melon pulp in a blender and blend to make a smooth, liquid purée. There should be approximately 2⅔ cups of purée. Add the cold milk-sugar mixture to the blender as well as 2 tablespoons of rum, and blend for 15 seconds to make a homogeneous mixture. Pour the contents of the blender into an ice-cream freezer, start the motor, and freeze for 20 to 25 minutes. The mixture will thicken and "catch" in the freezer.

TO SERVE:

Remove the emptied melons from the refrigerator, fill them halfway with the melon sherbet, then sprinkle in a layer of strawberries (do not add the rum they soaked in), then fill each melon with more sherbet. Put the tops of the melons back into place, and decorate by sticking a few mint leaves into each top.

Serve the melons on a large serving platter that has been covered with a bed of strawberry or other leaves. Serve the **strawberry sauce** separately so that it can be spooned over the sherbet at the table.

NOTE: *If wild strawberries are not available, ordinary strawberries that are either very small or have been cut into quarters can be used instead.*

Although the sherbet may be made and kept in the freezer well in advance, the melons should be garnished and served only at the last moment; otherwise the strawberries will freeze and turn to ice. Twenty to 30 minutes before serving, remove the sherbet from the freezer and place it in the refrigerator to soften, then garnish the melon shells as described. Ed.

130 *Granité au vin de Saint-Émilion*
BORDEAUX RED-WINE ICE

(color picture VIII)

Ingredients for 6 to 8 servings:

1 cup water
1 cup granulated sugar
1 bottle or 3¼ cups red bordeaux wine, preferably a Saint-Émilion
Juice of 1 orange
Juice of 1 lemon
6 to 8 fresh mint leaves (optional)

UTENSILS:

Saucepan
Medium-size bowl
Wire whisk
Rectangular cake pan or roasting pan 8 inches by 11 inches (capacity of 5 cups)
To serve: 6 to 8 wine glasses

MAKING THE ICE:

Place the water and sugar in a saucepan, bring to a boil, and boil for 1 minute, then pour into a bowl and allow to cool completely.

Once the syrup has cooled, add the wine, orange juice, and lemon juice to the bowl, stirring with a wire whisk to mix all the ingredients. Pour the mixture into the cake pan or roasting pan and place the pan in the freezer. Since the liquid in the pan is not very deep, it will freeze relatively quickly. About once every hour, stir the liquid with a fork; make sure to mix in what has frozen around the edges of the tray with the liquid that has not yet frozen in the center. After 5 to 6 hours, the liquid will be the consistency of a soft sherbet with little crystals in it, thanks to the frequent stirring. It is then ready to serve.

TO SERVE:

Use a spoon to fill stemmed wine glasses with the ice; fill each glass and round the ice into a mound on top. Stick several fresh mint leaves into the ice and serve immediately.

COMMENTS:

This ice can be made without an ice-cream freezer, but, because of the time needed for the ice to "catch," it must be begun well in advance.

A delicious variant of this recipe can be made using very small fresh peaches (see color picture VIII):

Drop the peaches into a pot of boiling water, boil for 15 seconds, drain, and rinse under cold running water; the skins will peel off easily. Peel the peaches but do not remove the pits. Place the whole peaches in a saucepan with a syrup made by boiling 4 cups of water with 2⅔ cups of granulated sugar. Add a vanilla bean split open lengthwise and poach the fruit for 15 minutes. Lift the peaches out of the syrup and allow to cool completely. Once the glasses have been filled with the red-wine ice as described earlier, place a peach on top, put several mint leaves where the stem of the peach was, and serve.

The orange juice can be replaced by tangerine juice, creating an unusual combination full of flavor.

NOTE: *This ice may be made a day in advance, but since it will harden completely in the freezer overnight, it must be removed from the freezer and placed in the refrigerator to soften for 30 minutes before serving. Stir to mix the sherbet and ice crystals, then serve as described. Ed.*

Granité de chocolat amer
BITTER CHOCOLATE AND COFFEE SHERBET 131

Ingredients for making approximately 1 quart of sherbet, or 6 servings:

FOR THE COFFEE ICE:

- 1 cup water
- 2 tablespoons granulated sugar
- 1 heaping tablespoon freeze-dried instant coffee

FOR THE CHOCOLATE SHERBET:

2 cups milk
Scant ½ cup granulated sugar
3½ ounces semisweet chocolate, broken into several pieces
¾ cup unsweetened Dutch cocoa
1 cup *crème fraîche* (*see p. 352*) or heavy cream

UTENSILS:

Saucepan
Wire whisk
Ice tray
Fork
Bowl
Sieve
Electric ice-cream freezer

To serve: 6 champagne glasses (tulip-shaped *flutes*)

MAKING THE COFFEE ICE (*a day in advance*):

Place the water and 2 tablespoons of sugar in a saucepan, bring to a boil, and immediately remove from the heat. Using a wire whisk, stir in the freeze-dried instant coffee. Mix well, then pour into an empty ice tray and place in the freezer. Stir the mixture frequently with a fork while it freezes so that little ice crystals form in it; see procedure in **Bordeaux red-wine ice (130).** Leave the ice in the freezer overnight.

MAKING THE CHOCOLATE SHERBET:

Place the milk and a scant ½ cup of granulated sugar in a saucepan, bring to a boil, and add the chocolate, stirring constantly with a wire whisk until the chocolate has melted and mixed well into the milk. Then place the cocoa in a bowl and stir in enough of the chocolate milk, little by little, to form a smooth, thick liquid. Mix well to remove as many lumps as possible, then pour this mixture into the pot with the chocolate milk. Have the saucepan over very low heat as the cocoa mixture is being added; stir constantly with a wire whisk to make a smooth, homogeneous mixture. Pour through a sieve into a large bowl, rubbing any remaining lumps through the sieve with a wooden spoon.

Using the whisk, stir the cream into the other ingredients and allow to cool completely before freezing.

Pour the cold chocolate mixture into an ice-cream freezer, start the motor, and freeze for about 20 to 25 minutes or until the sherbet "catches" and thickens to the proper consistency. Then, using a fork, mix half of the coffee ice into the sherbet. Fill champagne glasses with the sherbet, top each portion with some of the remaining coffee ice, and serve.

NOTE: *Since the amount of coffee ice made is very small, it freezes very quickly, in about an hour. Therefore, it is necessary to stir it very frequently indeed, about every 10 or 15 minutes. For this reason, it is not really necessary to make the coffee ice a day in advance; several hours is sufficient.*

If desired, both the sherbet and the ice can be made well in advance and kept in the freezer. But in this case they must both be removed from the freezer and placed in the refrigerator to soften about 45 minutes before serving. Ed.

Glace au miel
HONEY ICE CREAM 132

Ingredients for making approximately 1 pint ice cream, or 3 servings:

2 egg yolks
⅔ cup *crème fraîche* (*see p. 352*) or heavy cream
1 cup milk
½ cup honey (avoid honeys made from only one flower, such as rosemary, thyme, etc.)

UTENSILS:

2 bowls
Wire whisk
Saucepan
Sieve
Electric ice-cream freezer

Place the egg yolks in a bowl and beat with a wire whisk for 1 minute, then add the cream and continue beating until a homogeneous mixture is formed.

Place the milk in a saucepan and bring to a boil; as soon as the milk starts to rise in the pan, stir in the honey with a wire whisk. Beat vigorously, bring the milk-honey mixture back to a boil, then pour into the bowl with the egg yolks, whisking constantly as the liquid is being added. Once the ingredients are well mixed, pour the contents of the bowl through a sieve into another bowl and allow the mixture to cool completely before freezing.

Once the mixture is cold, pour it into an ice-cream freezer, start the motor, and freeze for 20 to 25 minutes or until the ice cream has thickened to the proper consistency. This ice cream is best when served immediately after being made, but it can be stored in the freezer in a tightly closed container or ice-cream mold.

Serve honey ice cream alone or in one of the dessert combinations suggested below.

COMMENTS:

Honey ice cream can be used instead of vanilla ice cream to enliven many traditional desserts. Strawberries, raspberries, or poached cherries served with honey ice cream and topped with a **Raspberry or strawberry sauce (124)** is a delicious dessert.

Honey ice cream with stewed pears and hot **Chocolate sauce (127)** is another treat.

But for those who want a truly magnificent dessert, nothing rivals *profiteroles* made with honey ice cream and served with **Chocolate sauce (127)**. To prepare this sumptuous dessert, make and bake cream puffs; see **Cream-puff pastry (119)**. Once they have cooled, split each one open with a serrated knife and fill with a spoonful of honey ice cream. Place the *profiteroles* on chilled plates, pour the hot chocolate sauce over them, and serve immediately.

Soufflé aux framboises
RASPBERRY SOUFFLÉ 133

Ingredients for 10 individual soufflés:

1½ tablespoons melted butter
2 tablespoons granulated sugar
1½ pints fresh raspberries
Juice of ¼ lemon
6 tablespoons granulated sugar
3 egg yolks
12 egg whites
A pinch of salt
⅓ cup confectioner's sugar
Raspberry sauce (**124**) (optional)

UTENSILS:

Pastry brush
10 soufflé molds, 4 inches in diameter and 2 inches deep
Electric blender
Large bowl
Copper basin or large bowl
Wire whisk
Wooden spatula
Long flexible-blade spatula or knife

Preheat the oven to 425° F.

Lightly butter the inside of each soufflé mold, using the melted butter and a pastry brush. Sprinkle some sugar (approximately 2 tablespoons in all) into the buttered molds, then turn them so that the sides and bottom are coated with a thin layer of sugar, as though you were flouring the molds. Tap the molds gently so that all the excess sugar will fall out.

Place the raspberries, lemon juice, and 6 tablespoons of sugar in the blender, and blend to form a smooth purée, then add the egg yolks and blend for 15 seconds more. Pour the resulting mixture into a large bowl.

Place the egg whites and a pinch of salt in a second large bowl or a copper basin and beat them with a wire whisk until stiff. Be careful not to make them too stiff, though; when they begin to peak, sprinkle in the confectioner's sugar and continue beating just long enough to mix the sugar in completely with the egg whites.

Using a wooden spatula, place a quarter of the egg whites in the bowl with the fruit purée. Carefully fold the egg whites into the fruit, cutting and lifting the mixture with the spatula to make it as light and airy as possible. Continue adding and folding in the egg whites, about a quarter at a time; then once all the egg whites have been completely incorporated and a homogeneous mixture has been formed, pour it into the soufflé molds prepared earlier. Fill the molds completely, smoothing the top of each soufflé with a flexible-blade spatula or a knife. Wipe off any of the soufflé batter that touches the rim of the mold, then run your thumb around the interior edge of the rim to make a little groove. This will help the soufflé rise more evenly. Immediately place the soufflés in the oven and bake for 12 minutes. Serve immediately, as soon as they come from the oven, either as they are or accompanied by a sauceboat of **raspberry sauce.**

COMMENTS:

Buttering the molds is essential since it permits the soufflés to rise straight up when baked. The sugar gives the outside of the soufflé a hint of crispness that is quite pleasant. Be very careful not to touch the inside of the molds once they have been buttered and sugared.

The top of each soufflé can be glazed by sprinkling a little confectioner's sugar over each soufflé 3 minutes after they go into the oven.

134 *Soufflé léger aux poires*
PEAR SOUFFLÉ

Ingredients for 10 individual soufflés:

1½ tablespoons melted butter
2 tablespoons granulated sugar
4 cups water
Scant ½ cup granulated sugar

1 vanilla bean, split open lengthwise
4 pears weighing a total of 1¼ pounds, peeled, stemmed, cored, and cut into quarters, or 3 cups canned pear halves
¼ cup granulated sugar
1½ tablespoons pear brandy (*alcool de poire*)
5 egg yolks
12 egg whites
A pinch of salt
2 tablespoons confectioner's sugar
Apricot sauce (125) (optional)

UTENSILS:

Pastry brush
10 soufflé molds 4 inches in diameter and 2 inches deep
Saucepan
Colander
Electric blender
Large bowl
Copper basin or large bowl
Wire whisk
Wooden spatula
Long flexible-blade spatula or knife

Preheat the oven to 425° F.

Using a pastry brush, lightly butter the inside of each soufflé mold with the melted butter. Sprinkle some sugar (approximately 2 tablespoons in all) into the molds, then turn them so that the sides and bottom are covered with a thin layer of sugar. Tap the molds to make any excess sugar fall out.

Place the water, a scant ½ cup of sugar, and the vanilla bean in a saucepan and bring to a boil. Drop the pears into the boiling liquid and poach for 15 minutes, then drain in a colander. (If using canned pears, do not poach them, simply drain them.) Place the pears in a blender with ¼ cup of sugar, the pear brandy, and the egg yolks. Blend for 1 minute or until perfectly homogeneous, then pour the mixture into a large bowl.

Place the egg whites and salt in a second large bowl or a copper basin. Beat the whites with a wire whisk until they stiffen; be careful not to beat them too long, they should be just stiff enough to peak. Then add the confectioner's sugar and beat just long enough to mix it into the egg whites.

Using a wooden spatula, place a quarter of the beaten egg whites in the bowl with the fruit purée. Gently fold in the egg whites by cutting and lifting the fruit purée over them with the spatula. Continue adding the egg whites a quarter at a time, folding, cutting, and lifting the mixture to incorporate as much air as possible. When the batter is perfectly homogeneous, fill the soufflé molds with it. Fill each mold to the brim, then smooth the surface of each soufflé with a flexible-blade spatula or a knife. Wipe off any of the soufflé batter that touches the rim of the mold, then run your thumb around the inside edge of the mold to make a little groove. Immediately bake the soufflés for 12 minutes and serve them as soon as they come from the oven. The soufflés can be served as they are or accompanied by **apricot sauce** served from a sauceboat or bowl.

COMMENTS:

The secret of making perfect soufflés is not to beat the egg whites too long. They should peak, but not be too stiff; this way they will rise much better when baked.

The salt will dissolve some of the albumen in the egg whites which often makes for lumpy soufflés; using it will make the egg whites smoother.

Rather than add the pear brandy directly to the pear purée, it can be incorporated into the soufflé in the following manner:

Cut four ladyfingers into 3 pieces each, soak them in the pear brandy, then fill the molds only half full and place a piece of ladyfinger into each mold. Finish filling the mold and bake. The taste of the pear brandy will be appreciated even more in this added tidbit.

Crêpes à la paresseuse
CRÊPES WITH ALMOND BUTTER 135

Ingredients for 10 small crêpes, or 5 servings:

FOR THE BATTER:

¾ cup flour
2 generous tablespoons granulated sugar
⅛ teaspoon salt
1 egg
1 egg yolk
Skin of ½ orange, finely grated
1 cup milk
3½ tablespoons butter

FOR THE ALMOND BUTTER:

⅔ cup powdered caramelized almonds (*see Note*)
¼ pound softened butter
1 tablespoon Grand Marnier liqueur or Cointreau

2 tablespoons cooking oil (for the crêpe pans)
3½ tablespoons softened butter for the 10 dessert plates (1 teaspoon per plate)
10 teaspoons armagnac or cognac

UTENSILS:

Electric blender
Small saucepan
2 bowls
2 small crêpe pans 6 inches in diameter (*see Note*)
Flexible-blade metal spatula
Dinner plate
To serve: 10 small dessert plates

THE CRÊPE BATTER:

Place the flour, sugar, salt, egg, egg yolk, and grated orange peel in the blender. Blend and start pouring in the milk little by little. Blend until all the milk has been added and a smooth batter has formed.

Heat 3½ tablespoons of butter in a small saucepan over moderate heat and cook until it begins to color slightly; the butter has cooked enough when it no longer sizzles (this means that the water it contained has evaporated). Pour the butter into the blender with the other ingredients and continue blending for 15 seconds, then pour the batter into a bowl and leave to rest for 30 minutes before using.

THE ALMOND BUTTER:

Clean the blender and place the powdered caramelized almonds, 1/4 pound of butter, and the Grand Marnier or Cointreau in it. Blend until a smooth and homogeneous paste is formed, then empty it into a bowl.

COOKING THE CRÊPES:

Lightly oil each crêpe pan, and place over moderate heat. Stir the crêpe batter with a small ladle, then place a little batter (approximately 2 1/2 tablespoons) in each pan. Tip the pans as the batter is added so that the bottom of the pans is completely covered by a layer of batter. Cook each crêpe for 1 minute, then, using a flexible-blade spatula, turn them over and cook for a minute more. The crêpes should be golden brown on each side. Remove the crêpes from the pans and place them on a dinner plate. Continue making crêpes in this way until you have a total of 10 crêpes.

TO REHEAT AND SERVE:

Preheat the oven to 475° F.

Spread one side of each crêpe with a thin layer of the almond butter; do *not* fold the crêpes.

Lightly butter 10 small dessert plates. Place each crêpe on its own small plate, almond-butter side up, then place the plates in the oven for just 30 seconds before serving. This short time in a very hot oven will be long enough to heat the crêpes. (You will have to do this either in two batches of 5 crêpes each or by using two shelves in the oven.) As the crêpes come from the oven, spoon a teaspoon of armagnac or cognac over each one and serve immediately; *don't* light the armagnac to flambé the crêpes. Each person should be served two crêpes, each on its own plate.

COMMENTS:

The crépe batter can be made up to a day ahead of time. If this is done, be sure to beat the batter well with a wire whisk before using so that the butter that has surfaced will be mixed back into it.

Since the final cooking of the crêpes in a hot oven is basically a reheating technique, the crêpes can in fact be cooked up to a day in advance as well. If this is done, they should be placed on a cake rack to cool as soon as they come from the pan; once cooled they should be placed on a plate in a pile, then covered with aluminum foil or another plate turned upside down. The crêpes must then be refrigerated. Thirty minutes before reheating and serving them, take them out of the refrigerator; they should have time to soften to their original consistency and be at room temperature before being spread with the almond butter and reheated.

Note: *Powdered caramelized almonds are called* praline *in French. To make 2½ cups use:*

1 cup granulated sugar
¼ cup water
1¾ cups shelled almonds

Boil the sugar and water until the mixture reaches the hard-ball stage on a candy thermometer, add the almonds, and remove from the heat. Stir with a wooden spoon until the sugar becomes grainy, then place the pan back over moderate heat and continue cooking for 10 to 15 minutes longer. Stir constantly while the sugar is melting to prevent its sticking to the bottom of the saucepan. When ready, the sugar should be a dark-caramel color. Pour the mixture onto a greased baking sheet and leave to cool completely.

To powder this nut brittle, break it into pieces and grind in a food processor or heavy-duty blender, or pound it in a mortar. Grind or pound it just enough to make a coarse powder; if ground too long, it will be reduced again to a syrupy liquid. Powdered caramelized almonds can be kept in a tightly closed container for up to 3 months.

Hazelnuts may be used instead of almonds.

The almond butter used to cover the crêpes will blend more easily if the powdered nut brittle and the butter are mixed together before being placed in the blender.

Five large crêpes (1 per person) may be made instead of 10 small ones. In this case, spoon 2 teaspoons of armagnac over each one before serving. Ed.

Crêpes soufflées

136 CRÊPES WITH SOUFFLÉ FILLING

(color picture VII)

Ingredients for 8 servings:

Crêpe batter; the full recipe as given in **Crêpes with almond butter (135)**

FOR THE PEAR-SOUFFLÉ FILLING:

4 cups water
Scant ½ cup granulated sugar
1 vanilla bean, split lengthwise
3 pears weighing a total of ¾ pound, peeled, quartered, and cored, or 6 canned pear halves
¼ cup granulated sugar
1 tablespoon pear brandy (*alcool de poire*)
6 egg yolks
10 egg whites
A pinch of salt
2 tablespoons confectioner's sugar

Butter (for the baking sheet)
Confectioner's sugar
1 cup **raspberry sauce (124)**

UTENSILS:

2 crêpe pans 6 inches in diameter
Spatula
Baking sheet
Sugar sifter for confectioner's sugar
To serve: 8 hot dessert plates

PRELIMINARY PREPARATIONS:

Prepare the crêpe batter as described in **Crêpes with almond butter (135)**. Prepare the soufflé mixture as described in the recipe for **Pear soufflé (134)**, but use the ingredients listed here.

COOKING AND SERVING THE CRÊPES:

Preheat the oven to 450° F.

Cook the crêpes in the small crêpe pans as described in **crêpes with almond butter.** Make 16 crêpes and place them, not overlapping, on a lightly buttered baking sheet; it may be necessary to use two sheets or to bake the crêpes in two batches. Place 3 tablespoons of the pear-soufflé mixture in the center of each crêpe, then fold the crêpe over the soufflé filling. Sprinkle them with confectioner's sugar and place them in the oven. Bake for 6 to 8 minutes, then remove from the oven. Use a spatula to lift the crêpes carefully off the baking sheet and place two of them on each dessert plate, with the folded sides touching each other. Spoon **raspberry sauce** around the crêpes and serve immediately.

COMMENTS:

Practice making the recipe for **Pear soufflé (134)** before trying this recipe; once you have mastered the soufflé (you'll soon be expert at it), making these crêpes will be extremely simple. Guests are always surprised and pleased when they are served this dessert—your friends will be green with envy. Even though the baking time may seem short, it is exactly what it should be; soufflés should always be slightly creamy in the middle.

Pommes bonne femme à l'amande d'abricot
BAKED APPLES WITH APRICOT FILLING 137

Ingredients for 4 servings:

8 almonds, fresh or dried
4 dried apricots
1 teaspoon granulated sugar
2 tablespoons rum

4 large apples weighing approximately 7 ounces each
4 heaping teaspoons butter
4 heaping teaspoons granulated sugar
8 tablespoons water

4 teaspoons butter
4 heaping teaspoons granulated sugar or **almond cream (123)** (*see Comments*)

1 cup **apricot sauce (125)**

UTENSILS:

Small bowl
Apple corer
Baking dish
Double boiler

MAKING THE FILLING:

If the almonds are still in their shells, crack the shells and remove the almonds. If the almonds are very fresh, the skin that surrounds each one can be removed with the aid of a small knife. Dried almonds, once shelled, must be dropped into boiling water for 2 minutes, then drained and cooled under running water; the skin will then come off easily. Split the almonds open lengthwise, using a paring knife; the halves should separate easily. Then place them in a bowl and reserve.

Rinse the dried apricots under cold running water, then cut them into ¼-inch squares. Place the apricots in the bowl with the almonds and add a teaspoon of sugar and 2 tablespoons of rum. Leave the apricots and almonds to marinate for 1 hour before using.

TO BAKE AND SERVE:

Preheat the oven to 425° F.

Peel the apples, but do not remove their stems. Cut off the top of each apple just under the stem and reserve. Use an apple corer or small knife to remove the seeds; try not to pierce the bottoms of the apples. Fill each apple with the almond-apricot mixture, place the apples in a baking dish, and pour the rum used to marinate the almonds and apricots over them. Place a heaping teaspoon of butter on top of each apple, then cover each one with its top. Sprinkle each apple with a teaspoon of sugar and add 8 tablespoons of water and 4 teaspoons of butter to the baking dish. Place the apples in the oven and bake for 30 to 40 minutes; they should be cooked but not be too soft or mushy. Halfway through their cooking time, baste the apples with the liquid in the baking dish and sprinkle each one once more with a teaspoon of sugar.

Just before they are ready to come from the oven, warm the **apricot sauce** gently in a double boiler or *bain-marie.*

To serve, either spoon the apricot sauce over the apples in the baking dish and serve immediately, or spoon apricot sauce onto 4 dessert plates, place the apples in the center, spoon the juice the apples cooked in over them, and serve.

COMMENTS:

A delicious change can be made in this recipe by adding 4 teaspoons of **Almond cream (123)** instead of sugar to each apple halfway through the baking time.

Fresh fruits can be used instead of the dried apricots and almonds for making the filling, such as pitted cherries, strawberries, raspberries, etc. If fresh fruit is used, make a **Raspberry sauce (124)** to spoon over the apples when they come from the oven.

This dessert is delicious served cold, especially in the summertime.

Tarte fine chaude aux pommes acidulées
HOT APPLE TARTS 138

Ingredients for 4 individual tarts:

- 8 very small cooking apples weighing approximately 1¼ pounds in all (*see Note*)
- Juice of 1 lemon
- 14 ounces **puff pastry (118)** (*see Comments and Note*)
- 6½ tablespoons softened butter
- ¼ cup granulated sugar
- *Crème fraîche* (*see p. 352*) or **whipped cream (121)** (optional)

UTENSILS:

- Paring knife
- Bowl
- Rolling pin
- Baking sheet
- *To serve*: 4 hot dessert plates

PRELIMINARY PREPARATIONS:

Preheat the oven to 425° F.

Peel, core, and seed the apples. Cut each apple in half, each half into quarters, and each quarter into eighths; thus each apple will have been cut into eight wedges a little more than ½ inch thick. Place them in a bowl with the lemon juice and rub all the pieces with the lemon juice to prevent discoloration.

Lightly flour a clean table. Roll out and shape the dough in the following manner:

Divide the dough into four equal pieces and form each piece into a ball. Roll out each ball of dough to form a circle approximately 6¾ inches in diameter and 1/16 inch thick.

If your circles are not perfectly round, roll them out slightly larger than the circle needed, place a plate the diameter of the circle required (6¾ inches) on each piece of dough, and cut around the edge of the plate with a sharp knife.

Place the circles of dough on a baking sheet, and, using a sharp knife, make a light incision about ½ inch from the edge of each circle, making a concentric circle inside the full circumference. In between the incision and the edge of the tart, the dough will rise, forming the border.

TO BAKE AND SERVE:

Place the apples on each tart inside the line drawn with the knife. The pieces should be arranged like the petals of a flower in a circular pattern and cover all the dough in the center of the tart. Dot the tarts with half the butter and sprinkle them with half the sugar, then place them in the preheated oven and bake for 30 minutes. Halfway through their baking time, dot again with the remaining butter and sprinkle with the remaining sugar. When they have finished baking, the surface of each tart should be beautifully colored and the sugar should have begun to caramelize. Serve the tarts immediately, as they come from the oven, either plain or accompanied by a saucer of *crême fraîche* or **whipped cream.**

COMMENTS:

The puff pastry can be rolled out to form the circles as described above, garnished with the apples, and then frozen for later use. In this case, the uncooked frozen tart can be taken from the freezer and baked immediately, anytime it is wanted, according to the directions given above.

Other fruits can be used to make tarts in the same way. However, red-fleshed fruits and berries should *not* be frozen. Following the instructions given here, use pitted cherries, apricots, peaches or pears (the last three cut in half) to make delicious hot fruit tarts.

Sweet short pastry (115) can be used instead of puff pastry to make any of these tarts (*see Note*).

NOTE: *The puff pastry can also be rolled out into circles or squares, the incision made to form the border, then frozen without being garnished. When needed, these frozen tart bottoms can simply be garnished as they come from the freezer with the fruit of your choice, dotted with butter and sugar, and immediately baked as described in the recipe.*

If using short pastry dough, use 1 pound 1½ ounces of dough, divide it into four pieces, and roll each into a circle 7½ inches in diameter, then fold the edges over to form the borders of the tarts. Ed.

Charlotte aux pêches
PEACH CHARLOTTE 139

Ingredients for one charlotte, 6 servings:

- 1 tablespoon gelatin
- 3 tablespoons cold water
- 2 cups milk
- 1 vanilla bean, split lengthwise
- 1 cup granulated sugar
- 5 egg yolks
- 2 poached or canned peaches (4 halves)
- 18 ladyfingers
- 1 cup heavy cream, chilled in a mixing bowl for at least 1 hour before using
- 2 cups **caramel and peach sauce (126)**

UTENSILS:

Large mixing bowl (for the cream)
Saucepan with cover
Large bowl
Wire whisk
Wooden spatula or wooden spoon
Charlotte mold 6¼ inches in diameter, 4 inches high
To serve: Round serving platter

PREPARING THE CHARLOTTE-CREAM FILLING:

Moisten the gelatin with 3 tablespoons water. Place the milk, vanilla bean, and half the sugar in a saucepan, place over high heat, and, when the milk starts to boil and rise, cover the pan and remove from the heat immediately. Leave the milk to infuse away from the heat for 5 minutes.

Place the egg yolks and the remaining sugar in a large bowl and beat with a wire whisk for 2 minutes or until the mixture lightens and becomes pale yellow.

Remove the vanilla bean from the milk and start pouring the milk slowly into the bowl with the egg yolk-sugar mixture. Whisk vigorously as the milk is being added. When all the ingredients are well mixed, pour them back into the saucepan and place over low heat. Stir constantly with a wooden spatula or spoon and cook for 6 to 8 minutes, but do *not* let the mixture boil. To check the consistency of the cream, remove the spatula, and, holding it at a sharp tilt, draw a line in the cream on the spatula with your finger: The cream is thick enough if the top edge of the line does not run down and cover the line itself. Once the cream has cooked, pour it immediately into a clean bowl, add the moistened gelatin, and stir to incorporate the gelatin, which should dissolve quickly. Leave the cream to cool completely before assembling the charlotte. Stir the cream occasionally as it cools to keep lumps from forming. (To speed cooling, place the bowl in a larger bowl half filled with cold water and ice cubes.)

ASSEMBLING THE CHARLOTTE:

Drain the peaches and cut them into ¾-inch squares. Line the bottom and sides of the mold with the ladyfingers; place them as close together as possible with the flat side (bottom) of each one against the mold. Cut off the ends of the ladyfingers if they stick up higher than the top of the mold. (See Note.)

Take the bowl of heavy cream from the refrigerator and beat it slowly for 1 minute with a wire whisk, then start whisking faster and continue beating for 5 minutes or until the cream stiffens and peaks almost like egg whites. Stir the peaches into the cold charlotte-cream filling, then pour the whipped cream on top. Use a flat wooden spatula to fold the whipped cream in by cutting, lifting, and folding the charlotte cream over it. When all the ingredients are perfectly mixed and homogeneous, pour them into the lined mold; it should be filled to the top. Place the mold in the refrigerator and leave for at least 1½ hours before serving; the charlotte will in fact be even better if refrigerated a day or two before serving.

TO SERVE:

Place a round serving platter on top of the charlotte mold, hold the platter in place, then turn both upside down so that the mold is sitting on the plate. Carefully lift off the mold. Spoon the **caramel and peach sauce** over the charlotte and serve.

COMMENTS:

Strawberries, raspberries, or poached pears can be used instead of peaches to make charlottes. Even apples can be used: Peel, core, and dice them, then poach them for 1 minute in a syrup made of sugar and water. Drain them and leave them to marinate for several hours in a tablespoon of apple brandy (Calvados), then use just like the peaches to make a charlotte.

Note: *To line the round bottom of the mold, the ladyfingers may simply be laid across it and trimmed to fit the circle. For a prettier, more professional effect, see the instructions in the following recipe for* **Chocolate charlotte with coffee sauce (140).**

As a precaution, to ensure that the charlotte turns out perfectly, the bottom of the mold can be lined with parchment paper and the sides lightly buttered before the mold is lined with the ladyfingers. In this case, dip the mold in hot water for a few seconds before turning it out. Ed.

140 *Marquise fondante au chocolat* CHOCOLATE CHARLOTTE WITH COFFEE SAUCE

Ingredients for 1 charlotte, 5 to 6 servings:

5 ounces semisweet chocolate
7 egg yolks
1 cup granulated sugar
½ pound plus 5 tablespoons softened butter
1⅓ cups unsweetened Dutch cocoa
4 cups **whipped cream (121)**
18 ladyfingers
½ cup strong black coffee, cold and unsweetened
Coffee sauce (128)

UTENSILS:

Double boiler
2 bowls
Wooden spoon
Wire whisk
Pastry brush
Straight-sided charlotte mold 6¼ inches in diameter (*see Note*)
To serve: Chilled round serving platter

PREPARING THE CHOCOLATE FILLING:

Melt the chocolate in the top of a double boiler or in a saucepan in a 350° F oven. Place the egg yolks in a bowl with the granulated sugar and beat with a whisk for 2 minutes or until the mixture lightens to a pale yellow.

Carefully stir the warm melted chocolate into the egg yolk-sugar mixture. Use a wooden spoon or spatula to lift and fold the chocolate in and to incorporate as much air into the mixture as possible.

In a second bowl, beat the butter with a wooden spoon until it is very creamy and smooth, then sprinkle the cocoa into it little by little, beating each addition of cocoa into the butter completely before adding more. When all the cocoa has been added, beat until a completely homogeneous, creamy mixture is formed. Pour it into the first bowl with the chocolate/egg-yolk mixture, and stir well until smooth. Now add the **whipped cream** to the bowl and beat vigorously with a wire whisk until all the ingredients are well mixed together.

ASSEMBLING THE CHARLOTTE:

Cut 7 ladyfingers in half diagonally from corner to corner. Then cut each one diagonally in the other direction, forming two triangles, pointed at one end and rounded at the other. Place the ladyfingers in the bottom of the mold with the pointed ends meeting in the center. Cut and shape the ladyfingers as necessary so that they fit perfectly in a geometric "flower" pattern.

Using a pastry brush, brush all of the ladyfingers with the cold black coffee. It is not necessary to use all of the coffee, but both the ladyfingers already in the mold and the whole ones to be used for the sides should all be lightly soaked with the coffee. Now line the sides of the mold with the whole ladyfingers, placing them as close together as possible. Pour the chocolate filling into the mold, then cut off the ladyfingers that are higher than the rim of the mold. Place the charlotte in the refrigerator for 2 or 3 hours to settle and set before serving.

TO SERVE:

Place a round serving platter on top of the mold, hold the platter in place, turn both upside down so that the mold is sitting on the platter, and remove the mold. Spoon some of the **coffee sauce** around the charlotte and serve the remaining sauce in a sauceboat. (This sauce is marvelous with chocolate.)

Note: *To ensure that the charlotte will turn out perfectly, the bottom of the mold can be lined with parchment paper before lining with the ladyfingers. Ed.*

COMMENTS:

When the whipped cream is added to the other ingredients and beaten in, the resulting cream may seem too compact, but this is perfectly normal. The mixture of the cream and chocolate makes the finished filling rich and luscious.

For an even more spectacular version of this recipe, add to the chocolate cream some fine *julienne* strips of candied orange peel (see page 348 for the method) and pieces of ladyfinger soaked in a rum syrup before filling the mold.

The chocolate-cream filling can be used to make another version of this dessert in the following manner:

Feuilleté de marquise
141 PUFF-PASTRY MARQUISE

Make and bake the squares of puff pastry as for **Puff pastry with asparagus and chervil (43)**. When the pastries come from the oven, cut them open with a serrated knife and fill them with the chocolate-cream filling. Serve with **coffee sauce** to make a truly sumptuous dessert.

Feuillantines de poires caramélisées
142 CARAMELIZED PEAR PASTRIES

Ingredients for 4 individual pastries:

1 lemon
2 small pears
3 cups water
Scant ½ cup granulated sugar
½ vanilla bean, split lengthwise

7 ounces **puff pastry (118)** (*see Note, p. 299*)
1 small egg, beaten

4 tablespoons **pastry cream (122)**
1 teaspoon pear brandy (*alcool de poire*)
Whipped cream (121) made with 4 tablespoons heavy cream and 1 tablespoon confectioner's sugar or granulated sugar
4 tablespoons granulated sugar (to caramelize)

UTENSILS:

Large bowl
Large saucepan with cover
Clean cloth or towel
Salamander (*see Comments and Note*)
Rolling pin
Ruler
Large sharp knife
Pastry brush
Small bowl
Serrated knife
Flexible-blade spatula
To serve: 4 hot dessert plates

POACHING THE PEARS:

Fill a large bowl with cold water, add the juice of half the lemon, and place the bowl on the table near the cutting board. Peel the pears, split them open from top to bottom, and remove the stem and seeds. Rub each half pear with the remaining half lemon, then place them in the bowl of cold water to keep them from discoloring.

Place the 3 cups of water in a saucepan with the sugar and vanilla bean, bring to a boil, then lower the heat. Drain the pears and add them to the pan. Cover the pan with a clean cloth or towel, then place the cover of the pan on top of the towel; this is to make sure that no steam escapes while the pears are cooking. The pears should simmer gently, not boil, for 15 minutes; then remove the pan from the heat and leave the pears to cool in their syrup.

MAKING THE PASTRIES:

Preheat the oven to 425° F.

Lightly flour the table and roll out the puff pastry into a square about 5 inches on a side and 1/8 inch thick. Using a large sharp knife, cut the square in half, then cut each half crosswise in half again, thus making 4 squares of pastry about 2½ inches on a side. Turn each square of pastry upside down on a baking sheet and brush with a little beaten egg; the egg will brown the pastries when they are baked. Be careful not to let any of the egg touch the edges of the dough or it will not rise properly. Bake for 12 to 15 minutes or until a rich golden brown.

While the pastry is baking, heat the salamander by placing it directly in the flame of a gas burner. The metal should be heated for 15 to 20 minutes.

TO GARNISH THE PASTRIES AND SERVE:

Mix the **pastry cream** in a bowl with the pear brandy. Lift the pears from their syrup and cut them crosswise into thin slices.

When they have finished baking, remove the pastries from the oven. Using a serrated knife, cut each pastry in half, forming a top and bottom. Place the bottom of each pastry on an individual dessert plate.

Using a flexible-blade metal spatula, spread the tops of each pastry with pastry cream. Set the sliced pears in the pastry cream so that they cover the top of each pastry. Sprinkle each of the garnished pastry tops with a tablespoon of sugar, then touch the hot salamander to the sugar, which will immediately harden and caramelize.

Garnish the pastry bottoms on each plate with several spoonfuls of **whipped cream,** then carefully place the caramelized tops onto the cream and serve immediately.

COMMENTS:

Another version of this dessert can be made with slices of oranges from orange marmalade instead of poached pears. If orange slices are used, bake and assemble the pastries as described here but do *not* caramelize the oranges.

NOTE: *A salamander is an instrument used for browning or caramelizing outside of the oven; it is composed of a wooden handle attached to a long metal rod that ends in a small, thick, round disk. The round end is heated and touched to the sugar to caramelize it. Ed.*

Millefeuille à la crème légère
MILLEFEUILLE WITH CREAM FILLING 143

Ingredients for 1 large pastry, 4 servings:

Flour
$12\frac{2}{3}$ ounces **puff pastry** (**118**) (*see Note, p. 299*)
1 cup **pastry cream** (**122**)
Whipped cream (**121**) made with $\frac{1}{3}$ cup heavy cream and 1 tablespoon confectioner's sugar
Confectioner's sugar to sprinkle on top

UTENSILS:

Rolling pin
Ruler
Baking sheet
Fork
Bowl
Wooden spatula
Sugar sifter
To serve: Long serving platter
Serrated knife

TO MAKE THE PASTRY:

Preheat the oven to 425° F.

Lightly flour the table, then roll out the **puff pastry** to make a rectangle 8 inches long, 18 inches wide, and $\frac{1}{16}$ inch thick. Cut this piece of dough into three equal strips each 6 inches wide and 8 inches long.

Slightly dampen the baking sheet, then lay the strips of dough on it. Prick each piece of dough all over with the prongs of a fork; this will keep the dough from rising too much. Place the dough in the oven and bake for 20 minutes. If the oven is not large enough for all three pieces of dough to bake at the same time, they will have to be baked separately. Once baked, the pastry should be nicely browned; remove from the oven and place on a cake rack to cool completely before assembling with the other ingredients.

TO ASSEMBLE AND SERVE:

Spoon the **pastry cream** into a bowl with the **whipped cream.** Mix the two together, using a wooden spatula to lift and cut the creams as though mixing with beaten egg whites. Folding and lifting the creams to mix them will mean that air is being incorporated as well, making the final mixture light and delicate.

Place one of the rectangles of pastry on the serving platter, spread half the cream over it, place a second rectangle of pastry on top of this, and spread it with the remaining cream. Top this with the last rectangle, sprinkle confectioner's sugar over the top of the assembled pastry, and serve. Use a serrated knife to cut and serve this pastry at the table.

COMMENTS:

Puff pastry tends to shrink when baked; this can be avoided by rolling out and cutting the dough a day before it is needed, and refrigerating the dough, wrapped in plastic, for 24 hours. Bake when taken from the refrigerator.

Two cups of fresh raspberries or strawberries can be delicately stirred into the cream that is used to garnish the pastry; save a few of the berries for decorating the top of the pastry.

Those who are willing to give it a try can crisscross the top of the assembled pastry with caramelized lines burned into the confectioner's sugar with a hot, thin metal rod: Each time the metal touches the sugar, it will immediately caramelize it, thus a pattern can be made by touching the sugar several times in succession.

Note: *It is very important that the prongs of the fork go all the way through the pastry when pricking it before baking. You should feel the fork hit the baking sheet. Ed.*

Ali Baba
ALI BABA CAKE 144

Ingredients for 2 cakes, 4 servings each:

3 tablespoons candied fruit
½ cup candied orange peel
2½ tablespoons raisins
1 cup **baba or savarin dough (120)**

¾ cup granulated sugar
1 cup water
3 tablespoons rum

1¼ cups **pastry cream (122)**
1 cup **almond cream (123)**, at room temperature
Confectioner's sugar to sprinkle on top

Raspberry sauce (124), or
Caramel and peach sauce (126)

UTENSILS:

Large bowl
Wooden spoon
2 round cake pans 5½ inches in diameter
Baking sheet
Cake rack
Small saucepan
Long serrated knife
Flexible-blade metal spatula
Sugar sifter
To serve: Large serving platter
Sauceboat

FIRST BAKING (*a day before serving*):

Cut the candied fruit and orange peel into squares about ½ inch on a side.

Rinse the raisins under cold running water and drain.

Place the baba or savarin dough in a large bowl and add the candied fruit, orange peel, and raisins (see Note). Mix these ingredients together, using a wooden spoon, then place the bowl of dough in a warm place to rise for 20 minutes. After it has risen a bit, punch it down by beating it with the wooden spoon, then flatten it with the palm of your hand.

Preheat the oven to 400° F.

Lightly butter the two small cake pans and divide the dough between them; they should be about half full. Place the pans in a warm place and leave the dough to rise for 40 minutes to an hour, or until it reaches the rims of the pans (the fruit in the dough slows its rising).

Place the cake pans in the oven and bake for 18 to 20 minutes. Remove from the oven and turn the cakes out immediately onto a rack to cool.

While the cakes are baking, prepare a rum syrup: Place the sugar and water in a saucepan over high heat. As soon as the water boils, remove it from the heat and allow to cool; while it is still lukewarm, add the rum to the syrup.

Place the rack supporting the cakes over a large bowl and spoon the rum syrup over the cakes. Some of the syrup will drip through the rack into the bowl; continue spooning it back over the cakes until they are thoroughly soaked with the syrup. Place the cakes in the refrigerator overnight before finishing their preparation.

FINISHING AND SERVING THE CAKES:

Preheat the oven to 425° F.

Remove the cakes from the refrigerator and carefully cut them into two layers, horizontally through the middle, using a long serrated knife.

Place the bottom layer of the cakes on the baking sheet, then spread the **pastry cream** over them. Put the top layers back in place to cover the pastry cream. Using a flexible-blade spatula, spread the **almond cream** all over the top and sides of each cake as though you were icing them. Sprinkle the top of each cake generously with confectioner's sugar and place them in the oven for 10 minutes. When finished baking, the cakes will still be white, but will have been somewhat "marbled" by the baking.

Place the cakes on a serving platter and refrigerate until ready to serve. These cakes are always eaten cold. Serve accompanied by a sauceboat of either **raspberry sauce** or **caramel and peach sauce.**

COMMENTS:

As with savarin cakes (see page 302), Ali Babas can be baked in advance and refrigerated or frozen before being soaked in the rum syrup. The cakes should be sealed in plastic bags as soon as they come from the oven, then refrigerated or frozen. Refrigerated cakes can be kept up to 12 days; frozen cakes can be kept 2 months, but should be left in the refrigerator to thaw for 24 hours before using. When needed, the cakes should be soaked with the rum syrup and finished as described in this recipe.

Once they have been finished, the Ali Babas can be kept refrigerated for 2 or 3 days before serving; they are even better this way, since all the flavors have had time to ripen and mix within the cake.

NOTE: *The raisins and candied fruit may be rolled in flour before being mixed with the dough; this will keep them from sinking to the bottom as the dough rises.*

Do not be alarmed when the almond cream melts in the oven and begins to slide down the sides of the cake. This is supposed to happen and adds to the charm of the cake. Ed.

Les Eugénies
CHOCOLATE-ORANGE EUGÉNIES 145

Ingredients for 4 servings:

- 2 oranges weighing approximately 7 ounces each; if possible, use oranges that have not been sprayed with pesticides
- 2 cups water
- 2¾ cups granulated sugar

- 5 ounces semisweet chocolate
- 4 tablespoons unsweetened Dutch cocoa

UTENSILS:

Vegetable peeler
Saucepan
Colander

Cake rack
Double boiler
Fork
Large shallow dish
To serve: Serving platter covered with a paper doily

TO CANDY THE ORANGE PEEL:

Place the oranges on a cutting board; using a sharp knife, cut off one end of each orange so that it will stand upright on the cutting board by itself. Use a vegetable peeler to shave off strips of the zest about 1 inch wide. Make these strips by holding the oranges upright on the cutting board and peeling from top to bottom. Remove only the colored part (the zest); there should be little or no white inner skin on the peels. The oranges themselves are not used in this recipe, but they can be saved for other uses. Cut each strip of zest into squares about an inch on a side.

Fill a saucepan with water (approximately 1 quart) and bring to a boil. Drop the squares of orange peel into the boiling water and boil for 3 minutes, then drain in a colander. Repeat this operation two more times, draining and using fresh water each time, to eliminate any bitterness from the peels.

Place the 2 cups of water and the sugar in a saucepan, bring to a boil, then add the drained orange peels. Stir the peel into the syrup, then lower the heat and simmer over very low heat for 3 hours. The surface of the liquid should barely quiver; it is essential that the peels cook *very* slowly.

Once they are cooked, drain the orange peels and place them on a cake rack to dry for another 3 hours before finishing. In this uncoated form, the candied peel has other uses; see Comments on **Chocolate charlotte with coffee sauce (140)**.

TO COAT THE PEELS WITH CHOCOLATE:

Break the chocolate into pieces and place it in a double boiler to melt; stir the melted chocolate to make it smooth.

Lift each piece of candied peel from the cake rack on the prongs of a fork (do *not* prick them), and dip them into the melted chocolate one by one. Each piece of orange peel should be completely coated with chocolate, then replaced on the cake rack. When all the pieces of peel have been coated, leave them on the rack until the chocolate begins to grow dull and can be handled. When this happens, place each piece of chocolate-covered peel in a shallow dish containing the cocoa, and turn it over to coat both sides. Leave the candies in the cocoa until they have cooled completely, then lift each piece out, shaking gently to remove the excess cocoa.

Serve on a plate lined with a paper doily, with coffee, after the meal.

COMMENTS:

Chocolate-orange Eugénies can be kept refrigerated for 8 days if they are left completely covered by the cocoa and lifted out only when ready to serve.

NOTE: *It is important to let the chocolate harden just enough, but not too much, before coating the peels with cocoa. If too soft, the chocolate will melt when you try to pick it up, but if allowed to harden completely, it will stick to the rack and crack when you try to lift it off. Ed.*

Ingredients & Procedures

ARMAGNAC: This is a spirit much like cognac but with a slightly different flavor. Cognac can be used instead, but it is preferable to use armagnac when it is specifically called for.

BUTTER: Unless otherwise indicated, unsalted (sweet) butter is used in these recipes. Salted butter may be used, but the dish should subsequently be salted less; this is especially important when a specific measurement for salt has been indicated in the recipe.

Softened butter means butter that has been left at room temperature until it can be easily separated into soft but consistent pieces with your hands. Generally, an hour at room temperature produces this effect.

CRAYFISH: Crayfish are found in streams, lakes, and ponds from the Great Lakes to the Gulf of Mexico and from the Atlantic to the Pacific. They are plentiful from September to April. Nevertheless, few people fish for them, and many cooks are unaware that they are to be found not far from their own homes, since crayfish are not sold commercially in many of the regions where they exist in abundance. Varieties and the size of crayfish may differ from one area to the next, but they are all edible and easy to catch. For those who are not so adventurous as to go fishing for them, the address of a well-known mail-order supplier of live crayfish is: Battistela's Sea Foods, Inc., 910 Touro Street, New Orleans, Louisiana 70116. They come by air, in large quantities only, and are somewhat expensive, so best plan ahead before placing an order.

CREAM: Many recipes call for "*crème fraîche* or heavy cream." When this is the case, it is preferable to make your own *crème fraîche*, but heavy cream can be used if no *crème fraîche* is at hand. Narcisse Chamberlain's recipe for *crème fraîche,* from the American edition of *Michel Guérard's Cuisine Minceur*, is given below.

Some recipes simply call for heavy cream (*crème fleurette*). These are usually recipes in which the cream is whipped and in which *crème fraîche* must be diluted with ¼ its volume of water for use instead.

Crème fraîche

Ingredients for 2 generous cups:

- 1 cup sour cream
- 1 cup heavy sweet cream

Put the sour cream into a bowl or wide-mouthed glass jar. With a fork, gradually stir in the sweet cream and stir until the mixture is smoothly blended. Cover and leave at room temperature for 8 to 12 hours. Stir again, and store in the refrigerator for 24 hours before using.

EGGS: Unless otherwise indicated, all eggs used should weigh 1¾ ounces each on the average (21 ounces per dozen). In the United States, these eggs are labeled "medium." If larger eggs are used, fewer are needed; it is preferable to use the size and number of eggs indicated in the recipe when possible. This is especially true of the dessert recipes.

FOIE GRAS: *Foie gras d'oie* is the enlarged liver of a force-fed goose. *Foie gras de canard* is the enlarged liver of a force-fed duck. Michel Guérard uses only *foie gras de canard* in his kitchens at Eugénie-les-

Bains; this is because they are a specialty of the region in which he lives and cooks. Michael Guérard can have fresh *foie gras de canard* all year round—few people are so privileged. Fresh *foie gras* of either duck or goose is difficult, if not impossible, to procure for most cooks. Unfortunately, canned *foie gras* does not have the same taste and often cannot be treated like fresh *foie gras.* Consequently Michel Guérard has suggested substitutions for fresh *foie gras* in those recipes where the canned product is of no use. In some cases, canned *foie gras* certainly can be used. Whenever this is called for, it means *foie gras au naturel* or *mi-cuit;* in both cases, whole pieces of *foie gras* are meant. They are not to be confused with *pâté, mousse,* or *bloc* of *foie gras,* each an entirely different preparation and never used. If available, *foie gras* sold as *mi-cuit* (partially cooked) is always preferred to canned *foie gras au naturel,* as it is the closest thing to the fresh product. Unfortunately, *foie gras mi-cuit* can be kept for only a short time and is therefore difficult to find. For specific substitutions and suggestions, see the individual *foie gras* recipes.

GOOSE FAT: This is sold in cans or jars in France. There is no substitute for its inimitable taste, but lard, although much less flavorful, may be used instead, and so may fresh chicken fat.

JULIENNE: To cut into *julienne* strips means to cut into strips about the size of a matchstick, or sometimes finer. First cut the food into thin slices, then cut through the slices to make the strips.

MEASURING: One cannot overemphasize the importance of carefully measuring ingredients in these *cuisine gourmande* recipes. At first, some measurements seem absurdly specific, but they must be respected. Because they are often numerous, preparation and measurement of most ingredients should be done before the cooking begins. In a chef's kitchen, this advance preparation is called the *mise en place,* and it is a boon to orderly cooking procedure.

MUSHROOMS: Unless otherwise indicated, "mushrooms" mean fresh ordinary (button) mushrooms. They should be very fresh and white.

The stems may be used if they are firm and white; all dirt should be removed from them.

Some wild mushrooms are used in the recipes; they are the *cèpes* (*Boletus*), *morilles* (morels), and *mousserons* (fairy-ring mushrooms). These are all available fresh in France at certain times of the year and can also be purchased dried or canned.

In the United States, many excellent wild mushrooms can be gathered by those experienced enough to identify them (and to identify the many varieties that are poisonous). *Cèpes* (*Boletus*), morels, and chanterelles all grow in the United States, but are seldom sold commercially. Canned morels and *cèpes* are sold in some specialty shops. Dried *cèpes* as well as dried chanterelles are imported from France and sold by specialty mail-order food suppliers as well as in shops.

All these wild mushrooms have their own distinct flavors. Nevertheless, if, for example, dried or canned *cèpes* are available and a recipe calls for morels, it is preferable to use the *cèpes* instead of the morels, rather than simply to use ordinary button mushrooms.

Narcisse Chamberlain has suggested that certain Japanese and Chinese mushrooms (dried or canned) are good substitutes for the wild mushrooms mentioned here. She suggests using Japanese *nameko* mushrooms for *mousserons*, and Japanese dried *shiitake* mushrooms for morels and *cèpes*. She points out that *shiitake* mushrooms should only be used cut into strips, *never* puréed.

All dried mushrooms need to be soaked before using; generally 30 minutes in lukewarm water is sufficient, but consult the instructions on the packages for further details.

SWIRL: This is the technique used when adding butter to thicken and enrich a sauce. It is done by adding softened butter in little nut-size pieces to a warm liquid and shaking the pan with a circular motion so that the sauce swirls, or spins, around the inside of the pan, thus combining the ingredients to make a sauce. While the butter is being swirled in, the pan should be held just above, or away from, the heat so that the liquid is warm but never boiling. The pan is placed back on the heat for a few seconds from time to time to make sure it doesn't cool too much, however. As the butter melts, the sauce becomes thicker and opaque. This type of sauce is made only at the last minute.

TRUFFLES: Although fresh truffles are available in France, canned truffles must often be used instead. Whole canned truffles are to be preferred to pieces, and those labeled *de première cuisson* are preferable to the more common *de deuxième cuisson.* The juice in the can with the truffles should be saved as it is precious and can be used to flavor various dishes. It has been suggested that once the juice is gone, or no longer covers the truffles in the can, madeira can be added to cover the truffles and help preserve them; nevertheless, they do not keep long once the can has been opened.

VANILLA SUGAR: Vanilla-flavored sugar is sold commercially in France, but it is very easy to prepare at home. Your own will be of much better quality, since the commercial brands contain artificial vanilla flavoring rather than real vanilla.

To make vanilla sugar, you need 1 vanilla bean, 5 ounces of lump sugar, a pair of scissors, and a mortar and pestle (or a heavy-duty electric blender).

Hold the vanilla bean over the mortar and cut it into tiny slices, using the scissors. When the entire bean has been sliced, add half the sugar lumps, and begin pounding with the pestle. When the sugar is about as fine as granulated sugar (after about 10 minutes), pour the contents of the mortar into a fine sieve and shake the sieve over a piece of waxed paper until all the finest pieces have gone through. Place what is left in the sieve back in the mortar, add the remaining lump sugar, and pound again for another 10 minutes. Sift once more. What now remains in the sieve can be pounded once again, but no more sugar should be added.

Instead of being pounded in a mortar, the sliced vanilla bean and the sugar lumps may be ground for 1 to 2 minutes in a heavy-duty blender, but the mixture should still be sifted and only half the sugar added at a time, as described above.

Keep the vanilla sugar in a tightly closed jar or other container to be used when needed. It is seldom used in large quantities. If none is available, a few drops of vanilla extract can often be used instead.

WINE: Unless otherwise indicated, the red and white wines used in these recipes should be table wines of good quality, preferably the French wine if an exact label is mentioned. When you choose a wine for cooking, it must always be one that is pleasing to drink. Expensive wines do not always add commensurately to the flavor of a dish, but a poor wine will ruin it.

Important Kitchen Utensils

BAIN-MARIE: This is not one specific utensil, but often an improvised arrangement designed to heat foods gently or to keep them warm. When foods, especially sauces, are kept warm in a *bain-marie*, this involves setting the pan containing the food in a large, shallow receptacle of hot water. The water should come about one-third of the way up the side of the pan. The *bain-marie* is put on the stove over very low heat or at the back of the stove—the water should *not* boil—and the contents of the saucepan are kept warm in this manner.

A similar arrangement, much more like a double boiler, is used for things such as melting chocolate. Here, a saucepan or pot is half-filled with water that is brought barely to a boil. A bowl is then placed in the pot so that it is supported by the sides of the pot and the bottom of the bowl does not touch the water, which should simmer, not boil, once the bowl is placed over it. This improvised double boiler is also called a *bain-marie*.

Finally, pâtés, *terrines*, and other foods are baked in the oven in a *bain-marie*. This again involves placing the dish or *terrine* containing the food to be baked in a receptacle such as a roasting pan, then pouring boiling water into the pan until it comes about halfway up the sides of the *terrine*. The pan is then placed in the oven and the food cooked in it.

COUSCOUS POT OR STEAMER: The couscous pot or steamer is composed of two parts: the bottom, in which water or another liquid is boiled; and the top, whose perforated bottom allows the steam to circulate around and cook the food that is placed in it. Pots of this type are useful for steaming all kinds of food, and it is best to have a very large one that can hold large quantities and big pieces.

Collapsible steaming racks can sometimes be used instead of the couscous pot or steamer, but only for foods that steam for a very short time, no more than 15 to 20 minutes.

An improvised steamer can be made by placing a colander or strainer in a pot that contains the boiling liquid. The colander should sit squarely on the rim of the pot; if it fits too loosely, wrap a clean cloth or towel around it to prevent steam from escaping between the sides of the colander and the sides of the pot. The boiling water in the pot should not touch the bottom of the colander.

ELECTRIC BLENDER: An electric blender is frequently used to purée ingredients in these recipes. Most blenders handle small quantities well, although often at least ½ cup of any given ingredient or liquid needs to be used for best results.

Follow the manufacturer's instructions on filling the blender; often soups will have to be blended in two or even three batches to avoid overflowing.

It is best to cut foods into ½- to 1-inch-long pieces or chunks before adding them to the blender.

Liquid may need to be added if foods being blended are too dry or compact.

ROASTING PANS: Rectangular, heavy-duty cast-aluminum roasting pans are the most commonly employed in France. Oval-shaped roasting pans are sometimes used, but the shape is usually of little importance. It is best to have two roasting pans, one about 14 inches by 10 inches and another 18 inches by 14 inches. Foods should fit flat on the bottom of the pan, and the pan that leaves the least room around the roast should be used whenever possible.

Since roasting pans are often deglazed and sometimes placed on the burners of the stove to reduce juices and make sauces, the thickness of the metal is important. Thin pans tend to warp and buckle when used on top of the stove; heavy-metal roasting pans are best.

SAUTEUSE: A *sauteuse* or *sauté* pan is basically a frying pan, but with straight sides a little more than 2 inches high. The large, flat bottom is good for browning, and the high sides allow room for various garnishes and liquids to be added during cooking. These pans are ideal for evaporating liquids (reducing) and can be used to cook all varieties of food. Two *sauteuses* are needed: one that is quite large, the other smaller. The inside measurements should be about 11 inches in diameter and 3¼ inches deep for the large one and 8½ inches in diameter and 2¾ inches deep for the small one. Both should have lids that fit perfectly.

Always use a pan that leaves little space around the food placed in it, but be sure all the food lies flat in the pan without crowding. Foods cooked in a *sauteuse* should never be piled on top of each other; contact with the bottom of the pan is essential.

In some cases, when little liquid is used, an ordinary frying pan can be used instead of a *sauteuse.*

SKIMMER OF SLOTTED SPOON: The perforated skimmer is ideal for removing foam from boiling liquids and lifting cooked ingredients out of pots and pans. A slotted spoon, though somewhat less efficient, can be used in the same way.

TERRINES: A *terrine* is an oval or rectangular high-sided utensil generally used for making pâtés. It is usually made of earthenware or porcelain, but it can be made of other materials such as Pyrex or enameled cast iron. A *terrine* should have a lid, although it is not always used in cooking. The approximate size and capacity of the *terrine* needed for any given recipe in this book is always indicated.

WIRE WHISKS: These are a must for making sauces and mixing in general. A small whisk, for use in saucepans and small bowls, should be about 8 to 10 inches long, including its wooden or metal handle. A large whisk 12 to 15 inches long is needed for larger quantities and for beating egg whites. Whisks that have numerous overlapping wires are to be preferred to ones that have only a few (usually far between and overly rigid).

Index

Index

Index

Index

Index